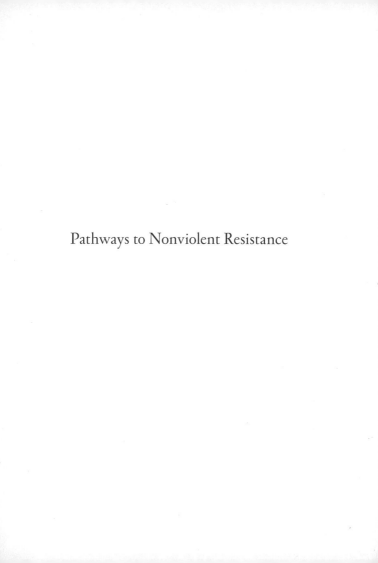

Pathways to Nonviolent Resistance

Pathways

TO

Nonviolent Resistance

BOLD-FACED WISDOM
from the EARLY WRITINGS

MAHATMA GANDHI

Edited by Laura Ross

STERLING
New York

STERLING
New York

An Imprint of Sterling Publishing
387 Park Avenue South
New York, NY 10016

ISBN 978-1-4549-0621-6

Distributed in Canada by Sterling Publishing
c/o Canadian Manda Group, 165 Dufferin Street
Toronto, Ontario, Canada M6K 3H6
Distributed in the United Kingdom by GMC Distribution Services
Castle Place, 166 High Street, Lewes, East Sussex, England BN7 1XU
Distributed in Australia by Capricorn Link (Australia) Pty. Ltd.
P.O. Box 704, Windsor, NSW 2756, Australia

Interior design by Ashley Prine

For information about custom editions, special sales, and premium and
corporate purchases, please contact Sterling Special Sales at 800-805-5489
or specialsales@sterlingpublishing.com.

Manufactured in China

2 4 6 8 10 9 7 5 3 1

www.sterlingpublishing.com

Contents

INTRODUCTION
7

Chapter One
SELF: RIGHTS AND DISCIPLINE
10

Chapter Two
SWADESHI: SELF-SUFFICIENCY
158

Chapter Three
SWARAJ: INDEPENDENCE
208

Chapter Four
SATYAGRAHA: SOUL FORCE
282

GLOSSARY 360
INDEX 361

INTRODUCTION

*"Life is greater than all art.
I would go even further and
declare the man whose life comes
nearest to perfection is the greatest
artist; for what is art without the
sure foundation and framework
of noble life?"*

India's political and spiritual leader, Mohandas Karamchand Gandhi (1869–1948), known out of respect as Mahatma ("Great Soul"), led his country's struggle for independence and crusaded for the basic human rights of people everywhere. His methods, honed over decades of firsthand engagement in struggles around the world, were based on nonviolent resistance and civil disobedience. His teachings and writings have had a profound influence on the most important civil rights leaders of our time, including Martin Luther King Jr. and Nelson Mandela. Upon Gandhi's death, Albert Einstein proclaimed, "generations to come . . . will scarce believe that such a one as this ever in flesh and blood walked upon this earth."

A prolific writer throughout his life, Gandhi's works comprise more than ninety volumes. From his early days as a law student in England and a young lawyer in India, through his twenty-one years as an activist in South Africa (a period crucial to the development of his political views, as well as his leadership skills), and following his return to his native country, Gandhi wrote heartfelt essays, articles, and speeches outlining his most deeply held beliefs. From an early age, he seemed to understand his own power to persuade and guide others, and clearly felt a strong personal responsibility to improve the world—by both influence and example.

Over the course of his lifetime—brutally ended in 1948 by an assassin's bullet—Gandhi campaigned fervently to eliminate poverty, improve the lot of women, build bridges between religious and ethnic groups, end the scourge of untouchability, promote economic self-reliance, and—above all—win the independence of India.

Much of Gandhi's work has been published, including an autobiography and various compilations of his speeches and political works. This volume takes a new approach. Focusing on his formative years, *Pathways to Nonviolent Resistance* features examples of Gandhi's early work—the foundation upon which his lifelong philosophy was built. In addition to excerpts from his published works, it brings together previously uncollected speeches, letters, articles, and other documents drawn from the first thirty years (from roughly 1893 to 1923) of his life as an activist, reformer, and thinker. Divided into chapters devoted to his most significant concepts, the goal of the book is to shed new light on Gandhi's revolutionary ideas by tracing them back to their earliest sources and influences.

As you immerse yourself in Gandhi's thoughts, pay particular attention to the passages and ideas that have been highlighted to assist you in understanding the most significant ideas and information. At regular intervals, "For Further Thought" passages comment on the text you've just read and offer questions to provoke contemplation of a variety of topics. You'll find that Gandhi's work has much to offer today's reader—and the lined pages following these prompts provide room to record your own thoughts.

Travel back to the early life and works of Mahatma Gandhi and consider not only the influence he had during his lifetime, but also how his beliefs are still being practiced around the world today. You are sure to emerge from the experience with a deeper appreciation for the work of one of the world's greatest humanitarians.

—Laura Ross

Chapter One

SELF: RIGHTS AND DISCIPLINE

*"It is beneath human dignity
to lose one's individuality and
become a mere cog in
the machine."*

Gandhi's struggle for his nation's rights and his relentless quest for personal human salvation were inextricably entwined. Throughout his life, he wrote about both—often within the same pieces. Dominion over the self, Gandhi believed, was the place to start and the key to freedom and responsibility in the world at large.

Many of his earliest writings focus on human rights and the imperiled dignity of Indians in the West. Yes, Indians had their own customs, beliefs, and languages—which he believed were critical to preserve—but couldn't they be accepted as they were, appreciated as different in demeanor but equally human? A deeply godly man, he was tolerant of all religions and spoke out against prejudice directed toward all races.

As he matured, Gandhi developed a series of rigorous—some would say onerous—disciplines for himself and others to follow. (He strove, always, to embody the perfect example of all that he asked of others.) Among these personal strictures were vegetarianism, celibacy, periodic fasting, and abstinence from alcohol, coffee, tea—even cocoa. In this chapter, you will find his earliest commentary on these practices—as well as the roots of his core beliefs about human rights and responsibilities.

"An Unwelcome Visitor"

(*The Natal Advertiser*, May 29, 1893)

Durban, May 26, 1893

To the editor, *The Natal Advertiser*

Sir,

I was startled to read a paragraph in your today's issue referring to myself, under the heading, "An Unwelcome Visitor." I am very sorry if His Worship the Magistrate looked at me with disapproval. It is true that on entering the Court I neither removed my head-dress nor salaamed, but in so doing I had not the slightest idea that I was offending His Worship, or meaning any disrespect to the Court. Just as it is a mark of respect amongst the Europeans to take off their hats, in like manner it is in Indians to retain one's head-dress. To appear uncovered before a gentleman is not to respect him. In England, on attending drawing-room meetings and evening parties, Indians always keep the head-dress, and the English ladies and gentlemen generally seem to appreciate the regard which we show thereby. In High Courts in India those Indian advocates who have not discarded their native head-dress invariably keep it on.

As to bowing, or salaaming as you would call it, I again followed the rule observed in the Bombay High Court. If an advocate enters the Court after the judge has taken his seat on the bench he does not bow, but all the advocates rise up when the judge enters the Court, and keep standing until the judge has taken his seat. Accordingly, yesterday when His Worship entered the Court I rose up, and took my seat only after His Worship had done so.

The paragraph seems to convey also that though I was told privately not to keep my seat at the horseshoe, I nevertheless "returned to the horseshoe." The truth is that I was taken by the chief clerk to the interpreters' room, and was asked not to take my seat at the horseshoe the next time I came unless I produced my credentials. To make assurance doubly sure I asked the chief clerk if I could retain my seat for the day, and he very kindly said "yes." I was therefore really surprised to be told again in open court that in order to be entitled to the seat I had to produce credentials, etc.

Lastly, I beg His Worship's pardon if he was offended at what he considered to be my rudeness, which was the result of ignorance and quite unintentional.

I hope, in fairness, you will extend me the favor of finding the above explanation a space in your paper, as the paragraph, if unexplained, would be likely to do me harm.

I am, etc.,
M. K. Gandhi

A PLEA FOR VEGETARIANISM

(*Guide to London*, 1893–94, a never-published handbook)

As to the wines, [i]t is not necessary to quote extracts to prove that wines are injurious and that we are not required to drink wines in England. There are hundreds of societies to convince you of the fact that wines are not necessary. There are many members of Parliament who do not drink at all. In fact, there is a teetotalers party in the Commons, with which are prominently associated the names W. S. Caine and Sir Wilfred Lawson. We have temperance societies in Bombay and many parts of India. There are even Anglo-Indians who are teetotalers. In spite of all this, persons there are, enlightened by then, who believe and refuse to disbelieve, even though convinced, that wines are absolutely necessary in England. A gentleman said: "After reaching England, you may not require them, but somewhere in the Mediterranean sea, I am told you die without them." He was told, I may be allowed to tell him that if the wines were so very necessary, the P. & O. Company would provide wines together with the food for the fees they charge and not make the passengers pay separately for the wines they consume. If the wines were to be taken in England, and that regularly, 9s[hillings] would be used up simply in drinking and it would be impossible to make the two ends meet for the estimate given by me.

So, then, it is absolutely necessary to exclude wines and tobacco from the estimate and advisable to exclude tea and coffee, as the latter can be used at a sacrifice of far more substantial drink: milk.

Now we come to the question of flesh foods which, I think, must be abandoned if 9[shillings] are to be sufficient so as not to injure health. *How would the Mahommedans and Parsis do*, it may be asked in that case.

For them this guide is useless. Tarry a little. I would ask: Are there not many Mahommedans and Parsis who, on account of their poverty, get flesh foods only on rare occasions and some on none? These surely can manage without flesh foods which they get but rarely in India, not for the sake of religion or principles, but for the sake of economy. They are free to take meat whenever they can get it, e.g., in their Inn if they have gone for a Barrister's education. If it be true that one can live on vegetable foods without injuring one's health, why should not all live on a vegetable diet because it is more economical than a meat diet? That vegetarianism exists in England there are living examples to prove.

There are vegetarian societies and any quantity of vegetarian literature to testify to the existence of vegetarianism in England. There are living notable Englishmen who are vegetarians.

Lord Hannen of the H.M.'s Privy Council, better known as Sir James Hannen, the President of the late Parnell Commission, is a vegetarian.

Mr. Gotling of Bombay is a vegetarian.

John Wesley was a vegetarian. So was Howard the philanthropist and a host of others all men of light and learning. The poet Shelley was a vegetarian. It is impossible in the compass of a small book to so much as do justice to such a vast subject. I must content myself with referring the inquisitive reader to *The Perfect Way in Diet* by Dr. Anna Kingsford who says of herself:

> I cured myself of tubercular consumption by living on vegetable food.
> A doctor told me I had not six months to live. What was I to do? I was to eat raw meat and drink port wine. Well, I went into the country and ate porridge and fruit and appear today on this platform.

There is another advisable book to which the reader might be referred. It is entitled *A Plea for Vegetarianism* by H. S. Salt. Dr. Benjamin Ward Richardson, M.B., L.R.C.S., etc., himself not a vegetarian, has come to the following conclusions in his *Food for Man*.

> 1. Man, although possessing the capacity of existing on an animal diet in whole or in part, is by original cast adapted to a diet of grain and fruit and, on a scientific adaptation of his natural supplies, might easily be provided with all he can require from that source of subsistence.

> 2. The vegetable world is incomparable in its efficiency for supply of food for man when its resources are thoroughly understood and correctly applied.

3. The supplies of food for man are most economically and safely drawn direct from the vegetable world.

4. Diseases may be conveyed by both sources of supply, but need not be conveyed by either. Diseases may be generated by misuse of either source, of supply, but need not be, and under judicious management, would not be, generated by either.

5. Under a properly constituted fruit and vegetable diet, strength of mind and body may be as fully secured as under an animal or a mixed animal and vegetable system. He says also, "I admit that some of the best work has been done and is being done on a vegetarian regimen."

If so much is conceded by a thoughtful and cautious doctor not a vegetarian, the reader will easily guess how much must be claimed by vegetarians for their system. They claim that anatomically, physiologically, economically and morally vegetarianism is far superior to meat-eating.

From this it must be abundantly clear that vegetarianism is not only possible, but is really practiced by hundreds of people in England.

If, then, vegetarianism be as shown above as good as flesh-eating in other respects, I hope no man, not determined upon setting his face against vegetarianism at any cost, would hesitate to adopt it if it is cheaper than flesh-eating.

While a vegetable soup costs 3d[amidi] per plate, a meat soup costs from 9d to ⅓s and more. A mutton chop would cost at least three times as much as a vegetable chop, unless you go in for meat of the worst kind, and it must be borne in mind that there are more diseases lurking in cheap meat than in vegetables.

It would be futile for me to demonstrate an admitted fact, viz., that vegetarianism costs far less than meat-eating. If there be anyone who can contradict this, let him try to live on 9s per week and get flesh foods. I concede that, by a judicious management, it would be possible to have in that sum, if anyone thinks that he must have, not as a luxury but as a sheer medical necessity, meat once or twice a week.

Another fact is worth mentioning here. An ordinary vegetarian in England does not exclude eggs from his dietary, while an Indian vegetarian would. As a counterpart, there are vegetarians in England who do not take even milk and butter, they being animal products.

There is nowadays a tendency to do it easily, i.e., to work little and expect much. This ought to be avoided if we would not be thrown further downward. If our parents send us to England, or if we hold a scholarship, we have a sacred trust to perform. We have to account to our parents or patrons for the work we have done and for the money which [we] have spent. We ought to do unto them as we would be done by. If we were to send some one to England at our expense to become a Barrister, I suppose we would expect him to utilize every moment of his stay there and give us an account of how he passed his time. Exactly the same would be expected of us. Consciousness of this and work according to it are all that is required of us. If we do that, we shall have done our duty and will have no occasion to be sorry for having gone to England. When we go there to be Barristers, we ought to do there everything that would make of us good Barristers and not indulge in luxuries or pleasures.

I used to walk about 8 miles every day and in all I had three walks daily, one in the evening at 5:30 p.m. for an hour and the other always for 30 or 45 minutes before going to bed. I never suffered from ill health except once when I suffered from bronchitis owing to over-work and neglect of exercise. I got rid of it without having to take any medicine. The good health I enjoyed is attributable only to vegetable diet and exercise in the open air. Even the coldest weather or the densest fog did not prevent me from having my usual walks.

And under the advice of Dr. Allinson, the champion of open air, I used to keep my bedroom windows open about 4 inches in all weathers. This is not generally done by people in winter, but it seems to be very desirable. At any rate it agreed with me very well.

An Experiment in Vital Food

(*The Vegetarian*, March 24, 1894)

Before describing the experiment, if it may be called one, I would mention that I gave the vital food a trial in Bombay for a week; that I left it off only because at the time I had to entertain many friends, and because there were some other social considerations; that the vital food agreed with me very well then; and that, had I been able to continue it, very likely it would have suited me.

I give the notes as I took them while I was conducting the experiment.

> AUGUST 22ND, 1893: Began the vital food experiment. I have been having a cold for the last two days, with a slight cold in the ears too. Had two tablespoonfuls of wheat, one of peas, one of rice, two of sultanas, about twenty small nuts, two oranges, and a cup of cocoa for breakfast. The pulses and cereals were soaked overnight. I finished the meal in 45 minutes. Was very bright in the morning, depression came on in the evening, with a slight headache. For dinner had the usual things —bread, vegetables, etc.

> AUGUST 23RD: Feeling hungry, had some peas last evening. Owing to that I did not sleep well, and woke up with a bad taste in the mouth in the

morning. Had the same breakfast and dinner as yesterday. Though the day was very dull and it rained a little, I had no headache or cold. Had tea with Baker. This did not agree at all. Felt pains in the stomach.

August 24th: In the morning woke up uneasy, with a heavy stomach. Had the same breakfast, except that the one spoonful of peas was reduced to half. The usual dinner. Did not feel well. Had feeling of indigestion the whole day.

August 25th: Felt a heaviness in the stomach when I got up. During the day, too, did not feel well. Had no appetite for dinner. Still I had it. There were undercooked peas for dinner yesterday. That may have to do with the heaviness. Got headache in the latter part of the day. Took some quinine after dinner. The same breakfast as yesterday.

August 26th: Rose up with a heavy stomach. For breakfast I had half a tablespoonful of peas, half of rice, half of wheat, two and a half of sultanas, ten walnuts, and one orange. The mouth did not taste well throughout the day. Did not feel well either. Had the usual dinner. At 7 p.m. had an orange and a cup of cocoa. I feel hungry (8 p.m.), and yet no desire to eat. The vital food does not seem to agree well.

AUGUST 27TH: In the morning got up very hungry, but did not feel well. For breakfast had one-and-a-half tablespoonfuls of wheat, two of raisins, ten walnuts and an orange (mark, no peas and rice). Towards the latter part of the day felt better. The cause of yesterday's heaviness was perhaps peas and rice. At 1 p.m. had one teaspoonful of unsoaked wheat, one tablespoonful of raisins, and fourteen nuts (thus, the usual dinner was replaced by vital food). At Miss Harris's had tea (bread, butter, jam and cocoa). I enjoyed the tea very much and felt as if I was having bread and butter after a long fast. After tea felt very hungry and weak. Had, therefore, a cup of cocoa and an orange on returning home.

AUGUST 28TH: In the morning the mouth did not taste well. Had one and a half tablespoonfuls of wheat, two of raisins, twenty nuts, one orange and a cup of cocoa; except that I felt weak and hungry I felt all right. The mouth, too, was all right.

AUGUST 29TH: Woke up well in the morning. For breakfast had one-and-half tablespoonfuls of wheat, two of sultanas, one orange and twenty nuts. For dinner had three tablespoonfuls of wheat, two of currants and twenty nuts and two oranges. In the evening had rice, vermicelli and potatoes at Tyab's. Felt weak towards evening.

AUGUST 30TH: For breakfast had two tablespoonfuls of wheat, two of raisins, twenty walnuts, and one orange. For dinner had the same things with an addition of one more orange. Felt very weak. Could not take the usual walks without fatigue.

AUGUST 31ST: When I got up in the morning the mouth was very sweet. Felt very weak. Had the same quantity of food both for breakfast and dinner. Had a cup of cocoa and an orange in the evening. Felt extremely weak throughout the day. I can take the walks with much difficulty. The teeth, too, are getting weaker, the mouth too sweet.

SEPTEMBER 1ST: Got up in the morning quite tired. Had the same breakfast as yesterday, the same dinner. Feel very weak; teeth are aching. The experiment must be left off. Had tea with Baker as it was his birthday. Felt better after the tea.

September 2nd: Woke up fresh in the morning (the effect of last evening's tea). Had the old food (porridge, bread, butter, jam and cocoa). Felt ever so much better.

Thus ended the vital food experiment.

Under more favorable circumstances it might not have failed. A boarding-house, where one cannot control everything, where it is not possible to make frequent changes in the diet, is hardly a place where food experiments can be conducted successfully. Again, it will have been noticed that the only fresh fruit that I could get was oranges. No other fruits were to be had in the Transvaal then.

It is a matter of great regret that, although the Transvaal soil is very fruitful, the fruit cultivation is very much neglected. Again, I could not get any milk, which is a very dear commodity here. People generally use condensed milk in South Africa. It must, therefore, be admitted that the experiment is entirely useless to prove the value of vital food. It were sheer audacity to venture any opinion on the vital food after an eleven days' trial under adverse circumstances. To expect the stomach, used for twenty years and upwards to cooked food, to assimilate, at a stroke, uncooked food, is too much, and yet I think the experiment has its value. It should serve as a guide to others, who would embark upon such experiments, attracted to them by some of their charms, but have not the ability, or the means, or the circumstances, or the patience, or the knowledge to carry them to a successful issue. I confess I had none of the above qualifications.

Having no patience to watch the results slowly, I violently changed my diet. From the very start, the breakfast consisted of the vital food, while four or five days had hardly passed when the dinner, too, consisted of vital food. My acquaintance with the vital food theory was very superficial indeed. A little pamphlet by Mr. Hills, and one or two articles that recently appeared from his pen in *The Vegetarian* were all I knew about it. Anyone, therefore, not possessing the necessary qualifications, is, I believe, doomed to failure, and will hurt both himself and the cause he is trying to investigate into and advance.

And after all, is it worthwhile for an ordinary vegetarian to devote his attention to such pursuits—a vegetarian who enjoys good health and is satisfied with his diet? Would it not be better to leave it to the adepts who devote their lives to such researches? These remarks apply especially to those vegetarians who base their creed on the grand basis of humanitarianism—who are vegetarians because they consider it wrong, nay, even sinful, to kill animals for their food.

That the ordinary vegetarianism is possible, is conducive to health, he who runs may see. What more, then, do we want? Vital food may have its grand possibilities in store; but it will surely not make our perishable bodies immortal. That any considerable majority of human beings would ever do away with cooking does not seem feasible. The vital food will not, cannot, as such, minister to the wants of the soul. And if the highest aim, indeed, the only aim of this life, be to know the soul, then, it is humbly submitted, anything that takes away from our opportunities of knowing the soul, and therefore, also playing with the vital food and other such experiments, is playing away, to that extent, the only desirable aim in life.

If we are to eat that we may live to the glory of Him, of whom we are, then, is it not sufficient that we eat nothing that, to Nature, is repulsive, that requires the unnecessary spilling of blood? No more, however, of this while I am yet on the threshold of my studies in that direction. I simply throw out these thoughts, which were passing through the mind while I was conducting the experiment, so that some dear brother or sister may find, perchance, an echo of their own in this.

The reasons which led me to try the vital food were its extreme simplicity. That I could dispense with cooking, that I could carry about my own food wherever I went, that I should not have to put up with any uncleanness of the landlady or those who supplied me with food, that, in traveling in such countries as South Africa, the vital food would be an ideal food, were charms too irresistible for me. But what a sacrifice of time and trouble to achieve what is after all a selfish end, which falls short of the highest! Life seems too short for these things.

Vegetarianism and Children
(*The Vegetarian*, May 5, 1894)

Recently a grand convention of Keswick Christians was held in Wellington, under the presidency of Rev. Andrew Murray. I attended it in the company of some dear Christians; they have a boy six or seven years old. He came out with me for a walk one day during the time. I was simply talking to him about kindness to animals. During the talk we discussed vegetarianism. Ever since that time, I am told, the boy has not taken meat. He did watch me, before the above conversation, taking only vegetables at the dinner table, and questioned me why I would not take meat. His parents, though not themselves vegetarians, are believers in the virtue of vegetarianism, and did not mind my talking to their boy about it.

I write this to show how easily you can convince children of the grand truth, and induce them to avoid meat if their parents are not against the change. The boy and I are thick friends now. He seems to like me very much.

Another boy, about 15, I was talking to, said he could not himself kill or see a fowl killed, but did not object to eating it.

⇛ For Further Thought ⇚

At age twenty-four, Gandhi was already espousing vegetarianism and abstinence from alcohol and tobacco. Clearly, he believed in the health benefits of these prohibitions, as well as their spiritual dimension: "If we are to eat that we may live to the glory of Him, of whom we are, then, is it not sufficient that we eat nothing that, to Nature, is repulsive, that requires the unnecessary spilling of blood?" On another level, he insisted that disciplining the body could be an end in itself, making us better human beings: "There is nowadays a tendency to do it easily, i.e., to work little and expect much. This ought to be avoided if we would not be thrown further downward."

What are your feelings about disciplining the body—particularly in relation to diet and health? Do you live according to any personal dietary restrictions, and if so, what is at the heart of that decision? Take some time to reflect on the relationship between what you eat and drink, and how that affects you physically, morally, and spiritually. To what extent do you share Gandhi's views on the connection between the substances we take into our bodies and the way we live our lives?

Contempt for the Indian
(Letter to *The Times of Natal*, Durban, October 25, 1894)

To the Editor,

I would, with your permission, venture to make a few remarks on your leader, entitled "Rammysammy," in your issue of the 22nd instant.

I have no wish to defend the article in *The Times of India* noticed by you; but is not your very leader its sufficient defense?

Does not the very heading "Rammysammy" betray a studied contempt towards the poor Indian? Is not the whole article a needless insult to him? You are pleased to acknowledge that "India possesses men of high culture, etc." and yet you would not, if you could, give them equal political power with the white man. Do you not thus make the insult doubly insulting? If you had thought that the Indians were not cultured, but were barbarous brutes, and on that ground denied them political equality, there would be some excuse for your opinions. You, however, in order to enjoy the fullest pleasures derived from offering an insult to an inoffensive people, must needs show that you acknowledge them to be intelligent people and yet would keep them under foot.

Then you have said that the Indians in the Colony are not the same as those in India; but, Sir, you conveniently forget that they are the brothers or descendants of the same race whom you credit with intelligence, and have, therefore, given the opportunity, the potentiality of becoming as capable as their more fortunate brethren in India, just as a man sunk in the depth of ignorance and vice of the East End of London has the potentiality of becoming Prime Minister in free England.

You put upon the franchise petition to Lord Ripon an interpretation it was never meant to convey. The Indians do not regret that capable Natives can exercise the franchise. They would regret if it were otherwise. They, however, assert that they too, if capable, should have the right. You, in your wisdom, would not allow the Indian or the Native the precious privilege under any circumstances, because they have a dark skin. You would look to the exterior only. So long as the skin is white it would not matter to you whether it conceals beneath it poison or nectar. To you the lip-prayer of the Pharisee, because he is one, is more acceptable than the sincere repentance of the publican, and this, I presume, you would call Christianity. You may; it is not Christ's.

And in spite of such opinions held by you, a respectable newspaper in the Colony, you impute falsehood to *The Times of India*.

It is one thing to formulate a charge, it is another to prove it. You end with saying that "Rammysammy" may have every right a citizen can desire, with one exception, viz., "political power."

Are the heading of your leader and its tenor consistent with the above opinion? Or is it un-Christian, un-English to be consistent? "Suffer little children to come unto me," said the Master. His disciples(?) in the Colony would improve upon the saying by inserting "white" after "little." During the children's fete, organized by the Mayor of Durban, I am told there was not a single colored child to be seen in the procession. Was this a punishment for the sin of being born of colored parents? Is this an incident of the qualified citizenship you would accord to the hated "Rammysammy."

If He came among us, will he not say to many of us, "I know you not"? Sir, may I venture to offer a suggestion? Will you reread your New Testament? Will you ponder over your attitude towards the colored population of the Colony? Will you then say you can reconcile it with the Bible teaching or the best British traditions? If you have washed your hands clean of both Christ and British traditions, I can have nothing to say; I gladly withdraw what I have written. Only it will then be a sad day for Britain and for India if you have many followers.

Yours, etc.,
M. K. Gandhi

"Whence come we? What are we? Whither go we?"

(Letter to *The Natal Mercury*, December 3, 1894)

Durban

To the Editor,

You will greatly oblige me by allowing me to draw the attention of your readers to an advertisement that appears in your advertisement columns with regard to the Esoteric Christian Union. The system of thought expounded by the books advertised is not, by any means, a new system but a recovery of the old, presented in a form acceptable to the modern mind. It is, moreover, a system of religion which teaches universality, and is based on eternal verities and not on phenomena or historical facts merely. In that system, there is no reviling Mahomed or Buddha in order to prove the superiority of Jesus. On the other hand, it reconciles the other religions with Christianity which, in the opinion of the authors, is nothing but one mode (among many) of presentation of the same eternal truth. The many puzzles of the Old Testament find herein a solution at once complete and satisfactory.

If there is anyone of your readers who has found the present day materialism and all its splendor to be insufficient for the needs of his soul, if he has a craving for a better life, and if, under the dazzling and bright surface of modern civilization, he finds that there is much that is contrary to what one would expect under such a surface, and above all, if the modern luxuries and the ceaseless feverish activity afford no relief, to such a one I beg to recommend the books referred to. And I promise that, after a perusal, he will find himself a better man, even though he may not thoroughly identify himself with the teaching.

If there is anyone who would like to have a chat on the subject, it would afford me the greatest pleasure to have a quiet interchange of views. In such a case, I would thank any such gentleman to correspond with me personally. I need hardly mention that the sale of the books is not a pecuniary concern. Could Mr. Maitland, the President of the Union, or its agent here, afford to give them away, they would gladly do so. In many cases, the books have been sold at less than cost price. In a few, they have even been given away. A systematic distribution for nothing has been found impossible. The books will be gladly lent in some cases.

I would try to conclude with a quotation from a letter of the late Abbe Constant to the authors: "Humanity has always and everywhere asked itself these three supreme questions: Whence come we? What are we? Whither go we? Now these questions at length find an answer complete, satisfactory, and consolatory in *The Perfect Way*."

I am, etc.,
M. K. Gandhi

"What the best men do the multitude will follow"

(Pamphlet circulated among Europeans in Natal, December 19, 1894)

Durban

To
The Hon. Members Of
The Hon. The Legislative Council And
The Hon. The Legislative Assembly

Sirs,

Were it possible to write to you anonymously, nothing would have been more pleasing to me. But the statements I shall have to make in this letter will be so grave and important that it would be considered a sheer act of cowardice not to disclose my name. I beg, however, to assure you that I write not from selfish motives, nor yet from those of self-aggrandizement or of seeking notoriety.

The one and only object is to serve India, which is by accident of birth called my native country, and to bring about better understanding between the European section of the community and the Indian in this Colony.

The only way this can be done is to appeal to those who represent and, at the same time, mold public opinion.

Hence, if the Europeans and the Indians live in a perpetual

state of quarrel, the blame would lie on your shoulders. If both can walk together and live together quietly and without friction, you will receive all the credit.

It needs no proof that masses throughout the world follow, to a very great extent, the opinions of the leaders. Gladstone's opinions are the opinions of half England, and Salisbury's are those of the other half. Burns thought for the strikers during the dock laborers' strike.

Parnell thought for almost the whole of Ireland. The scriptures—I mean all the scriptures of the world—say so. Says *The Song Celestial* by Edwin Arnold: "What the wise choose the unwise people take; what the best men do the multitude will follow."

This letter, therefore, needs no apology. It would hardly be called impertinent.

For, to whom else could such an appeal be more aptly made, or by whom else should it be considered more seriously than you?

To carry on an agitation in England is but a poor relief when it can only create a greater friction between the two peoples in the Colony. The relief, at best, could only be temporary. Unless the Europeans in the Colony can be induced to accord the Indians a better treatment, the Indians have a very bad time before them under the aegis of the Responsible Government, in spite of vigilance of the Home Government.

Without entering into details, I would deal with the Indian question as a whole.

I suppose there can be no doubt that the Indian is a despised being in the Colony, and that every opposition to him proceeds directly from that hatred.

If that hatred is simply based upon his color, then, of course, he has no hope. The sooner he leaves the Colony the better. No matter what he does, he will never have the white skin. If, however, it is based upon something else, if it is based upon an ignorance of his general character and attainments, he may hope to receive his due at the hands of the Europeans in the Colony.

The question what use the Colony will make of the 40,000 Indians is, I submit, worthy of the most serious consideration by the Colonists, and especially those who have the reins of Government in their hands, who have been entrusted by the people with legislative powers. To root out the 40,000 Indians from the Colony seems, without doubt, an impossible task. Most of them have settled here with their families. No legislation that could be permissible in a British Colony would enable the legislators to drive these men out. It may be possible to devise a scheme to effectively check any further Indian immigration. But apart from that, the question suggested by me is, I submit, sufficiently serious to warrant my encroaching upon your attention and requesting you to pursue this letter without any bias.

It is for you to say whether you will lower them or raise them in the scale of civilization, whether you will bring them down to a level lower than what they should occupy on account of heredity, whether you will alienate their hearts from you, or whether you will draw them closer to you—whether, in short, you would govern them despotically or sympathetically.

You can educate public opinion in such a way that the hatred will be increased day by day; and you can, if you chose so to do, educate it in such a way that the hatred would begin to subside.

I now propose to discuss the question under the following heads:

1. Are the Indians desirable as citizens in the Colony?

2. What are they?

3. Is their present treatment in accordance with the best British traditions, or with the principles of justice and morality, or with the principles of Christianity?

4. From a purely material and selfish point of view, will an abrupt or gradual withdrawal of them from the Colony result in substantial, lasting benefit to the Colony?

I

In discussing the first question, I will deal, first of all, with the Indians employed as laborers, most of whom have come to the Colony under indenture.

It seems to have been acknowledged by those who are supposed to know, that the indentured Indians are indispensable for the welfare of the Colony; whether as menials or waiters, whether as railway servants or gardeners, they are a useful addition to the Colony. The work that a Native cannot or would not do is cheerfully and well done by the indentured Indian. It would seem that the Indian has helped to make this the Garden Colony of South Africa. Withdraw the Indian from the sugar estate, and where would the main industry of the Colony be? Nor can it be said that the work can be done by the Native in the near future. The South African Republic is an instance in point.

In spite of its so-called vigorous Native policy, it remains practically a desert of dust, although the soil is very fruitful. The problem how to secure cheap labor for the mines there has been daily growing serious. The only garden worthy of the name is that on the Nelmapius Estate, and does it not owe its success entirely to the Indian labor?

II

The second head of the enquiry is the most important, viz., what are they, and I request you to peruse it carefully. My purpose in writing on this subject will have been served if only it stimulates a study of India and its people; for, I thoroughly believe that one half, or even three-fourths, of the hardships entailed upon the Indians in South Africa result from want of information about India.

No one can be more conscious than myself of whom I am addressing this letter to. Some Honorable Members may resent this portion of my letter as an insult. To such I say with the greatest deference: "I am aware that you know a great deal about India. But is it not a cruel fact that the Colony is not the better for your knowledge? Certainly the Indians are not, unless the knowledge acquired by you is entirely different from and opposed to that acquired by others who have worked in the same field. Again, although this humble effort is directly addressed to you, it is supposed to reach many others, in fact all who have an interest in the future of the Colony with its present inhabitants."

In spite of the Premier's opinion to the contrary, as expressed in his speech at the second reading of the Franchise Bill, with the utmost deference to His Honor, I venture to point out that both the English and the Indians spring from a common stock, called the Indo-Aryan.

I would not be able, in support of the above, to give extracts from many authors, as the books of reference at my disposal are unfortunately very few. I, however, quote as follows from Sir W. W. Hunter's *Indian Empire*:

This nobler race (meaning the early Aryans) belonged to the Aryan or Indo-Germanic stock, from which the Brahman, the Rajput, and the Englishman alike descend. Its earliest home visible to history was in Central Asia. From that common camping ground certain branches of the race started for the East, others for the West. One of the Western offshoots founded the Persian Kingdom; another built Athens and Lacedaemon, and became the Hellenic nation; a third went on to Italy and reared the city on the seven hills, which grew into Imperial Rome. A distant colony of the same race excavated the silver ores of prehistoric Spain; and when we first catch a sight of ancient England, we see an Aryan settlement, fishing in wattle canoes and working the tin mines of Cornwall. The forefathers of the Greek and the Roman, of the Englishman and the Hindoo, dwelt together in Asia, spoke the same tongue and worshipped the same gods. The ancient religions of Europe and India had a similar origin.

Thus, it will be seen that the learned historian, who must be supposed to have consulted all the authorities, without a shadow of doubt makes the above unqualified assertion. If then I err, I err in good company. And the belief, whether mistaken or well-founded, serves as the basis of operations of those who are trying to unify the hearts of the two races, which are, legally and outwardly, bound together under a common flag.

A general belief seems to prevail in the Colony that the Indians are little better, if at all, than savages or the Natives of Africa. Even the children are taught to believe in that manner, with the result that the Indian is being dragged down to the position of a raw Kaffir.

Such a state of things, which the Christian legislators of the Colony would not, I firmly believe, wittingly allow to exist and remain, must be my excuse for the following copious extracts, which will show at once that the Indians were, and are, in no way inferior to their Anglo-Saxon brethren, if I may venture to use the word, in the various departments of life—industrial, intellectual, political, etc.

As to Indian philosophy and religion, the learned author of the *Indian Empire* thus sums up:

> The Brahmin solutions to the problems of practical religion were self-discipline, alms, sacrifice to and contemplation of the Deity. But, besides the practical questions of the spiritual life, religion has also intellectual problems, such as the compatibility of evil with the goodness of God, and the unequal distribution of happiness and misery in this life. Brahmin philosophy has exhausted the possible solutions of these difficulties, and of most of the other

great problems which have since perplexed the Greek and Roman sage, mediaeval schoolman and modern man of science. The various hypotheses of creation, arrangement and development were each elaborated and the views of physiologists at the present day are a return with new lights to the evolution theory of Kapila. The works on religion published in the native language in India in 1877 numbered 1192, besides 56 on mental and moral philosophy. In 1882 the total had risen to 1545 on religion and 153 on mental and moral philosophy.

Max Müller says with regard to Indian philosophy (the following, and a few more that will follow, have been partly or wholly quoted in the Franchise petition):

If I were asked under what sky the human mind has most fully developed some of its choicest gifts, has most deeply pondered on the greatest problems of life, and has found solutions of some of them which well deserve the attention even of those who have studied Plato and Kant—I should point to India; and if I were to ask myself from what literature we have here in Europe, we who have been nurtured almost exclusively on the thoughts of Greeks and Romans, and of one Semitic race, the Jewish, may draw that corrective which is most wanted in order to make our inner life more perfect, more comprehensive, more universal, in fact, more truly human—a life not for this life only, but a transfigured and eternal life—again I should point to India.

The German philosopher, Schopenhauer, thus adds his testimony to the grandeur of Indian philosophy as contained in the Upanishads:

> From every sentence deep, original and sublime thoughts arise, and the whole is pervaded by a high and holy and earnest spirit. Indian air surrounds us, and original thoughts of kindred spirits. . . . In the whole world there is no study, except that of the originals, so beneficial and so elevating as that of the Oupnek'hat1. It has been the solace of my life; it will be the solace of my death.

Coming to science, Sir William says:

> The science of language, indeed, had been reduced in India to fundamental principles at a time when the grammarians of the West still treated it on the basis of accidental resemblances, and modern philosophy dates from the study of Sanskrit by European

scholars. . . . The grammar of Panini stands supreme among the grammars of the world. . . . It arranges in logical harmony the whole phenomena which the Sanskrit language presents, and stands forth as one of the most splendid achievements of human invention and industry.

Speaking on the same department of science, Sir H. S. Maine, in his Rede lecture, published in the latest edition of the *Village-Communities*, says:

India has given to the world Comparative Philosophy and Comparative Mythology; it may yet give us a new science not less valuable than the sciences of language and of folklore. I hesitate to call it Comparative Jurisprudence because, if it ever exists, its area will be so much wider than the field of law. For India not only contains (or to speak more accurately, did contain) an Aryan language older than any other descendant of the common mother tongue, and a variety of names of natural objects less perfectly crystallized than elsewhere into fabulous personages, but it includes a whole world of Aryan institutions, Aryan customs, Aryan laws Aryan ideas, Aryan, beliefs, in a far earlier stage of growth and development than any which survive beyond its borders.

Of Indian astronomy the same historian says:

> The astronomy of the Brahmins has formed alter-
> nately the subject of excessive admiration and of mis-
> placed contempt. . . . In certain points the Brahmins
> advanced beyond Greek astronomy. Their fame
> spread throughout the West, and found entrance
> into the Chronicon Paschale. In the 8th and 9th
> centuries the Arabs became their disciples.

I again quote Sir William:

> In algebra and arithmetic the Brahmins attained a
> high degree of proficiency independent of Western
> aid. To them we owe the invention of the numerical
> symbols on the decimal system. . . .

> The Arabs borrowed these figures from the Hindus,
> and transmitted them to Europe. . . . The works on
> mathematics and mechanical science, published in
> the native languages in India in 1867, numbered 89,
> and in 1882, 166.

> The medical science of the Brahmins (continues the
> eminent historian) was also an independent develop-
> ment. . . . The specific diseases whose names occur in

Panini's grammar indicate that medical studies had made progress before his time (350 B.C.). . . . Arabic medicine was founded on the translations from the Sanskrit treatises. . . . European medicine down to the 17th century was based upon the Arabic. . . . . The number of medical works published in the native languages of India in 1877 amounted to 130, and in 1882 to 212, besides 87 on natural science.

Writing of the art of war, the writer proceeds:

The Brahmins regarded not only medicine but also the arts of war, music, and architecture as supplementary parts of their divinely inspired knowledge. . . . The Sanskrit epics prove that strategy had attained to the position of a recognized science before the birth of Christ, and the later Agni Purana devotes long sections to its systematic treatment.

On architecture the same author says:

The Buddhists were the great stone-builders of India. Their monasteries and shrines exhibit the history of the art during twenty-two centuries, from the earliest cave structures of the rock temples to the latest Jain erections dazzling in stucco, over-crowded with ornament. It seems not improbable that the churches of Europe owe their steeples to the Buddhist topes. . . . Hindu art has left memorials which extort the admiration and astonishment of our age.

The Hindu palace architecture of Gwalior, the Indian Mahommedan mosques, the mausoleums of Agra and Delhi, with several of the older Hindu temples of Southern India, stand unrivalled for grace of outline and elaborate wealth of ornament.

English decorative art in our day has borrowed largely from Indian forms and patterns. . . . Indian artworks, when faithful to native designs, still obtain the highest honors at the international exhibitions of Europe.

Here is what Andrew Carnegie in his *Round the World* says about the Taj of Agra:

There are some subjects too sacred for analysis, or even for words. And I now know that there is a human structure so exquisitely fine or unearthly, as to lift it into this holy domain. . . . The Taj is built of a light creamy marble, so that it does not chill one as pure cold white marble does. It is warm and sympathetic as a woman. . . . One great critic has freely called the Taj a feminine structure. There is nothing masculine about it, says he; its charms are all feminine. This creamy marble is inlaid with fine black marble lines, the entire Koran, in Arabic letters, it is said, being thus interwoven. . . Till the day I die, amid mountain streams or moonlight strolls in the forest, wherever and whenever the moon comes, when all that is most sacred, most elevated and most pure recur to shed their radiance upon the tranquil mind, there will be found among my treasures the memory of that lovely charm—the Taj.

Nor has India been without its laws, codified or otherwise. The Institutes of Manu have always been noted for their justice and precision. So much does Sir H. S. Maine seem to have been struck with their equity that he calls them "an ideal picture of that which, in the view of the Brahmins, ought to be the law." Mr. Pincott, writing in 1891 in *The National Review*, alludes to them as "the philosophical precepts of Manu."

Nor have the Indians been deficient in the dramatic art. Goethe thus speaks of *Shakuntala*, the most famous Indian drama:

Wouldst thou the young year's blossoms, and the fruits of its decline,

And all by which the soul is charmed, enraptured,
  feasted, fed.
Wouldst thou the earth, and heaven itself in one sole
  name combine?
I name thee, O Shakuntala! and all at once is said.

Coming to the Indian character and social life, the evidence is voluminous. I can only give meager extracts. I take the following again from Hunter's *Indian Empire:*

> The Greek ambassador (Megasthenes) observed with admiration the absence of slavery in India, and the chastity of the women and the courage of the men. In valor they excelled all other Asiatics; they required no locks to their doors; above all, no Indian was ever known to tell a lie. Sober and industrious, good farmers and skilful artisans, they scarcely ever had recourse to a lawsuit, and lived peaceably under their native chiefs. The kingly government is portrayed almost as described in Manu, with its hereditary castes of councillors and soldiers. . . . The village system is well described, each little rural unit seeming to the Greek an independent republic.

Bishop Heber says of the people of India:

> So far as their natural character is concerned, I have been led to form on the whole a very favorable opinion. They are men of high and gallant courage, courteous, intelligent, and most eager after knowledge and improvement. . . . They are sober, industrious, dutiful to their parents, and affectionate to their children; of tempers almost uniformly gentle and patient, and more easily affected by kindness and attention to their wants and feelings than almost any men whom I have met with.

Sir Thomas Munro, sometime Governor of Madras, says:

> I do not exactly know what is meant by civilizing the people of India. In the theory and practice of good government they may be deficient, but if a good system of agriculture, if unrivalled manufacturers, if a capacity to produce what convenience and luxury demand, if the establishment of schools for reading and writing, if the general practice of kindness and hospitality, and, above all, if a scrupulous respect and delicacy towards the female sex, are amongst the points that denote a civilized people, then the Hindus are not inferior in civilization to the people of Europe.

Sir George Birdwood gives the following opinion on the general character of the Indians:

> They are long-suffering and patient, hardy and enduring, frugal and industrious, law-abiding and peace-seeking. . . . The educated and higher mercantile classes are honest and truthful, and loyal and trustful towards the British Government, in the most absolute sense that I can use, and you understand the words. Moral truthfulness is as marked a characteristic of the Settia (upper) class of Bombay as of the Teutonic race itself. The people of India, in short, are in no intrinsic sense our inferiors, while in things measured by some of the false standards—false to ourselves—we pretend to believe in, they are our superiors.

Sri C. Trevelyan remarks that:

> They have very considerable administrative qualities, great patience, industry, and great acuteness and intelligence.

Of the family relations, thus speaks Sir W. W. Hunter:

> There is simply no comparison between Englishmen and Hindus with respect to the place occupied

by family interests and family affections in their minds. The love of parents for children and of children for parents has scarcely any counterpart in England. Parental and filial affection occupies among our Eastern fellow-citizens the place which is taken in this country by the passion between the sexes.

And Mr. Pincott thinks that:

In all social matters the English are far more fitted to sit at the feet of Hindus and learn as disciples than to attempt to become masters.

Says M. Louis Jacolliot:

Soil of ancient India, cradle of humanity, hail! Hail, venerable and efficient nurse, whom centuries of brutal invasions have not yet buried under the dust of oblivion. Hail, fatherland of faith, of love, of poetry, and of science! May we hail a revival of thy past in our Western future!

Says Victor Hugo:

These nations have made Europe, France and

Germany. Germany is for the Occident that which India is for the Orient.

Add to this the facts that India has produced a Buddha, whose life some consider the best and the holiest lived by a mortal, and some to be second only to that lived by Jesus; that India has produced an Akbar, whose policy the British Government have followed with but few modifications; that India lost, only a few years ago, a Parsee Baronet who astonished not India only, but England also, by his munificent charities; that India has produced Christodas Paul, a journalist, whom Lord Elgin, the present Viceroy, compared with the best European journalists; that India has produced Justices Mahomed and Muthukrishna Aiyer, both Judges of High Courts in India, whose judgments have been pronounced to be the ablest delivered by the judges, both European and Indian, who adorn the Indian Bench; and, lastly, India has in Baddruddin, Banerji, and Mehta, orators who have on many an occasion held English audiences spellbound.

Such is India. If the picture appears to you to be somewhat overdrawn or fanciful, it is nonetheless faithful. There is the other side. Let him who takes delight in separating, rather than in uniting, the two nations give the other side. Then, please, examine both with the impartiality of a Daniel, and I promise that there will yet remain a considerable portion of what has been said above untouched, to induce you to believe that India is not Africa, and that it is a civilized country in the truest sense of the term civilization.

Before, however, I can quit this subject, I have to crave leave to be allowed to anticipate a possible objection. It will be said: "If what you say is true, the people whom you call Indians in the Colony are not Indians, because your remarks are not borne out by the practices prevailing among the people whom you call Indians. See how grossly untruthful they are." Everyone I have met with in the Colony has dwelt upon the untruthfulness of the Indians. To a limited extent I admit the charge. It will be very small satisfaction for me to show, in reply to the objection, that other classes do not fare much better in this respect, especially if and when they are placed in the position of the unfortunate Indians. And yet, I am afraid, I shall have to fall back upon argument of that sort. Much as I would wish them to be otherwise, I confess my utter inability to prove that they are more than human. They come to Natal on starvation wages (I mean here the indentured Indians).

They find themselves placed in a strange position and amid uncongenial surroundings. The moment they leave India they remain throughout life, if they settle in the Colony, without any moral education. Whether they are Hindus or Mahommedans, they are absolutely without any moral or religious instruction worthy of the name. They have not learned enough to educate themselves without any outside help. Placed thus, they are apt to yield to the slightest temptation to tell a lie. After some time, lying with them becomes a habit and a disease. They would lie without any reason, without any prospect of bettering themselves materially, indeed, without knowing what they are doing. They reach a stage in life when their moral faculties have completely collapsed owing to neglect. There is also a very sad form of lying. They cannot dare tell the truth, even for their wantonly ill-treated brother, for fear of receiving ill-treatment from their master. They are not philosophic enough to look with equanimity on the threatened reduction in their miserable rations and serve corporal punishment, did they dare to give evidence against their master. Are these men, then, more to be despised than pitied? Are they to be treated as scoundrels, deserving no mercy, or are they to be treated as helpless creatures, badly in need of sympathy? Is there any class of people who would not do as they are doing under similar circumstances?

But I will be asked what I can have to say in defense of the traders, who, too, are equally good liars. As to this, I beg to submit that the charge against them is without foundation, and that they do not lie more than the other classes do for the purposes of trade or law. They are very much misunderstood; in the first place, because they cannot speak the English language, and secondly, because the interpretation is very defective, through no fault of the interpreters. The interpreters are expected to perform the Herculean task of interpreting successfully in four languages, viz., Tamil, Telugu, Hindustani and Gujarati. The trading Indian invariably speaks Hindustani or Gujarati.

Those who speak Hindustani only, speak high Hindustani. The interpreters, with one exception, speak the local Hindustani, which is a grotesque mixture of Tamil, Gujarati and other Indian languages, clothed in extremely bad Hindustani grammar. Very naturally, the interpreter has to argue with the witness before he can get at his meaning. While the process is going on, the judge grows impatient, and thinks that the witness is prevaricating. The poor interpreter, if questioned, true to human nature, in order to conceal his defective knowledge of the language, says the witness does not give straight answers. The poor witness has no opportunity of setting himself right.

In the case of the Gujarati speakers the matter is still more serious.

There is not a single Gujarati interpreter in the Courts. The interpreter, after great difficulty, manages to get at the sense only of what the witness is speaking. I have myself seen a Gujarati-speaking witness struggling to make himself understood, and the interpreter struggling to understand the Gujarati-Hindustani. Indeed, it speaks volumes for the acuteness of the interpreters in extracting even the sense from a forest of strange words, but all the while the struggle is going on, the Judge makes up his mind not to believe a word of what the witness says, and puts him down for a liar.

III

In order to answer the third question, "Is their present treatment in accordance with the best British traditions, or with the principles of justice and morality, or with the principles of Christianity?" it will be necessary to enquire what their treatment is. I think it will be readily granted that the Indian is bitterly hated in the Colony. The man in the street hates him, curses him, spits upon him, and often pushes him off the footpath. The Press cannot find a sufficiently strong word in the best English dictionary to damn him with. Here are a few samples:

> "The real canker that is eating into the very vitals of the community"; "these parasites"; "Wily, wretched, semi-barbarous Asiatics"; "a thing black and lean and a long way from clean, which they call the accursed Hindoo"; "he is chock-full of vice, and he lives upon rice. . . . I heartily cuss the Hindoo"; "squalid coolies with truthless tongues and artful ways." The Press almost unanimously refuses to call the Indian by his proper name. He is "Ramsamy"; he is "Mr. Sammy"; he is "Mr. Coolie"; he is "he black man."

And these offensive epithets have become so common that they (at any rate one of them, "coolie) are used even in the sacred precincts of the Courts, as if "the coolie" were the legal and proper name to give to any and every Indian. The public men, too, seem to use the word freely. I have often heard the painful expression "coolie clerk" from the mouths of men who ought to know better. The expression is a contradiction in terms and is extremely offensive to those to whom it is applied. But then, in this Colony the Indian is a creature without feelings!

The tramcars are not for the Indians. The railway officials may treat the Indians as beasts. No matter how clean, his very sight is such an offense to every white man in the Colony that he would object to sit, even for a short time, in the same compartment with the Indian.

The hotels shut their doors against them. I know instances of respectable Indians having been denied a night's lodging in an hotel.

Even the public baths are not for the Indians, no matter who they are.

If I am to depend upon one-tenth of the reports that I have received with regard to the treatment of the indentured Indians on the various estates, it would form a terrible indictment against the humanity of the masters on the estates and the care taken by the Protector of Indian immigrants. This, however, is a subject which my extremely limited experience of it precludes me from making further remarks upon.

The Vagrant Law is needlessly oppressive, and often puts respectable Indians in a very awkward position.

Add to this the rumors that are rife in the air, to the effect that they should be made, or induced, to live in Locations. It may be merely an intention; nonetheless, it is an index of the feeling of the

European Colonists against the Indians. I beseech you to picture to yourself the state the Indian would be in Natal if it were possible to carry out all such intentions.

Now, is this treatment in consonance with the British traditions of justice, or morality, or Christianity?

I would, with your permission, quote an extract from Macaulay, and leave it to you to answer the question as to whether the present treatment would have met with his approval. Speaking on the subject of the treatment of the Indians, he expressed the following sentiments:

> We shall never consent to administer the pousta to a whole community, to stupefy and paralyze a great people whom God has committed to our charge, for the wretched purpose of rendering them more amenable to our control. What is that power worth which is founded on vice, on ignorance, and on misery, which we can hold by violating the most sacred duties which as governors we owe to the governed, which as a people blessed with far more than an ordinary measure of political liberty and of intellectual light we owe to a race debased by three thousand years of despotism and priestcraft? We are free, we are civilized, to little purpose, if we grudge to any portion of the human race an equal measure of freedom and civilization.

I have but to refer you to writers like Mill, Burke, Bright, and Fawcett, to further show that they, at any rate, would not give countenance to the treatment accorded to the Indians in the Colony.

To bring a man here on starvation wages, to hold him under bondage, and when he shows the least signs of liberty, or, is in a position to live less miserably, to wish to send him back to his home where he would become comparatively a stranger and perhaps unable to earn a living, is hardly a mark of fair play or justice characteristic of the British nation.

That the treatment of the Indians is contrary to the teaching of Christianity needs hardly any argument. The Man, who taught us to love our enemies and to give our clock to the one who wanted the coat, and to hold out the right cheek when the left was smitten, and who swept away the distinction between the Jew and the Gentile, would never brook a disposition that causes a man to be so proud of himself as to consider himself polluted even by the touch of a fellow-being.

IV

The last head of the enquiry has, I believe, been sufficiently discussed in discussing the first. And I for one would not be much grieved in an experiment were tried to drive out each and every Indian from the Colony. In that case, I have not the slightest doubt that the Colonists would soon rue the day when they took the step and would wish they had not done it. The petty trades and the petty avocations of life would be left alone. The work for which they are specially suited would not be taken up by the Europeans, and the Colony would lose an immense amount of revenue now derived from the Indians. The climate of South Africa is not such as would enable the Europeans to do the work that they can easily do in Europe. What, however, I do submit with the greatest deference is this, that if the Indians must be kept in the Colony, then let them receive such treatment as by their ability and integrity they may be fit to receive, that is to say, give them what is their due, and what is the least that a sense of justice, unalloyed by partiality or prejudice, should prompt you to give them.

It now remains for me only to implore you to give this matter your earnest consideration, and to remind you (here I mean especially the English) that Providence has put the English and the Indians together, and has placed in the hands of the former the destinies of the latter, and it will largely depend upon what every Englishman does with respect to the Indian and how he treats him, whether the putting together will result in an ever lasting union brought about by broad sympathy, love, free mutual intercourse, and also a right knowledge of the Indian character, or whether the putting together will simply last so long as the English have sufficient resources to keep the Indians under check, and the naturally mild Indians have not been vexed into active opposition to the foreign yoke. I have, further, to remind you that the English in England have shown by their writings, speeches and deeds that they mean to unify the hearts of the two peoples, that they do not believe in color distinctions, and that they will raise India with them rather than rise upon its ruins. In support of this I beg to refer you to Bright, Fawcett, Bradlaugh, Gladstone, Wedderburn, Pincott, Ripon, Reay, Northbrooke, Dufferin, and a host of other eminent Englishmen who represent public opinion. The very fact of an English constituency returning an Indian to the British House of Commons, in spite of the expressed wish to the contrary of the then Prime Minister, and almost the whole British Press, both Conservative and Liberal, congratulating the Indian member on the success, and expressing its approval of the unique event, and the whole House again, both Conservative and Liberal, according him a warm welcome—this fact alone, I submit, supports my statement. Will you, then, follow them, or will you strike out a new path? Will you promote unity, "which is the condition of progress," or will you promote discord, "which is the condition of degradation"?

In conclusion, I beg of you to receive the above in the same spirit in which it has been written.

I have the honor to remain,
Your obedient servant,
M. K. Gandhi

⇢ For Further Thought ⇠

"I thoroughly believe that one half, or even three-fourths, of the hardships entailed upon the Indians in South Africa result from want of information about India," Gandhi wrote in a widely circulated 1894 pamphlet addressed to the legislative bodies of that country. Rather than railing against the injustices suffered by his people there, he patiently outlined the many services Indians performed within South Africa, as well as the myriad contributions of Indians throughout history to art, literature, government, science, and more (even producing testimonials of well-known Western figures as to the beauty and importance of the Indian nation and its people).

Even before he had formulated his concept of nonviolent resistance, Gandhi was quietly attempting to create change peacefully—through reason and education rather than a call to arms.

As you read through his simple yet heartfelt arguments on behalf of his people, think about the racial, religious, and/or national prejudices you have witnessed or experienced in your own life. Have you been the victim of prejudice based on your background or beliefs? Have you found yourself making judgments of others based on these things? How have you dealt with this? What do you think is the best way to rise above it?

_____

_____

_____

_____

_____

_____

_____

_____

_____

_____

_____

_____

INDIANS AND COMPETITION

(Interview in *The Englishman*, November 14, 1896)

There has always been a dislike of the Indian from the first days of their migration to Africa, but it was only when our people began to trade that the antipathy became marked and took shape in the imposition of disabilities.

Q. Then all these grievances you speak of are the outcome of commercial jealousy and prompted by self-interest?
A. Precisely. That is just the root of the whole matter. The Colonists want us cleared out because they do not like our traders competing with them.

Q. Is the competition a legitimate one? I mean, is it entered into and conducted on a fair and open basis?
A. The competition is an open one and conducted by the Indians in a perfectly fair and legitimate manner. Perhaps a word or two as to the general system of trading may make matters clear. The bulk of Indians engaged in trafficking are those who get their goods from the large European wholesale houses, and then go about the country hawking them. Why, I may say that the Colony of Natal, of which I speak particularly from knowledge and experience, is practically dependent for its supplies on these traveling traders. As you know, shops are scarce in those parts, at least away from the towns, and the Indian gets an honest livelihood by supplying the deficiency. It is

said that the petty European trader has been displaced. This is true to a certain extent; but then it has been the fault of the European trader. He has been content to stop in his shop, and customers have been compelled to come to him. It is not to be wondered at, therefore, that when the Indian, at no small trouble, takes the goods to the customers, he readily finds a sale. Moreover, the European trader, no matter in however small a way, will not hawk his goods about. Perhaps the strongest proof of the trading capabilities of the Indian and, generally speaking, of his integrity, is to be found in the fact that the great houses will give him credit, and, in fact, many of them do the bulk of their trade through his agency. It is no secret that the opposition to the Indian in Natal is but partial, and by no means represents the real feelings of a good portion of the European community.

Q. What, briefly, are the legal and other disabilities placed upon the Indian residents in Natal?
A. Well, first there is the 'curfew' law which prohibits all 'colored' persons being out after 9 o'clock at night without a permit from their master, if indentured servants, or unless they can give a good account of themselves. The great cause of complaint on this score is that this law may be used by the police as an engine of oppression. Respectable, well-dressed, educated Indians are sometimes subjected to the humiliation of arrest by a policeman, being marched to the lock-up, incarcerated for the night, brought before the magistrate next morning and dismissed without a word of apology when their

bona fides have been established. Such occurrences are by no means rare. Then there is the deprivation of the franchise, which was brought out in the article you published. The fact is the Colonists do not want the Indian to form part of the South African nation—hence the taking away from him of franchise rights. As a menial he can be tolerated, as a citizen never.

Q. What has been the attitude of the Indians on this question of the exercise of political rights in an alien country?

A. Simply that of the person who claims to enjoy the same rights and privileges in a country as those who are not native to the country freely enjoy. Politically speaking, the Indian does not want the vote; it is only because he resents the indignity of being dispossessed of it that he is agitating for its restitution. Moreover, the classifying of all Indians in one category and the non-recognition of the just place of the better class is felt to be a great injustice. We have even proposed the raising of the property qualifications and the introduction of the education test, which would surely give the hallmark of fitness to every Indian voter, but this has been contemptuously rejected, proving that the sole object is that of discrediting the Indian and depriving him of all political power, so that he will be forever helpless. Then there is the crippling imposition of the £3 poll tax per annum on all who remain in the country after fulfilling their indenture. Again, the Indian has no social status; in fact, he is regarded as a social leper—a pariah. Indignities of all kinds are heaped upon him. No matter what his station may be, an Indian throughout South Africa is a coolie, and as such he is treated. On the railway he is restricted to a certain class, and, although in Natal he is permitted to walk on the foot-path, this is refused to him in other States.

Q. Will you tell me something about the treatment of Indians in these States?
A. In Zululand no Indians can buy landed property in the townships of Nondweni and Eshowe.

Q. Why was the prohibition imposed?
A. Well, in the township of Melmoth, which was the first established in Zululand, there were no regulations and the Natal Indians availed themselves of the right to buy landed property, which they did to the extent of over £2,000 worth. Then the prohibition was passed and made to apply to townships subsequently founded. It was purely trade jealousy, the fear being that the Indians would enter Zululand for trade purposes as they had done in Natal.

In the Orange River Free State, the purchase of any property by an Indian has been made impossible by simply classifying him with the Kaffir. It is not permitted him to hold immovable property, and every Indian settler in the State has to pay an annual tax of ten shillings. The injustice of these arbitrary laws may be gauged from the fact that when they were promulgated the Indians, mostly traders, were compelled to leave the State without the slightest compensation, causing losses to the extent of £9,000. Matters in the

Transvaal are hardly any better. Laws have been passed which prohibit the Indian from engaging in trade or residing otherwise than in specific localities. On the latter point, however, proceedings are pending in the law-courts. A special registration fee of £7 has to be paid, the 9 o'clock rule is operative, walking on the foot-path is forbidden (at least this is so in Johannesburg), and traveling first and second class on the railways is not permitted. So you will see that the Indian's life in the Transvaal is not altogether a pleasant one. And yet, in spite of all these disabilities, nay, unwarrantable indignities and insults, the Indian, unless Mr. Chamberlain interferes, will be liable to compulsory military service.

According to the Commandeering Treaty, all British subjects were exempted from this service, but, when the Transvaal Volksraad was considering the point, they added a resolution to the effect that the British subjects means "whites" only. The Indians, however, memorialized the Home Government on this question. Cape Colony, following on the same lines, has recently empowered the East London Municipality to prohibit trading by Indians, walking on the foot-paths and limiting them to residence in certain locations. So you see almost everywhere in South Africa there is a dead set against the Indians. Yet we ask no special privileges, we only claim our just rights.

Political power is not our ambition, but to be let alone to carry on our trading, for which we are eminently suited as a nation, is all we ask. This is, we think, a reasonable demand.

Q. So much for these grievances, which seem to be general through out South Africa. Now tell me, Mr. Gandhi, how do Indian advocates fare in the lawcourts?

A. Oh! there is no distinction between advocates and attorneys of whatever race; in the courts, it is only a question of ability. There are many lawyers in the Colony, but, on the whole, forensic talent cannot be said to be of a very high order. A good many European pleaders are to be found, and it goes without saying that those with English training and degrees monopolize the practice of the courts.

But I suppose it is the English degree, for those of us who have taken it, which places us more on a level footing. Those with an Indian degree only would be out of place. There is scope, I believe, for Indian lawyers in South Africa, if at all sympathetically disposed to their fellow-countrymen.

As to the political aspect of affairs in South Africa, Mr. Gandhi preferred not to commit himself.

AN EVIL TO THE COLONY?

(Letter to *The Natal Mercury*, April 13, 1897)

Durban
April 13, 1897

To the Editor,

As this will be my first contribution after my return from India, on the Indian question, and a great deal has been said about me, much as I would like to avoid it, it seems to be necessary that I should say a few words on the matter. The following charges have been laid against me: (1) That I blackened the character of the Colonists in India, and made many misstatements; (2) that there is an organization under me to swamp the Colony with Indians; (3) that I incited the passengers on board the *Courland* and *Naderi* to bring an action against the Government for damages for illegal detention; (4) that I have political ambition, and the work I am doing is done in order to fill my pocket.

As for the first charge, I believe I need not say anything since you have absolved me from it. I venture, however, to deny formally that I ever did anything to merit it. As to the second, I repeat what I have said elsewhere: that I have no connection with any organization, nor, so far as I know, is there any organization to swamp the Colony with Indians. As to the third, I have denied and again deny most emphatically that I incited a single passenger to bring an action for damages against the Government. As to the fourth, I may state that I have no political ambition whatever. Those who know me personally know well in what direction my ambition lies. I do not aspire to any Parliamentary honors whatever, and, though three opportunities passed by, I deliberately refrained from getting myself placed on the Voters' List. I receive no remuneration for the public work that I am doing. If the European Colonists can believe me, I beg to assure them that I am here not to sow dissensions between the two communities, but to endeavor to bring about an honorable reconciliation between them. In my humble opinion, much of the ill feeling that exists between the two communities is due to misunderstanding of each other's feelings and actions. My office, therefore, is that of an humble interpreter between them. I have been taught to believe that Britain and India can remain together for any length of time only if there is a common fellow feeling between the two peoples. The greatest minds in the British Isles and India are striving to meet that ideal. I am but humbly following in their footsteps, and feel that the present action of the Europeans in Natal is calculated to retard, if not altogether to frustrate, its realization. I feel, further, that such action is not based on good grounds, but rests on popular prejudice and preconceived notions. Such being the case, I venture to trust that, however much the European Colonists may differ from the above opinion, they would be gracious enough to show a spirit of toleration thereof.

There are several Bills before the Natal Parliament prejudicially affecting the interests of the Indians. They are not supposed to represent final legislation with regard to the Indians, but the Honorable the Prime Minister has stated that more stringent measures may be adopted after the forthcoming Conference of the Colonial Premiers has taken place. This is a gloomy outlook for the Indians, and if, in order to avert it, they put forth all the legitimate resources at their disposal, I venture to think that they should not be blamed. It seems that everything is being hurried on as if there was any danger of thousands of Indians of all sorts and conditions pouring into Natal. I submit that there is no such danger and the late quarantine would serve as an effective check, if there was any. The suggestion that there should be an inquiry as to whether the Indian is an evil or a benefit to the Colony has been pooh-poohed and an opinion expressed that he who has eyes can see how the Indians are ousting the Europeans in every direction. With deference, I beg to differ. The thousands of free Indians, apart from the indentured, who have developed the large estates in Natal and given them a value, and turned them from jungles into productive soil, I am sure you will not call an evil to the Colony. They have not ousted any Europeans; on the contrary, they have brought them prosperity and considerably increased the general wealth of the Colony. Will the Europeans—can they?—perform the work done by those Indians? Have not the Indians very much helped to make this the Garden Colony of South Africa? When there were no free Indians, a cauliflower sold at half a crown; now, even the poorest can buy it. Is this a curse? Has the working man been injured in any way thereby? The Indian traders are said to "have eaten into the very vitals of the Colony." Is it so? They have made it possible for the European firms to extend their business in the way they have done. And these firms, because of this extension, can find employment for hundreds of European clerks and book keepers. The Indian traders act as middlemen. They begin where the Europeans leave. It is not to be denied that they can live cheaper than Europeans; but that is a benefit to the Colony. They buy wholesale from European stores, and can sell with a trifling addition to the wholesale prices, and are thus a benefit to the poor Europeans. It might be said in answer to this that the work now done by the Indian storekeepers could be done by Europeans. This is a fallacy. The very Europeans who are now wholesale dealers would be retail dealers but for the presence of the Indian storekeepers, except in isolated instances. The Indian storekeepers have, therefore, raised the Europeans a stage higher. It has, further, been said that, in time to come, Indians may usurp the wholesale trade also from the Europeans. This supposition is not borne out by facts, because the wholesale prices in Indian and European stores are, if not exactly, almost the same, thus showing the competition in the wholesale lines cannot by any means be said to be unfair. The cheaper living of the Indian is not an important factor in determining the wholesale price, because the cheaper living of the one is counterbalanced by the more methodical business habits and the mercantile "home connections" of the other. It is objected, on the one hand, that the Indians buy landed property in Natal and, on the other, that their money does not circulate in the Colony but goes to India, because "they wear no boots, no

European-made clothing, and send their earnings to India," thus constituting a terrible drain on the Colony. These two objections completely answer each other. Assuming that the Indians wear no boots and European-made clothing, they do not send the money thus saved to India, but invest it in buying landed property. What, therefore, they earn with one hand in the Colony they spend with the other. All, then, that the Indians send to India can only be a portion of the interest in the shape of rents received from such property. The purchase of landed property by the Indians is a double benefit. It increase the value of land, and gives work to the European builders, carpenters, and other artisans. It is a mere chimera to say that European workmen have anything whatever to fear from the Indian community. There is absolutely no competition between the European artisans and the Indian, of whom there are very few, and the few are indifferent workmen. A project to import Indian artisans to construct an Indian building in Durban failed. No good Indian artisans would come to the Colony. I do not know of many Indian buildings which have been constructed by Indian artisans. There is a natural division of work in the Colony, without any community encroaching upon the work of the other.

If there is any reason whatever in the views put forward above, I beg to submit that legislative interference is unjustifiable. The law of supply and demand will naturally regulate the supply of free Indians.

After all, if the Indian is really a canker, the more dignified course, since it has been admitted that the Indians can thrive because of the European support, will be that such support should be withdrawn. The Indians, then, may fret awhile, but cannot legitimately complain. But it should appear unfair to anybody that legislation should interfere with the supported on the complaint of the supporters. All, however, I venture to claim on the strength of the above argument is that there is sufficient in it to justify the inquiry hereinbefore suggested. No doubt there would be the other side of the question. If there was an inquiry, both sides could thoroughly be thrashed out and an unbiased judgment obtained. Then there would be some good material for our legislators to go on with and for Mr. Chamberlain to guide him. The opinion pronounced 10 years ago by a Commission of Inquiry, consisting of Sir Walter Wragg and other Commissioners, is that the free Indian is a benefit to the Colony. That is the only reliable material at present before the legislators, unless it is proved that the conditions during the last 10 years have so far changed as to prevent them from accepting that opinion. These, however, are local considerations. Why should not Imperial considerations also guide the Colonist? And if they should, then, in the eye of the law, the Indian is to have the same rights as all other British subjects. India benefits hundreds of thousands of Europeans; India makes the British Empire; India gives an unrivalled prestige to England; India has often fought for England. Is it fair that European subjects of that Empire in this Colony, who themselves derive a considerable benefit from Indian labor, should object to the free Indians earning an honest livelihood in it? You have said that the Indians want social equality with the Europeans; I confess I do not quite understand the phrase; but I know that the Indians have never asked

Mr. Chamberlain to regulate the social relations between the two communities; and so long as the manners, customs, habits, and religions of the two communities differ, there will, naturally, be a social distinction. What the Indians fail to understand is, why that difference should come in the way of the two living cordially and harmoniously in any part of the world without the Indians having to accept a degradation of their status in the eye of the law. If the sanitary habits of the Indian are not quite what they ought to be, the Sanitary Department can, by strict vigilance, effect the needed improvement. If Indians have not got decent-looking stores, licensing authorities can soon turn them into decent-looking ones.

These things can only be done when European Colonist, as Christians, look upon the Indians as brethren, or, as British subjects, look upon them as fellow-subjects. Then, instead of cursing and swearing at the Indians as now, they would help them to remove any defects that there may be in them, and thus raise them and themselves also in the estimation of the world.

I appeal to the Demonstration Committee, who are supposed more particularly to represent the working men. They now know that the Courland and Naderi did not bring 800 passengers for Natal, and that, in what they did bring, [there] was not a single Indian artisan. There is no attempt on the part of the Indians "to put the Europeans in the kitchen, and to become masters themselves." The European working man can have no complaint against the Indian. Under the circumstances, in my humble opinion, it behooves them to reconsider their position and direct the energy at their disposal in such channels that all sections of Her Majesty's subjects in the Colony may live in harmony and peace, instead of under a state of excitement and friction. Information has appeared in the papers that a gentleman is shortly to proceed to England on behalf of the Indians and the evidence against the Colony is being collected. In order that there may be no misunderstanding about the matter, I may state that, in view of the approaching Conference, a gentleman is going to London on behalf of the Indian community in South Africa, to place the Indian side of the question before their sympathizers and the general public, as also, if necessary, Mr. Chamberlain. He is to receive no remuneration for his services but passage and expenses. The statement that evidence is being collected against the Colony is very ugly and, unless it were true, could only be made by a person writing under an assumed name. The gentleman in question will certainly be put in possession of all the information about the Indian question in South Africa, but that appears in the papers already published. The Indians never have wished, and do not now wish, to make out a charge of brutality or general bodily ill-treatment by the Europeans towards them. Nor do they wish to make out that the treatment of the indentured Indians in Natal is worse than elsewhere. Therefore, if collecting evidence against the Colony is meant to convey some such impression, it is a groundless statement.

Your, etc.,
M. K. Gandhi

INDIAN AMBULANCE CORPS IN NATAL

(*The Times of India* (weekly edition), June 16, 1900)

Durban

Since sending my last contribution, I have been twice to the front; and though what General Olpherts said of the dhoolie-bearers could not be said of all the Indian Ambulance Corps, I have no doubt that the Corps has done a work that was absolutely necessary, and that would do credit to any Ambulance Corps in the world. I referred in my letter, dated October 27th, to the unconditional offer, without pay, of the English-speaking Indians of Durban to do service on the battlefield. Since then, events have happened which resulted in its acceptance. It was anticipated that the battle of Colenso would claim not a few lives, and that the safe carrying of the seriously wounded would be a grave problem, as the limited number of European ambulance bearers would not be equal to the required strain. General Buller, therefore, wrote to the Natal Government, asking them to raise an Indian Ambulance Corps, which would not be required to work within the range of fire. The managers of the various plantations (which control much Indian labor), as well as the leaders of the Indian community, were approached by the Government, and the response was prompt. A Corps of over 1,000 Indian stretcher-bearers was formed in less than three days, the bearers receiving 20s[hillings]. per week as against 35s. per week received by the European bearers.

The Corps reached Chieveley at about 3:30 p.m. on December 15, and as soon as they were detrained, the bearers were given their redcross badges and ordered to march to the field hospital—a distance of over 6 miles. The conditions under which this Corps worked were possibly somewhat more arduous than is usual. Wherever they went, they carried rations for a month or a fortnight, as; the case might be, including firewood, and, at first, without wagons or a water-cart. The Chieveley district is extremely dry, and there is hardly any water to be found within easy distances. The roads all over Natal are rugged and more or less hilly. On reaching the field hospital, we heard of the battle at Colenso. We saw the wounded being brought by the ambulance wagons and the European bearers from the base of operations to the field hospital, and the men as well as the leaders fully realized the situation. Before the tents could be pitched (I mean the tents for the leaders and not for the bearers— the latter had to sleep as they could, in the open, in some cases even without blankets), or the men could have anything to eat or drink, the Medical Officer wanted over 50 wounded men carried to Chieveley station. By 11 o'clock at night, all the wounded the Medical Officer could get ready were taken as directed, and it was only after that time that the Corps could get a meal. After this, the Superintendent of the Corps went to the Medical Officer and offered to carry more stretchers, but he was thanked and told to keep the men in readiness at 6 o'clock next morning. Between that time and noon, over 100 stretcher cases were disposed of by the men. While they were returning from their work, orders were received to strike camp and march to Chieveley immediately to entrain there for Estcourt. This was, of course, a retreat. It was wonderful to see how, with clockwork regularity, over 15,000 men with heavy artillery and transports broke camp and marched off, leaving behind nothing but empty tins and broken cases. It was an extremely hot day for marching—this portion of Natal is treeless as well as waterless. The Corps commenced its march at noon under these trying conditions.

On reaching the railway station at about 3 o'clock, the station-master informed the Superintendent that he could not say definitely when he could place the carriages—I mean open trucks in which the men were to be packed like sardines—at his disposal. The European Ambulance men and the Indians had to remain about the station yard till 8 p.m.

The former were then entrained for Estcourt, and the latter were told to shift for the night as best they could on the veldt. Tired, hungry, and thirsty (there was no water available at the station except for the hospital patients and the station staff), the men had to find means of satisfying both hunger and thirst, and of obtaining some rest. They brought dirty water from a pool about half a mile from the station, cooked rice and by midnight, after partaking of what was, under the circumstances, regarded as an excellent repast, wanted to sleep.

Practically the whole of General Buller's Cavalry passed by during the night, and the men had very little rest. Next day the men were closely packed in the trucks, and, after five hours' waiting, the train proceeded to Estcourt where, in a violent storm, exposed to the sun and wind, without shelter, the Corps had to remain for two days, after which orders were received to temporarily disband it. General Wolf-Murray had officially recognized the services rendered by the Corps.

The Indian merchants had supplied the leaders with large quantities of cigarettes, cigars, pipes, and tobacco for the wounded, and these were freely distributed among them. Of course, they were very much appreciated, especially as no cigarettes, etc., could be had in or near the camp. The leaders and the bearers were by no means satisfied with having carried their charge safely and well to their destination; but, at each stopping place during the long marches, even neglecting their own comforts, they left no stone unturned to attend to the wants of the wounded, e.g., helping them to tea and fruit—often doing so with their own money, or from their own rations.

Nor is this the only part the Indian community has taken in the war. All the leaders who went without pay were not capable of maintaining their dependents during their absence. The Indian merchants, therefore, started a fund which contributed to the support of the families of such leaders as needed it, and at no inconsiderable cost fully equipped the volunteers. In order to still more effectively identify themselves with the patriotic wave, and to show that they are capable of sinking their differences in the face of a common danger, they have subscribed a respectable sum of £65 to the Durban

Women's Patriotic League, a local organization formed for the purpose of providing medical comforts for the wounded soldiers and volunteers, some of which latter are violent anti-Indian Colonists. the Indian ladies have come forward to prepare pillowcases and handkerchiefs for the same purpose, out of cloth furnished by the Indian merchants.

It may not be amiss to mention also a few instances of individual sympathy for the soldiers. An Indian woman who lives on the daily sale of her fruits is reported, on the soldiers landing at the Durban wharf, to have emptied the whole contents of her basket into Tommy's truck, saying that was all she could give that day. We are not told where the noble-hearted woman found her food for the day. Similarly, several Indians, in an outburst of enthusiasm are reported to have showered cigarettes and other delicacies on Natal's fighters from over the waters. When the joyful news of the relief of Kimberley and Ladysmith was flashed across the wire, the Indians vied with the Europeans in their patriotic zeal to celebrate the occasion by decorating their stores, etc. They also held, on the 14th instant, a meeting. The Hon. Sir John Robinson, K.C.M.G., the first Prime Minister of Natal under Responsible Government, was invited to preside on the occasion, and he very kindly accepted the invitation. Over a thousand Indians from all parts of the Colony and over sixty leading European citizens attended the meeting.

THE USES OF ADVERSITY

(*Indian Opinion*, August 20, 1903)

There can be no question that the British Indians in South Africa are hemmed in on all sides by restrictions more or less severe according to the Colonies in which they are imposed, and that they are also very much misunderstood. By this time, those of our readers who have followed these columns at all, attentively, would have noticed that there is ample proof for the two statements we have just made. The purpose of this article is to draw some lessons from these adverse circumstances. We are told "Sweet are the uses of adversity," which should be "the instructor of the wise." Let us see, then, whether we have learnt any lessons from adversity.

There are, in India, sharp divisions between the different races inhabiting it; for instance, the Tamils, the "Calcutta men," as the inhabitants of the upper provinces are called here, the Panjabis, the Gujaratis, etc. There are also the Mahomedans, the Hindus, the Parsis, and others, according to religions. Then, among the Hindus there are the Brahmans, the Kshatriyas, the Baniyas, and others.

Now, to our mind, if we have brought from India these divisions and differences as very valuable cargo to be treasured up all this distance, then there is no doubt that it would clog us at every step, and hinder our progress. South Africa ought to be to the British Indians a great Puri where all divisions are abolished and leveled up. We are not, and ought not to be, Tamils or Calcutta men, Mahomedans or Hindus, Brahmans or Baniyas, but simply and solely British Indians, and as such we must sink or swim together. That the interests of all the divisions are absolutely identical cannot be gainsaid. That being so, it is plain enough that our duty lies in doing away with any such prejudices. That is a preliminary step, and an indispensable one. We are quite aware that our people have made a very great advance in that direction, but in drawing general lessons from our difficulties, the statement would be incomplete without a warning.

It is also incumbent on every Indian not merely to be satisfied with having made sufficient to feed and clothe himself and his family; he must be prepared to put his hands deep into his pocket for the public weal, and here again we know that the community throughout South Africa has not altogether failed in its duty, but we have no hesitation in saying that it might have done much better.

Courage and patience are qualities which one needs very badly when one is placed in difficult circumstances. We had, during the late war, a precious opportunity of watching these two qualities at their best among Englishmen in South Africa. The history of the siege of Ladysmith and its relief will always be an example of invulnerable courage and inexhaustible patience.

Many Indians who took part as stretcher-bearers will be able to recollect the scenes that they were witnesses to at the fights of Colenso and Spion Kop. In spite of fearful odds and bad reverses, there was no yielding. When at one time, even General Buller was inclined to think that relief was impossible, the world knows that there flashed across the wire a message from the hero of Candahar, that as long as General Buller had one man left with him, he was not to give in. The great result we all know. Ours is not a struggle so difficult, or so heroic to contend against, but it teaches a lesson in courage and patience which we ought to learn. If no sum of money, no quantity of blood and no amount of time were considered too great for the honor of the British Empire to relieve what were, after all, a handful of the besieged in Ladysmith, shall we not think similarly when we are engaged in a struggle for our liberties, and come to the conclusion that we must have courage and patience enough to tide over passing misfortunes? We should not forget that "Calamity is man's true touchstone," and that "none can cure their harms by bewailing them."

But we require something more also. We are apt as a nation, and the Missionaries have brought it up against us as a charge, to look at things material with philosophical indifference, and make little of everyday comforts of life. Now, that is an attitude for which we have unbounded admiration; but it would be very much misplaced in South Africa. Such an attitude would be a credit to those who do not strive after material gain, but it becomes a misnomer in the case of those who strive their utmost in order to enrich themselves; and we do not know that there are many Indians in South Africa who have migrated with any other desire than that of bettering their material position. To such, then, it would be more philosophical to fall in with the natural order of things, and to be prepared to spend in proportion to their earnings. The charge, then, against the Indians that they live on nothing a year would be dispelled. At the same time, nothing can be further from our thoughts than to suggest that we, as a community, should give ourselves up to pleasure. What we do wish to emphasize is the fact that we ought, as far as may be, to "do in Rome as the Romans do," still retaining the attitude of mental indifference. If we can have such comforts, well and good; and if we cannot, well and good, also.

But, above all else, what is most needed in a community which considers itself to be ill-treated at the hands of others is the virtue of love and charity. It is well known that, after all, men, being creatures of circumstances, would do things which are unjustifiable quite unconsciously, owing to the control exercised over them by the circumstances in which they are placed. Is it not, then, necessary for us to be charitable in our judgments? We, as a people, are devoted to religious speculations, and to doctrines of non-resistance and of returning good for evil. We believe firmly in the fact of even our thought coloring the actions of those of whom we may think. We see such instances often in daily life. A great crime committed by a man has been known to change his face in such a way as to stamp the crime on it. Similarly, a great good act done by a man has produced the opposite effect on his features, and he has been known, as the case may be, either to attract to, or to repulse from, himself people by his very act. We then hold it to be our paramount duty not to think evil of those who we may consider are dealing unjustly by us. There is hardly any virtue in the ability to do a good turn to those that have done similarly by us. That even the criminals do. But it would be some credit if a good turn could be done to an opponent. If this very simple thing be always borne in mind, we do think that success will come to us far more quickly than we are likely to imagine. We hope, as time goes by, to develop more fully each one of the points cursorily touched upon in this article. At present, it is enough for us to ask our countrymen to ponder over what we have said, and to be always on the alert, otherwise, storm-tossed as we are, a surging wave may all of a sudden come upon us and engulf us, when any action we may wish to take will be *Too Late*.

From Slave to College President
(*Indian Opinion*, September 10, 1903)

Mrs. Besant has said somewhere that England owes her present position not to her warriors, but to her one great national act, namely, the emancipation of slaves. This truth is very strikingly realized in the life-story of Booker Washington. Mr. Rolland has contributed a very interesting article to the latest number of *East and West* on Booker T. Washington, which is worth bringing to the attention of our readers.

Booker, as he was known when yet a slave, was born about the year 1858, the exact date being unknown to him. "His lot," says Mr. Rolland, "was the average one. He did not fall under the tyranny of one of those brutes so forcibly depicted in Mrs. Beecher Stowe's novel. . . . Yet even those masters who were kind to their slaves, treated them like inferior beings—a kind of useful cattle which had to be well fed if they were to work well, and which had no need of comforts they would be unable to appreciate." When freedom for the slaves was proclaimed, Mr. Booker's family left the plantations and went to town. He had a very great desire, illiterate though he was, to learn and educate himself. He, therefore, set about learning the rudiments of the English language, and attended a night-school. In his uphill work towards mental progress, he was helped by many white patrons of his, chief among whom was General Armstrong who had served in the Civil War. "He was," proceeds Mr. Rolland, "a sort of apostle who devoted his life to the colored races, whose needs he thoroughly understood, and who founded in 1868 in Virginia the Hampton Normal and Agricultural Institute to train young men and women of the negro and (Red) Indian races to become teachers among their own people." Our hero longed to receive his education at the Institute; he, therefore, accepted service in a military officer's house, and after he had saved some money started for Hampton. The distance he had to cover was nearly five hundred miles. "The difficulties of the road were still further increased by his being a colored man who could not be received at the same hotel as white people. More than once, he had to sleep out of doors, and to work all day in order to get enough to eat, but he never hesitated. At last, he reached Hampton. His appearance was so wretched and disreputable that the gates would have been closed against him if the matron of the establishment had not thought he might be useful as a servant. Thus, he got permission to stay. He was able to pay for his board and teaching by fulfilling the duties of doorkeeper, room cleaner and man-of-all-work, Washington, manifold occupations did not prevent him from assiduous attention at the classes."

It was not likely that such marvelous industry would escape the sympathetic notice of General Armstrong, who bestowed special attention on him, with the result that Mr. Booker came out of the Institute as one of the most brilliant students. Having imbibed knowledge himself which enabled him to take a broader view of life and to fight poverty and all difficulties, he thought that he could not better devote his life than being instrumental in imparting a similar knowledge to his fellow-countrymen. With such a laudable aim, he opened a small school, first at Malden, then at Washington, until he was called back to Hampton to occupy the post of teacher to the Indians of the Institute. Being himself a negro, he had some difficulty with the American Indians, but by his gentleness and prudence he soon succeeded in disarming all opposition to himself. This humble beginning laid the foundation of what is now an ideal college at Tuskegee. He realized that "the one thing needed by negroes, for the time being, was to learn how to work to advantage in the trades and handicrafts; how to be better farmers; how to be more thrifty in their lives; how to resist the money-lenders' inducements to mortgage their crops before they were made."

With this resolution, he set out for Tuskegee, and began his teaching in 1881 in a shanty. He had, however, like many pioneers, not only to found a school but to attract pupils to it. His idea about combining industrial education with a knowledge of letters merely, as might be well imagined, was not taken up enthusiastically. He, therefore, traveled from place to place, lecturing to the people on the advantage of his system. In his struggle for reform, he found Miss Olivia Davidson to be a worthy helper, whom he afterwards married. The result was that the support he received as to the number of the pupils soon outgrew the capacity of his humble school building. But Booker, who by this time had added Washington to his name, was equal to the occasion. He borrowed money and purchased a plantation of a hundred acres. Here was an opportunity for him of putting into practice his theory of industrial training. His students were, therefore, set to work, and a suitable structure was built. The clay was dug by them, and the bricks, too, were burnt by them.

The Tuskegee College has now forty buildings and a beautiful library, a gift from Mr. Andrew Carnegie, on an estate of 2,000 acres, besides fifteen cottages belonging to it. It represents a value of £100,000, the annual cost is £16,000, the number of people about 1,100; the cost of each student is £10 per year, board being paid partly in money, partly in labor—£40 suffices to complete a four years' course, while £200 provides a permanent scholarship. A great number of donations from great philanthropists and voluntary contributions from all kinds of people have every year added to the funds of the College, and a grant of 25,000 acres of land in Alabama was given by the Government of the United States in 1898.

The students come from twenty different States and territories. There are eighty-six instructors in the college and twenty-six different industries taught, every student, man or woman, having to learn a trade in addition to his or her studies in the class-room. The men learn printing, carpentering, bricklaying (in which they have become so competent that they turn out a hundred thousand bricks of superior quality a month), and various agricultural processes. The women learn plain sewing, dressmaking, cooking, ironing, and all about dairy work and poultry, horticulture, which is now a special feature at Tuskegee, five thousand pear trees being grown on the farm. They have a market garden which they have planned and made themselves. They have constructed a cold farm house, doing the carpentry work themselves.

They keep an account of the expenses incurred in raising and amounts realized from the sale of all vegetables. A nurse-training department has lately been established, and there is now a Kindergarten in the College. A savings bank has been founded on the grounds, and a school Post Office recognized by the State and responsible to the Government. A newspaper is also issued every month.

Such is the work done by Mr. Booker T. Washington, single-handed, in the face of enormous odds, without a glorious past to look back upon as an incentive which more ancient nations can boast of.

His influence at present is so great and universal that he is liked by all, both black and white. We read some time ago in the newspapers that the President of the United States invited him to the White House—"an unprecedented event—a revolution in the States where, a short time ago, no white man would have touched the hand of a negro without thinking himself defiled by this contact." Harvard University has honored him with the degree of Master of Arts. In traveling through Europe, he has drawn crowds of appreciative audiences. A life such as this teaches a lesson to all of us. If it is one full of honors, the honors have been well earned, after patient toil and suffering. Mr. Washington might have chosen another career in which he might have shone perhaps better in the estimation of some, but he chose first of all to raise his people, to qualify them for the great task lying before them. With himself he has raised his own countrymen also immeasurably, and set to them, as indeed to all of us who care to study his life, an example worthy to be followed. One word to our own countrymen, and we have done.

We have in our midst in India men who have devoted their lives to the service of their country, but we make bold to say that the life of our hero would perhaps rank higher than that of any British Indian, for the simple reason that we have a very great past and an ancient civilization. What, therefore, may be and is undoubtedly natural in us, is a very great merit in Booker Washington. Be that, however, as it may, a contemplation of lives like this cannot fail to do good.

➤➤ For Further Thought ◄◄

As he developed his rhetorical style, Gandhi chose to educate by example rather than by simply preaching his beliefs. Among the positive examples he held up for his readers were his fellow members of the Indian Ambulance Corps in Natal and the accomplished African-American, Booker T. Washington. In his eyes, their achievements were all the more remarkable for what they had to overcome. Can you think of more recent examples of people who have overcome the obstacles of racism, sexism, and other prejudices to accomplish great things? Record your thoughts about someone you would consider to be a great role model based on all that he or she has surmounted in order to achieve greatness. Why do you admire this person in particular? How has he or she helped change the world while shaping the opinions of others?

_____

_____

_____

_____

The World's Religion

(*Indian Opinion*, August 26, 1905)

The time has now passed when the followers of one religion can stand and say, ours is the only true religion and all others are false.

The growing spirit of toleration towards all religions is a happy augury of the future. An article appeared recently in the columns of *The Christian World*, a London religious weekly, over the signature of "J.B.," one of that journal's regular contributors, on this question, extracts from which I intend to quote.

The writer, in a most liberal and generous spirit, reviews the question from the Christian standpoint, and shows how the world's religions are linked one with the other, each having characteristics common to all others. The appearance of such an article in the Christian Press is worth noting, and shows that it is moving with the times. A few years back, such an article would have been classed as heretical teaching, and its author denounced as a traitor to the cause.

After remarking upon the new spirit which was changing the attitude of Christians to other religions, and pointing out how, a few years ago, the idea prevailed of the Christian religion standing out [as] the only true religion amongst a multitude of false ones, he goes on to say:

> There has been an immense revulsion, and one of the
> features of it is the discovery, so vastly surprising to

the average man, that the doctrine he was brought up on was not the earlier Christian teaching at all. The noblest of the old apologists thought very differently, he finds, of the outside races and faiths, from what he had been led to imagine. He hears of Justin Martyr, standing so close to the apostolic age, who regards the wisdom of Socrates as inspired by the "Word"; of Origen, and Gregory of Nyssa, whose teaching is of this was published as "Specially Contributed"; the entire race of man as under the Divine tutorship; of Lactantius maintaining that belief in Providence was the common property of all religions. . . .

. . . The finer Christian minds have, in fact, in every age gone more or less along this line. It needed only that men should come into contact with these outside races, whether in their literature or face to face, to realize at once that the "impassable gulf" theory between one religion and another was false to life and to the soul. . . .

. . . Religion, by a hundred different names and forms, has been dropping the one seed into the human heart, opening the one truth as the mind was able to receive it.

"J.B." points out that many of the Christian institutions and doctrines were born of the knowledge of other religions. Many of the symbols are relics of ancient days.

> How marvelous, too, in this connection, is that ancient cult of Mithras in Persia, where, as M. Cumont says: "Like the Christians, the followers of Mithras lived in closely united societies, calling one another father and brother; like the Christians, they practiced baptism, communion and confirmation; taught an authoritative morality, preached continence, chastity and self-denial, believed in the immortality of the soul and the resurrection of the dead."

It is not surprising that the writer should claim for the Christian religion the premier position, but it is gratifying to find such a broadminded attitude taken up by Christian writers and the Christian Press.

To Europeans and Indians working together for the common good, this has a special significance. India, with its ancient religions, has much to give, and the bond of unity between us can best be fostered by a wholehearted sympathy and appreciation of each other's form of religion. A greater toleration on this important question would mean a wider charity in our everyday relations, and the existing misunderstandings would be swept away. Is it not also a fact that between Mahomedan and Hindu there is a great need for this toleration? Sometimes one is inclined to think it is even greater than between East and West. Let not strife and tumult destroy the harmony between Indians themselves. A house divided against itself must fall, so let me urge the necessity for perfect unity and brotherliness between all sections of the Indian community.

BRAVE WOMEN
(*Indian Opinion*, December 28, 1907)

Women in England have surpassed all expectations. When the Indian community started the struggle against the obnoxious law in the Transvaal, the suffragette movement in England was many months old. They are still continuing the struggle undaunted. The struggle of the Transvaal Indians is nothing when compared with the courage and the tenacity of these women. Moreover, they have to face opposition from many women. There is a much larger number of women against than in favor of franchise for themselves. Though a mere handful, these women do not admit defeat. The more they are repressed, the more the resistance they offer. Many of them have been to jail. They have borne being kicked and stoned by base and cowardly men.

There was a cable last week that they had resolved to intensify their struggle still further. There are taxes to be paid to the

Government by these women or their husbands. If they do not pay the taxes, whatever things they possess can be auctioned. They may even be imprisoned.

The women have now resolved that they will not pay any taxes or levies till they get their rights, but will rather allow their possessions to be auctioned, and they themselves will suffer imprisonment. This courage and tenacity deserves to be emulated by the Transvaal Indians, in fact, by the whole Indian community. The Natal Indians think it much of a hardship if their goods are to be auctioned for trading without a license. These people do not realize that the Government cannot auction the goods of a large number of people.

But what would it matter if it did? If women can sacrifice their possessions for a matter like franchise, cannot we put up with a similar hardship while fighting for our livelihood? The movement of the suffragettes will go on for a long time, and they will keep up the agitation, resolute and tireless. They fight on with faith in truth, persuaded that, though they will not be there to enjoy the rights, if only the succeeding generations enjoy them, it will be as good as if they had themselves done so. Indians have to fight with the same spirit.

BAD HABIT

(*Indian Opinion*, February 29, 1908)

A reader from Durban writes to say that many of us are in the habit of referring to Indians from Calcutta or Madras, in public as well as in private, as "coolya" or "coolie." The complaint appears to be justified. We have often heard well-bred Indians use such terms. We are annoyed when Mr. Smuts or other whites use the word "coolie," but ourselves frequently use the same word deliberately or unwittingly, referring to persons from Calcutta or Madras who may not be laborers. The correspondent informs us that he once heard an Indian businessman refer to a person from Calcutta as a "coolie" in the presence of a lawyer. We hope that every Indian who has this habit will give it up, if only because such behavior stands in the way of bringing all the Indians together.

INDIANS AND ALCOHOL

(*Indian Opinion*, April 10, 1909)

Pretoria Jail

I have seen your letter addressed to the British Indian Association regarding its evidence to be submitted to the Commission.

I have not been able, my movement[s] having been uncertain, to submit my statement earlier. Nor has it been possible to call a meeting of the Association to consider the evidence to be given. The Chairman and the Acting Chairman of the Association are in jail.

The statement, therefore, that I am about to submit represents my personal views only.

I have been in South Africa now for the last fifteen years, and having, almost throughout that period, been officially connected with Indian public bodies, I have come in contact with all classes of Indians. Since 1903, I have been practicing as an attorney in Johannesburg, and have held the office of Honorary Secretary of the British Indian Association.

The Transvaal has a population of not more than 13,000 adult male Indians. Indians actually resident in the Colony since the war have probably never been more than 10,000 at any time. At the present moment, owing to the Asiatic struggle, there are probably not more than 5,000 in the Colony. These are chiefly Mahomedans and Hindoos. For the purposes hereof, I do not consider the Christians and the Parsees, as they form, though important, a numerically small section of the Indian community.

Both Mahomedans and Hindoos are prohibited by their respective religions from taking intoxicating liquors. The Mahomedan section has very largely conformed to the prohibition. The Hindoo section, I am sorry to say, contains an appreciable number who, in this Colony, have disregarded the prohibition of religion.

The method adopted by Indians who indulge in alcoholic drinks is generally to secure the assistance of some unscrupulous whites. There are other methods, also, which I do not care to go into.

I am of opinion that the legal prohibition should continue. I think, however, that the prohibition has not succeeded in preventing Indians, who have wanted it, from obtaining liquor. The only use I see in continuing the prohibition is to let those of my countrymen, who indulge in it, retain the sense of shame they have in drinking liquor.

They know that it is wrong for them both in religion and in law to obtain and drink liquor. This enables temperance workers to appeal to their law-abiding sentiment. I draw a fundamental distinction between wrongful law-breaking and a conscientious breach of man-made law in obedience to a higher law. Happily, those Indians who break the liquor law know that it is wrong for them to do so.

I am aware that some of my countrymen—themselves ardent temperance men—see in the liquor legislation one more disqualification based on the ground of color. Superficially speaking, they would be right. But I believe that this legislation has little to do with color. It is, in my opinion, a recognition on the part of the predominant race that the drink habit is an evil which, while they themselves are yet unable to get rid of, they do not want other races to contract. Viewing the position in this manner, I believe liquor prohibition among the Asiatic and Colored races to be the forerunner of general prohibition.

Whether, however, general prohibition becomes an accomplished fact or not, so long as the predominant race continue to indulge in alcoholic drinks, be it ever so moderately, partial prohibition such as we now have cannot be of much practical use.

This, it is submitted, is a forcible illustration of one of the evil incidents of contact between the European and other races. And unless those who preach abstinence are themselves ready to practice it, all liquor legislation must largely be a makeshift. I wish the Commission could see their way to point out to the electors of the Transvaal what a serious responsibility rests on their shoulders. They make it impossible for their representatives to pass legislation that is so desirable.

It is they who must take the responsibility for the breaking up of many a home. I am writing under a full sense of my own responsibility. I know only too well how many Indian youths who never knew the taste of spirituous liquors have succumbed, after having come to South Africa or the Transvaal.

If the Commission desire me to answer any question, I shall be pleased to do so.

Color Prejudice

(Indian Opinion, February 7, 1910)

America is regarded as a free country. It is claimed that everyone enjoys the fullest freedom there. A great many people, we find, are inclined to imitate America. Men are dazzled by her industry. But, on deeper reflection, we shall see that there is not much in America worthy of imitation. The people there are given over to the worship of self and of mammon. For money they will do the meanest things.

There are reports now which suggest that even the freedom which the Americans boast of is vanishing. Color prejudice is on the increase. Indians have enjoyed voting rights till this day. An official has now discovered that the framers of the Constitution could never have intended the granting of the franchise to Asiatics. He believes that not only Indians but even Turks should be denied the right to vote. Though the vast majority of the Turkish people are white-skinned, the official has pointed out that they are, after all, Asiatics.

The agitation against Asiatics going on in the West is likely to have grave consequences. We are not thinking just now of what China and Turkey will do. It is the duty of every Indian to think of what India should do. Japan has shown one way, that of proving one's strength and defending one's land with [the power of] arms.

Following that way, Japan has become like America and the imitation will soon be perfect, if it is not already so. To us it appears that, if we wish to avoid being found in America's predicament, we had better refrain from training in the use of arms. Behind the venturesome spirit of America is her armed strength.

All that India has to do to hold her own is to preserve her ancient civilization, eliminating only its defects. The kind of racial discrimination which America practices, we have practiced against our own people in India. Once there were many reformers in the West who had hoped and desired that the people there would shun such discrimination, but that is no more so. They have now begun to say that there must be no mixing with the Colored races, that the Asiatics must be kept down. We think this movement will grow stronger rather than otherwise—it cannot but do so.

Where people are concerned only with self-interest, it is not possible that they will allow others a foothold. Since their selfishness is mounting, their hostility to us will also grow. Self-interest will make them fight among themselves, too—even today they are fighting. That is a characteristic aspect of Western civilization. If we imitate the Western people, we may succeed for a time in mixing with them but subsequently we would also be blinded by selfishness and fight with them and fight among ourselves, too.

Someone may argue that even today we are fighting among ourselves. True. but our fighting is of a different kind. We must of course put an end to this. But we should be careful to see that in our attempt to mend matters we do not cause greater harm instead.

GENERAL KNOWLEDGE ABOUT HEALTH, PART X

(Indian Opinion, March 8, 1913)

In considering what food we should eat, let us first ask what we should not eat. If we designate as food all that enters the body by way of the mouth, then alcohol, cigarettes, tobacco, hemp, tea, coffee, cocoa, spices—all are food.

All these should be avoided. The author has found this to have been borne out by experience. Some of these articles he has consumed himself; regarding the rest he has observed the experience of others.

It is necessary to write about alcohol and hemp. All religions regard them as bad. There is hardly anyone who will defend their consumption. Alcohol has brought destruction to entire families. Millions of drunkards have been ruined. Under the influence of drink a man ceases to be himself. Such a one sometimes forgets the difference between mother and wife. This vice corrodes the intestines and, in the final stages, the victim becomes a burden upon the earth.

Drunkards may be seen rolling in the gutters. A respectable man turns into a man of straw when he gets drunk. It is not that a person falls into such a state only when he drinks. An alcohol addict, one will observe, is feeble-minded even when sober. He has no control over his mind, which wanders like a child's. Alcohol, as also hemp, deserves to be entirely avoided. There is no room for two opinions on this. Some think alcohol may be taken as medicine.

However, doctors in Europe, which is the home of wine, say that even this is not necessary. At first alcohol was used there for many ailments, but that has now been stopped. As a matter of fact, this whole argument is advanced with dubious motives. If wine can be used for medicinal purposes [the argument runs], there can be no objection against its use as drink either; that is the game of these advocates of drink. But aloes and crotons are good medicine; yet no one suggests that they be used as food.

It is possible that alcohol may prove beneficial in certain illnesses, but the havoc that it has wrought is so great that it is the duty of every thoughtful person to give up even its medicinal use, at the cost of his life if need be. If, by using alcohol for preserving the body, we are likely to harm the best interests of hundreds of people, our duty requires that we sacrifice the body instead.

There are in India hundreds of thousands who do not take alcohol in spite of the doctor's orders. They are not willing to prolong their lives by taking alcohol or anything else to which they have an objection. The great people of China, enslaved by opium as they are, will soon perish in spite of the freedom that they have achieved. The garasias among us have lost their patrimony, thanks to their addiction to opium.

The reader will easily recognize the harm in alcohol, hemp, and opium, but not so readily that in cigarettes and tobacco. These have spread their tentacles so firmly over the human race that it will take ages to free it of them. Young and old, all alike have got into their clutches. Even people regarded as virtuous have taken to smoking, and the habit is not regarded as something to be ashamed of. It is quite a popular form of hospitality among friends. Instead of being checked, the habit is spreading. The ordinary man is not even aware of the fact that cigarette dealers use every kind of trick in the manufacture of cigarettes to confirm the hold of the addiction over its victims.

Various kinds of perfumed solutions and even opium water, are sprinkled on the tobacco. As a result of these practices, cigarettes acquire a stronger and stronger hold over us. Thousands of pounds are spent on advertisement in order to popularize them. Cigarette companies in Europe run their own printing presses. They purchase bioscopes and offer all kinds of prizes, start lotteries, and spend money like water on advertisements. The result is that even women have begun to smoke. Poems have been written about the cigarette, which has been called the poor man's friend.

It is impossible to estimate the harm done by smoking. A smoker becomes so brazen-faced that, indifferent to the feelings of others, he will light his cigarette even in another's house without so much as asking for permission to do so. He respects no one's presence.

It has been observed that cigarette or tobacco smokers will commit many other crimes in order to obtain these things. Children steal money from their parents. In jail, prisoners treasure stolen cigarettes at great risk. They can get on without food but not without cigarettes. During war, soldiers addicted to smoking are in a pitiable condition if they do not get cigarettes. They become practically useless.

The late Tolstoy, writing on this subject, tells the story of a man who planned to kill his beloved. He drew his knife and got ready to use it. Then he relented and turned back. After this, he sat down for a smoke. The fumes of the cigarette entered his head, the poison affected his brain, and he finally committed the murder. It was Tolstoy's firm belief that the cigarette is so subtle a form of intoxication that it should be regarded as in some ways a greater menace than even drink.

Smoking is also very expensive, and, indeed, every smoker feels the strain of the expense to a greater of lesser degree, depending on his means. Some people spend five pounds or seventy-five rupees a month on cigarettes. The author has himself come across such a case.

Smoking weakens the digestion, renders food tasteless so that more and more spices have to be added to it. The smoker's breath is offensive. The smoke that he exhales pollutes the atmosphere. At times he gets small ulcers in the mouth. Gums and teeth become black or yellow, and some persons have even contracted serious diseases in consequence. It seems strange that people who disapprove of drinking see nothing wrong in smoking; when, however we remember how subtle is the poison of smoking, we see easily enough why it is that men who hate alcohol are nevertheless ready to enjoy smoking. Those who wish to remain healthy should definitely give up the cigarette.

Drink, tobacco, hemp, etc., not only damage physical health, but also impair mental fitness and entail wasteful expenditure.

We lose all our moral sense and become slaves to our weakness. About tea, coffee and cocoa, however, it seems extremely difficult to explain the truth and convince anyone that they are harmful. One must say, all the same, that they, too, are harmful. These also contain some kinds of intoxicants. If milk and sugar were not added to tea and coffee, they would have no nutritional value whatever.

Experiments in living exclusively on tea and coffee indicate that they contain no nourishment for the blood. Only a few years ago, tea and coffee were generally not drunk among us. They were only taken on certain occasions or with medicine, but, tidy in the wake of modern progress, they have become a daily necessity. They are offered even to a casual visitor, and frequent tea-parties are given. During Lord Curzon's regime, tea wrought terrible havoc. That gentleman, seeking to promote the interests of tea merchants, introduced tea into every household so that those who were previously accustomed to wholesome drinks now take tea.

Cocoa has not yet become so popular because it is slightly more expensive that tea. Fortunately for us, we have not yet made friends with it, but it holds strong enough sway in fashionable homes.

Tea, coffee, and cocoa all have a certain property that weakens our digestive powers. They are intoxicants because they form a habit which cannot be broken. When the author was in the habit of drinking tea, he felt lethargic if he did not get tea at the usual hour—this is the conclusive test of an intoxicant. On one occasion, about 400 women and children were gathered together at a function.

The organizing committee had resolved not to provide tea or coffee. The women in the gathering were in the habit of taking tea at four every afternoon.

A message was soon conveyed to the organizers that, if tea was not served, the ladies would fall ill and be unable to move. And so the resolve had to be set aside. As arrangements were being make for serving tea, excited messages poured in demanding that the organizers should hurry up. The ladies' heads had begun to ache, and every moment felt like a month to them. It was only after they had their tea that these worthy ladies' faces brightened up and they calmed down.

This incident has been described exactly as it happened. One woman had suffered so much harm because of the tea habit that she could not digest any food and had constant headaches. Her health, however, has greatly improved since she, with a strong effort of will, gave up tea. A physician in the employ of Battersea Municipality in England has discovered that thousands of women in that area suffer from nervous disorders, which he ascribes to their addiction to tea. The author has come upon innumerable examples of the harm done to health by tea, and he is personally convinced, therefore, that tea is very injurious to health.

As regards coffee, there is a couplet which has become well known:

Counters phlegm and wind, but lower vigor and
strength

And turns blood to water—two merits against three
    faults.

This verse sounds quite convincing. Coffee may have the virtue of counteracting phlegm and wind. But so have some other substances. Those who wish to drink coffee for the first two reasons should take a little ginger juice; it will serve the same purpose as coffee. But a preparation detrimental to vigor which needs to be fully conserved, one reducing strength and turning blood into water, surely deserves to be wholly shunned.

Cocoa shares the defects of coffee. Like tea, it also contains a substance which has the effect of making the skin quite rough.

For those who include morals in their conception of good health, there is a further argument against these three beverages. Tea, coffee, and cocoa are produced for the most part by indentured labor. In cocoa plantations, Negro workers are subjected to such inhuman treatment that if we witnessed it with our own eyes we would have no desire to drink cocoa. Volumes have been written on the tortures inflicted in these plantations. To be sure, if we made searching inquiries regarding the origin of the various articles of our diet, we should feel called upon to reject 90 percent of them!

In place of these three drinks, a harmless and nourishing beverage can be prepared in the following manner. Those who like can certainly call it tea. Many coffee lovers cannot distinguish it from coffee. Wheat should be well cleaned and roasted in a pan. It should be kept on the fire till it becomes red and is about to turn black. It should then be taken off the fire and ground rough in a coffee-mill.

A teaspoon of this powder should be put into a cup and boiling water poured over it. Boiling this mixture for a minute improves the flavor.

Milk and sugar to taste may be added, but it can also be taken without them. Every reader will find it worthwhile to make this experiment. If he acquires this habit and gives up tea, coffee, and cocoa, he will save such money and also be spared the risk to his health. Those who do not want the bother of roasting and grinding the wheat may send 9d. to the Manager, and they will receive one lb. of the prepared wheat powder.

Indian Marriages
(Indian Opinion, March 29, 1913)

Last week we dwelt upon the marriage case in Cape Town. Another case of the same nature, regarding one Bai Janubie, has come to our knowledge. This lady is a widow, whose husband has left her his property by a will. The Master of the Supreme Court, however, refuses to execute the will. He states that Bai Janubie's marriage cannot be recognized as valid. The marriage question, thus, is assuming a serious aspect day by day, and we shall find ourselves quite helpless afterwards if we are not vigilant and fail to act in time.

The effects will be felt by all Indians. Some people argue, we hear, that there can be no satyagraha in a matter concerning women, for they cannot be asked to go to jail. We leave aside the question whether or not they can be. Cannot men go to jail for women's honor and their own? There may be no need whatever for women to go to jail or to be asked to do so. What is needed is that men should be men enough. Satyagraha, moreover, is far off yet. Where is the question of satyagraha in taking counsel together, parting with a little money, holding meetings and sending petitions? If we take cover behind the argument that there can be no satyagraha and sit back with folded hands, we shall only bring ridicule upon ourselves and our womenfolk.

GENERAL KNOWLEDGE ABOUT HEALTH, PART XXXIV (CONCLUSION)

(*Indian Opinion*, August 16, 1913)

These chapters on the subject of health have been appearing for the past few months. They have now come to an end. . . .

I have repeatedly asked myself why I wrote them. I am not a vaidya. My knowledge of the subject is but superficial. Is it not likely that my suggestions have been made after inadequate thought or observation? In truth, both study and observation are bound to be incomplete, a process without end. Every day new facts are observed, and new ideas emerge. Why, then, this effort? Thus has my mind been perplexed.

And yet, medical science is itself based on inconclusive experiments. Most of it is quackery, as I have shown. With so much of it about, if these chapters are also reckoned as such, no great harm will be done! They have been written from a worthy motive. The intention is not to recommend what medicines to take after the onset of a disease. The more immediate purpose, rather, has been to show how sickness may be averted. A little thought will show that the steps for prevention of diseases are easy enough. No specialized knowledge is necessary for this. The difficulty lies in taking to that way of life. I have felt it proper to write on certain diseases, but only in order to show that most ailments have a common origin and, as a result, the treatment also should be common to them all. Moreover, despite all precautions, the diseases mentioned in these chapters do occasionally occur. Some remedies for these, one finds, are known to all. If my experience is added to these, nothing is likely to be lost.

The main question, however, still remains to be considered. Why is good health necessary? We behave as if no such necessity exists. To be sure, rather than build a stout and healthy body and give it over to the enjoyment of luxuries, regard the body as the only thing worth preserving and be puffed up with pride to see it strong, it will be better to have it rotting with leprosy.

All religions have looked upon this body as a place where one may meet and recognize God. It is called the House of the Lord.

It has been leased to us, all the rent we have to pay being praises of the Master. Another condition in the rent note is that we must not misuse it. It should be kept clean and pure inside and out and returned to the Master in due course in the same condition in which it came to us. If all the conditions are duly fulfilled, the Master will reward us at the end of our tenure and will make us his heirs.

All living creatures have bodies alike in their design, in that they have organs for hearing, sight, smell, and pleasure. But the human body has been described in prose and verse as a *ratnachinta-mani*. The term signifies a jewel which secures to one anything one may wish for.

In an animal body, the soul cannot attain to the highest knowledge and cultivate devotion to God. Without these, there can be no freedom for the soul and, so long as the soul has not attained freedom, there can be no true happiness and no ending to our real suffering. This body is of some service only if it is well used, that is, made the abode of God. Otherwise, it is a filthy mass of bones, flesh and blood, and the breath and water that exude from it are full of poison. Of all the excreta coming out of the innumerable openings in the body, there is nothing that we would wish to retain. One is nauseated at the very thought or sight or touch of them. It is only with the greatest difficulty that we can prevent them from being infested with worms.

By means of the body, we practice a thousand things which we would do better to avoid, cunning, self-indulgence, deceit, stealing, adultery, etc. Its desires are endless. Even when they are all gratified, it is so like a glass bangle that it has less strength to resist a blow than has a broken vessel. It is destroyed in an instant.

Such a state is quite natural for the body. Anything that can be used for the highest purpose is also capable of being misused. Otherwise, it would be impossible to know or estimate its value. We can measure the value of sunlight because we experience the darkness that follows the sun's absence. In that same sun, without which we cannot live, resides the power to turn us to ashes. A king can be both magnanimous and wicked.

God is striving for mastery over the body, and so is Satan engaged in a desperate struggle for it. When it is under the control of God, it is like a jewel. When it passes into the control of the Devil, it is a pit of filth. If engrossed in pleasure, gorging itself the whole day with all variety of putrifying food, exuding evil odors, with limbs employed in thieving, the tongue uttering unworthy words and taking in unwholesome things, the ears hearing, the eyes seeing and the nose smelling what they ought not to, the body is worse than hell. Everyone recognizes hell for what it is. But though we use the body as if it were hell, we go on pretending that it is heaven. Such is our hypocrisy in regard to the body. Knowing a latrine for what it is, we shall know its right use. If a splendid hall, however, comes to be used as a lavatory, the result is bound to be evil. Therefore, if the body be in the Devil's control, it would be far better to desire its destruction, rather than its well-being.

In these chapters on health, an effort has been made to bring home the truth that the body can remain in health only by obeying the laws of God. It can never be healthy if it be given over to the Devil. Where there is real health, there alone is true happiness possible, and in order to achieve real health we must conquer the palate. If we succeed in this, all other organs will be automatically under our control and one who has this body under control can subdue the world because such a one becomes God's heir, a part of Him. Rama is not in the Ramayana, nor Krishna in the Gita. Khuda is not in the Koran, nor Christ in the Bible.

They all live and have their being in the purity of human conduct, which springs from morality. Morality consists in truth, which is the same as Shiva. You may know it by whatever name you please. That one may have a glimpse, if only occasional, of this truth in these chapters on health has been the underlying purpose of this effort.

A PRAYER FOR DISCIPLINE

(Johannesburg, May 23, 1914)

I shall not be pleased just because you recite verses from the Gita. I don't care whether or not you read history, do sums in arithmetic, or learn Sanskrit. What is necessary is that you should acquire self-control. That is what I want. I may agree to be someone's slave, but not that of my mind.

There is no sin as base as being the slave to one's mind. Be wise, therefore, and learn to discipline your mind. So you will be able to live with me. Otherwise I have no need of anyone. Nor am I conceited enough to want to teach you or anyone else. I have a pupil, to train whom is the most difficult task. It is only by training that pupil that I can do some good to you, to India or the world. That pupil is myself, what I call my mind. Only those who thus become their own pupils are fit to stay here. Others who cannot stand such a life had better not stay here. Such a person would do well to leave this place. It is a sin, however, to do anything blindly (without a purpose, mechanically). I want no such thing.

Gandhijini Sadhana

The Hindu Caste System

(*Bharat Sevak*, October 1916)

The Hindu social structure has endured, I believe, on the foundation of the caste system. Sir William Hunter says in his *History of India* that, thanks to the continuing existence of the institution of caste, there has been no need for any law for the poor (pauper law) in India. This seems to me a sound view. The caste system contains within it the seed of *swaraj*. The different castes are so many divisions of an army. The general does not know the soldiers individually but gets them to work through the respective captains. In like manner, we can carry out social reform with ease through the agency of the caste system and order through it our religious, practical and moral affairs as we choose.

The caste system is a perfectly natural institution. In our country, it has been invested with a religious meaning; elsewhere, its utility was not fully realized, and so it remained a mere form, with the result that the countries concerned did not derive much benefit from it. These being my views, I am opposed to the movements which are being carried on for the destruction of the system.

However, any defects in the caste system which we may find must certainly be removed, and for that purpose we must first study its real nature. As I pointed out earlier, we have given a religious meaning to the system. It is merely an agency for ensuring self-control.

The caste defines the limits within which one may enjoy life; that is to say, we are not free to seek any happiness outside the caste. We do not associate with members of other communities for eating or enter into marriage relationships with them. With an arrangement of this kind, there is a good chance that loose conduct will be kept down.

The idea that coming together for purposes of eating promotes friendship is contradicted by experience. If it did, the great war being waged today in Europe would never have started. The bitterest quarrels are among relatives. We have needlessly exaggerated the importance of eating.

The process of eating is as unclean as evacuation, the only difference being that, while evacuation ends in a sense of relief, eating, if one's tongue is not held in control, brings discomfort. Just as we attend to evacuation, etc., in private, we should likewise eat and perform other actions common to all animals always in private. The purpose of eating is to sustain the body. If this statement is correct, obviously, the less ostentation we make about it, the better.

The same thing is true of marriage. Prohibition of marriage with anyone not belonging to one's community promotes self-control, and self-control is conducive to happiness in all circumstances. The larger the area over which the net is cast, the greater the risk. That is the reason why I see nothing wrong in the practice of choosing the husband or the wife from among persons of equal birth. Even in countries where class differentiation does not rest on religion, they guard against hybrid unions. This is the meaning of the phrase "blue blood" in England. Lord Salisbury used to boast that he belonged to the same stock as Elizabeth. It was a fact which seemed to him and the British people worth being proud of.

In this way, the restrictions in regard to eating and marriage are, as a general rule, wholesome.

There is, of course, and there will always be, room for exceptions. This has been accepted by Hindu society, whether it knows the fact or not. Rightly considered, however, there are no exceptions. If I eat in the company of a *Bhangi*, there being, from my point of view, greater self-control in doing so, the community should have nothing to do in the matter. Or, if I fail to get a suitable bride from my own community and I am likely, if I remain unmarried, to contract vicious habits, it will, in these circumstances, be an act of self-control on my part to marry a girl of my choice from any community, and hence my action will not be a violation of the fundamental principle of the caste system. It would be for me to demonstrate that my purpose in taking such a step in disregard of the general rule was discipline of the flesh, and this would appear from my subsequent conduct. Meanwhile, however, I should not resent being denied the usual privileges that go with membership of a community but ought to continue doing my duty by it.

The caste system has other laws besides those relating to eating and marriage. It has, ready at hand, the means for providing primary education. Every community can make its own arrangements for [such] education. It has machinery for election to the Swaraj Sabha (Parliament). Every community with some standing may elect its own representatives. It has ready provision for arbitration and tribunals to solve disputes. Each community should itself resolve disputes among its own members. If it becomes necessary to raise an army for war, we have already as many battalions as we have communities. The caste system has struck such deep roots in India that I think it will be far more advisable to try to improve it, rather than uproot it.

Some may argue that, if these views about the caste system are right, one will have to admit that the more numerous the communities, the better it would be, and that, if that came about, every ten persons would form a community. There is no substance in this argument. The rise and disappearance of communities does not depend upon the will of particular individuals or groups. In Hindu society, communities have been formed, have disappeared, and have gone through improvements according to the needs of the times, and the process is taking place even today, visibly or invisibly. The Hindu caste system is not merely an inert, lifeless institution but a living one and has been functioning according to its own law. Unfortunately, today we find it full of evils like ostentation and hypocrisy, pleasure seeking and quarrels. But this only proves that people lack character; we cannot conclude from it that the system itself is bad.

FASTING AND PRAYER

(*Navajivan*, October 12, 1919)

It is my conviction and my experience that, if fasting and prayer are done with a sincere heart and in a religious spirit, marvelous results could be obtained from them. There is nothing as purifying as a fast, but fasting without prayer is barren; it may result in a diseased person being restored to health or may only mean a healthy person suffering unnecessarily. A fast undertaken purely for ostentation or to inflict pain on others is an unmitigated sin. Hence, it is only a prayerful fast undertaken by way of penance to produce some effect on oneself which can be called a religious fast. Prayer does not mean begging God for worldly happiness or for the things which advance one's interests; it is the earnest cry of a soul in anguish. It cannot but influence the whole world and cannot but make itself heard in the divine court. When an individual or a nation suffers because of a great calamity, the true awareness of that suffering is prayer; in the presence of this purifying knowledge, physical functions like eating, etc., become less urgent. A mother suffers when her only son dies. She has no desire for eating. A nation is born when all feel the same sort of grief at the suffering of any one among them; such a nation deserves to be immortal. We are well aware that quite a large number of our brothers and sisters in India live in great suffering, and so, truly speaking, we have occasion at every step for prayerful fasting. But our national life has not attained to this degree of intensity and purity.

Even so, occasions arise when we suffer acutely.

Such an occasion has arisen for our Muslim brethren. Readers of *Navajivan* know what it is: if Turkey is partitioned, the Khilafat will disappear. If the Khilafat disappears, Islam will lose its vitality. This the Muslims can never tolerate. Supporting my view, the good Mr. Andrews said that, if the Muslims feel they have not received justice, then Mr. Montagu and His Excellency the Viceroy should resign.

This remedy is essential, but external. A far, far more powerful remedy lies in the hands of our Muslim brethren themselves. It has been decided that on Friday, October 17, Muslims should observe a *roza*, that is, a fast of twenty-four hours; accordingly, beginning from the evening of the 16th, they should spend the whole of the 17th in prayers. This is a beautiful idea. The peace and the good that ensue from turning our thoughts to God in a time of sorrow are not to be had in any other way.

The duty of Hindus at such a time is obvious. If they regard the Muslims as their brethren, they should fully share their suffering. This is the best and the easiest method of promoting unity between Hindus and Muslims. Sharing another's sorrow is the only real sign of brotherly regard. I hope, therefore, that every man and woman in India will spend October 17 in prayer and fasting.

The *Gita* is universally accepted among Hindus. They should read it through from the beginning to the end, along with a rendering of its meaning.

This way the whole day will be spent in a religious spirit, and that will be the prayer of the Hindus.

I think we may, without fear, observe a *hartal* on that day. Those who are independent should stop their work. People in service, the laborers and those who serve in hospitals, etc., need not stop work. If people remain within doors on the day and take out no processions, there will be no cause for fear. There can be no coercion in fasting and prayer; and this should also be true about stopping work. A hartal can be effective only if it is purely voluntary. Such a hartal alone can provide the true measure of the feelings of Hindus and Muslims. In order that the hartal may remain voluntary, those who are appointed volunteers may move about. It should be their duty to see that no one offers violence to, or exerts undue pressure on, those who open their shops or attend to their work.

If the Government is wise, it will encourage the people in this step. It is the duty of His Excellency the Viceroy, if he would demonstrate to the Muslims his sympathy for them, to instruct the officers not to come in the way of the people observing a hartal. If His Excellency can go further, he could stop work on that day and thereby assuage the people a great deal. Whether the Government does this or not, the duty of the people is clear. Hindus and Muslims should unite to observe October 17 in the manner suggested above.

WRITING UNDER THE "WEIGHT OF SUPPRESSION"

(Speech at Gujarati Shaitya Parishad [Ahmedabad] April 4, 1920)

Let us consider what kind of literature should be produced if we are to educate the masses. The poet gave us today the right point of view on this. He was shrewd in taking the example of Calcutta. He saw that things are the same in Ahmedabad as in Calcutta and his verbal attacks were entirely for our benefit. Sydney Smith was skilled in the art of satire. By using the pronoun "we," he tried to soften the blow; but our poet has used the pronoun "we" to mean his own people. We should see, however, that his attack is against us. Describing Calcutta, he says that the banks of the sacred Ganga are covered with huge buildings and this has turned what should be a beautiful scene of nature into an eyesore. Such a spot should fill us with thoughts of nature.

Instead, when he thinks of Calcutta, his eyes fill with tears.

According to me, a laborer that I am, our duty is to realize God. Forgetting that, we have given ourselves to the worship of money and the pursuit of self-interest.

I ask writers: "Will you, through your creations, bring me sooner to God?" If their reply is in the affirmative, I will be a slave to their works. If the work of any writer bores me, it is not my dullness that is to blame but his art itself. A gifted writer should so perfect his art that the reader would be simply absorbed in his work. I am sorry that our literature has little of this kind of thing.

There is nothing the masses can learn from the literature of today. There is not one idea in this literature in virtue of which it may endure for a week, or a year or a whole age.

Let us, then, see what literature we possess in the holy books we have had with us from ancient times. The satisfaction they give we don't derive from our modern literature. Even a barely passable translation of any of those works is more interesting to read than anything of the latter. There is much indeed, some will say, in contemporary literature. That may be, but it is an exhausting task to search for that "much." Whoever gives us today anything like what Tulsidas and Kabir gave?

Live as you may,
Realize God anyhow, anyway.

We never see these days anything of this kind. Where do we find now what we received in the age of Akha?

I returned to India after twenty years in South Africa, and, looking round, I discovered that we lived in a state of fear. A people in such a state cannot express itself fearlessly. If we have to write under the weight of suppression, the springs of poetry in us will not flow, nor will truth come floating on the wave. The same is true about newspapers. With the Press Act hanging over him, the editor cannot write uninhibitedly. With the same Act hanging over the writers, not a single line is written in freedom, and hence it is that truth is not presented as it ought to be.

This is a period of transition in India. Crores of people feel that great changes are about to take place, that our poverty will give place to glory, that now the Age of Truth will dawn upon us. I hear these hopes expressed wherever I go. Large numbers of people think that India is about to turn a new leaf. If it does, what sort of writing shall we find on that new leaf? The Reforms which will have been granted will only prove to be a collar and we shall continue to be driven like bullocks, as we are driven today. At such a time, I ask the servants of literature nothing less than that they help us to a vision of God and Truth. They must demonstrate that India is not given to sinful ways, that she will not betray one's faith [in her].

No Indian in Madras has served South India so well as did Pope—not the Pope of the *Iliad* fame. I am ever in love with human beings and would, therefore, always want to steal people's hearts. In order that I might steal the hearts of my brothers of the South, I had to learn their language. I cannot just now quote anything from the writings of the Rev. Pope, but this I will tell you that the poems, or rather the poetry, in Tamil which even the peasant can enjoy as he waters his field is just superb. The watering of the field begins even before the sun has risen. *Bajri* and wheat, everything is covered with pearly dew.

The liquid drops on the tree leaves shine like pearls. This is what the men, these peasants, as they water the fields sing about. When I lived at Kochrab, I used to watch the peasants and listen to their songs. I found obscene words in their mouth. Why should this be so? I should like to have an answer to this from Shri Narasinhroa here and from the Chairman.

I say to the Sahitya Parishad that, unless you help remove the filthy language from the mouths of our peasants, the sin of our degradation will be on your heads. I want to know from the servants of literature what the condition of the majority of our people is and what they will write for this majority. I will say only this to the Sahitya Parishad and repeat it over and over again: rid yourselves of all your shortcomings.

Lewis thought of writing a book and wrote one for his children. They read it to their profit; men, women and children today may also read it and profit by it. I ask for such literature from our men of letters. I want, not Banabhatta's *Kadambari* but Tulsidas's *Ramayana*.

I have my doubts whether *Kadambari* will be with us forever, but Tulsidas's work will certainly endure. Let us at present get just *rotli*, ghee, and milk from our literature. Later on we shall add almonds, pistachio nuts, etc., and produce something like *Kadambari*.

If the meek people of Gujarati—a people filled with sweetness, whose goodness is without bounds, a people so very simple-minded and having unswerving faith in God—if these people are to go forward, their men of letters should sing and write for laborers and peasants in the fields.

It is my heartfelt prayer that people may learn to write the truth, speak the truth, and live the truth.

CURSE OF WIDOWHOOD

(*Navajivan*, May 9, 1920)

Mr. Kanchanlal Khandwala's letter is full of figures about widows. Anyone's heart will bleed to read them. Impatient reformers will merely say that remarriage of widows is the only straight and simple remedy for this. I cannot say so. I too have a family of my own. There are many widows in my family, but I can never bring myself to advise them to remarry, and they will not think of doing so either. The real remedy is for men to take a pledge not to remarry.

But there are other remedies, barring remarriage, which we do not adopt, or rather do not wish to adopt. Here they are:

1. Child-marriages should stop.

2. No boy and girl should be betrothed till they are of an age to live together.

3. Not only should a woman who has never lived with her husband be permitted to remarry, she should actually be encouraged to do so. Such women should not be classed with widows.

4. Those who became widows before the age of fifteen and who are still young should be free to remarry.

5. Instead of being regarded as a sign of ill fortune, widowhood should be looked upon as a holy state and respected accordingly.

6. The best arrangements should be made to educate widows and give them some occupation.

There is no doubt that, if these reforms are brought about, Hindu society would be rid of the evils arising from widowhood.

Every family and every community may adopt these reforms for themselves. Many reforms are delayed because everyone waits for someone else to make a start. It is a divine injunction that man should do a good deed the moment he sees it as such; about a sinful act, one should think, consult a fortune-teller and take advice from thousands of people, and ultimately refrain from it.

We become guilty in the sight of God if we delay in the performance of a good deed. But we act the opposite way. We are not afraid of doing anything sinful, but, when it comes to doing good, we wait for conferences.

DUTY OF WOMEN

(*Navajivan*, July 18, 1920)

At a meeting held under the presidentship of that good lady Mrs. Jaiji Jehangir Petit, the women of Bombay have given expression to their view on the atrocities committed in the Punjab. The meeting has served two purposes. In the first place, the women have joined the country in her suffering and understood what that suffering is.

Women ought not to remain unconcerned in the face of such atrocities. They cannot afford to keep silent when events happen which deprive women of their womanhood and men of their manhood. It is not men alone who have been humiliated in the Punjab. Women, too, have been humiliated. That arrogant officer, Mr. Bosworth Smith, left nothing undone in disgracing women in Manianwala in the Punjab. In holding the meeting, therefore, the women of Bombay have done nothing more than their duty. I hope the women of Gujarat, too, will hold similar meetings in the principal cities of the province and pass appropriate resolutions.

Women cannot disown such duties thinking that they are but weak creatures. The soul can never be described as weak; it is the body which may be so described. Even a little girl who has, and knows that she has, a soul of shining purity can stand up to an overbearing Englishman, six-and-a-half foot tall. A woman conscious of her dignity as woman sheds luster on her womanhood through soul-force.

The woman who, knowing that she is weak in body, becomes weak [in mind] cannot do this. Our shastras tell us how Sita, Draupadi, and other women filled the wicked with awe. Just as the strength of an elephant's body is unavailing before the power of human intelligence, so also a man's intellectual and physical strength is quite helpless before the soul-force either of a man or a woman.

I, therefore, want the women of India not to believe themselves weak and give up their right and privilege of protecting their progeny.

It is sheer ignorance to call woman weak, woman who has been the mother of mighty heroes like Hanuman. Maybe she has been so called simply in order to impress upon the male his duty towards her, to tell him that, being physically the stronger, he must not be a monster and, in his pride, oppress woman who is weak, but that, on the contrary, he must do her service by protecting her and providing her with the means through which she may cultivate strength of soul.

Victims of the illusion that this is an age of sheer physical power, we feel perplexed and puzzled and wonder what the weak and miserable people of India can do. Thinking thus, even our menfolk feel themselves quite as helpless as women. If only the country realized that this is not true at all! The day the people of India come to have self-respect, they will be strong, and no General Dyer will then remain in the country.

How may we acquire such strength? No elaborate training is necessary. We have only to put our trust in God and stop being afraid of anybody's physical strength. The physically strong have at the most, the power of destroying our body. When we shed all fear for the safety of our body, we become lions among men. Real power, therefore, consists not in having the physical strength of a giant but in strength of mind, knowledge of the Self and freedom from the fear of death.

On Celibacy
(*Young India*, October 13, 1920)

I receive so many letters questioning me regarding celibacy, and I hold such strong views upon it, that I may no longer, especially at this the most critical period of national life, withhold my views and results of my experiences from the readers of *Young India*.

The word in Sanskrit corresponding to celibacy is *brahmacharya*, and the latter means much more than celibacy.

Brahmacharya means perfect control over all the senses and organs.

For a perfect *brahmachari* nothing is impossible. But it is an ideal state which is rarely realized. It is almost like Euclid's line which exists only in imagination, never capable of being physically drawn.

It is nevertheless an important definition in geometry yielding great results. So may a perfect *brahmachari* exist only in imagination. But if we did not keep him constantly before our mind's eye, we should be like a rudderless ship. The nearer the approach to the imaginary state, the greater the perfection.

But for the time being I propose to confine myself to *brahmacharya* as in the sense of celibacy. I hold that a life of perfect continence in thought, speech and action is necessary for reaching spiritual perfection. And a nation that does not possess such men is the poorer for it. But my purpose is to plead for *brahmacharya* as a temporary necessity in the present stage of national evolution.

We have more than an ordinary share of disease, famines, and pauperism—even starvation among millions. We are being ground down under slavery in such a subtle manner that many of us refuse even to recognize it as such, and mistake our state as one of progressive freedom in spite of the triple curse of economic, mental and moral drain. The ever-growing military expenditure, and the injurious fiscal policy purposely designed to benefit Lancashire and other British interests, and the extravagant manner of running the various departments of the State constitute a tax on India which has deepened her poverty and reduced her capacity for withstanding disease.

Is it right for us who know the situation to bring forth children in an atmosphere so debasing as I have described? We only multiply slaves and weaklings if we continue the process of procreation whilst we feel and remain helpless, diseased, and famine-stricken. Not till

India has become a free nation, able to withstand avoidable starvation, well able to feed herself in times of famine, possessing the knowledge to deal with malaria, cholera, influenza, and other epidemics, have we the right to bring forth progeny. I must not conceal from the reader the sorrow I feel when I hear of births in this land. I must express that for years I have contemplated with satisfaction the prospect of suspending procreation by voluntary self-denial. India is today ill equipped for taking care even of her present population, not because she is overpopulated but because she is forced to foreign domination whose creed is progressive exploitation of her resources.

How is the suspension of procreation to be brought about? Not by immoral and artificial checks that are resorted to in Europe but by a life of discipline and self-control. Parents must teach their children the practice of *brahmacharya*. According to the Hindu Shastras, the lowest age at which boys may marry is 25. If the mothers of India could be inclined to believe that it is sinful to train boys and girls for a married life, half the marriages of India will automatically stop. Nor need we believe the fetish of early puberty among girls because of our hot climate. I have never known a grosser superstition than this of early puberty. I make bold to say that the climate has absolutely nothing to do with puberty. What does bring about untimely puberty is the mental and moral atmosphere surrounding our family life.

Mothers and other relations make it a religious duty to teach innocent children that they are to be married when they reach a particular age. They are betrothed when they are infants or even babes in arms. The dress and the food of the children are also aids to stimulating passions. We dress our children like dolls not for their but for our pleasure and vanity. I have brought up children by the score. And they have without difficulty taken to and delighted in any dress given to them. We provide them with all kinds of heating and stimulating foods. Our blind love takes no note of their capacity. The result undoubtedly is an early adolescence, an unmature progeny, and an early grave. Parents furnish an object lesson which the children easily grasp. By reckless indulgence in their passions they serve for their children as models of unrestrained license. Every untimely addition to the family is ushered in amid trumpets of joy, and feasting. The wonder is that we are not less restrained than we are, notwithstanding our surroundings. I have not a shadow of doubt that married people if they wish well to the country and want to see India become a nation of strong and handsome full-formed men and women, would practice perfect self-restraint and cease to procreate for the time being. I tender this advice even to the newly married. It is easy not to do a thing at all than to cease doing it, even as it is easier for a life-abstainer to remain a teetotaler than for a drunkard or even a temperate man to abstain. To remain erect is infinitely easier than to rise from a fall.

It is wrong to say that continence can be safely preached only to the satiated. There is hardly any meaning, either, in preaching continence to an enfeebled person. And my point is that whether we are young or old, satiated or not, it is our duty at the present moment to suspend bringing forth heirs to our slavery.

May I point out to parents that they ought not to fall into the argumentative trap of the rights of partners? Consent is required for indulgence, never for restraint, this is an obvious truth.

When we are engaged in a death-grip with a powerful Government, we shall need all the strength—physical, material, moral and spiritual. We cannot gain it unless we husband the one thing which we must prize above everything else. Without this personal purity of life, we must remain a nation of slaves. Let us not deceive ourselves by imagining that because we consider the system of Government to be corrupt, Englishmen are to be despised as competitors in a race for personal virtue. Without making any spiritual parade of the fundamental virtues, they practice them at least physically in an abundant measure. Among those who are engaged in the political life of the country there are more celibates and spinsters than among us.

Spinsters among us are practically unknown except the nuns who leave no impression on the political life of the country. Whereas in Europe thousands claim celibacy as a common virtue.

I now place before the reader a few simple rules which are based on the experience not only of myself but of many of my associates.

> 1. Boys and girls should be brought up simply and naturally in the full belief that they are and can remain innocent.

> 2. All should abstain from heating and stimulating foods, condiments such as chilies, fatty and

concentrated foods such as fritters, sweets, and fried substances.

3. Husband and wife should occupy separate rooms and avoid privacy.

4. Both body and mind should be constantly and healthily occupied.

5. "Early to bed early to rise" should be strictly observed.

6. All unclean literature should be avoided. The antidote for unclean thoughts is clean thoughts.

7. Theaters, cinemas, etc., which tend to stimulate passion should be shunned.

8. Nocturnal dreams need not cause any anxiety. A cold bath every time for a fairly strong is the finest preventive in such cases. It is wrong to say that an occasional indulgence is a safeguard against involuntary dreams.

9. Above all, one must not consider continence even as between husband and wife to be so difficult as

to be practically impossible. On the contrary, self-restraint must be considered to be the ordinary and natural practice of life.

10. A heartfelt prayer every day for purity makes one progressively pure.

"You Merely Wish to Imitate the West"
(Letter to Mahadev Desai, August 13, 1921)

Bhaishri Mahadev,

I have your letter. Self-surrender does not, should not, deprive one of one's originality. It only means that the person has realized his little-ness and, therefore, relies on somebody in whom he has faith. When in doubt, such a person does not insist on his own view but yields to the friend's. Arjuna harried Krishna with no end of questions. The tortoise was a lover of God. His wife would tempt God right till the last. Though [he] scorned the counselors and sent them away, she kept complaining to God all the time. Self-surrender does not mean giving up one's judgment. Sincere self-surrender is not inertia, it is energy; knowing that there is someone to whom to turn ulti-mately, the person undertakes, with due regard for his limitations, a thousand experiments one after another. But they are all undertaken with humility, knowledge, and discrimination. I count Maganlal's self-surrender to be of the highest order, but he has never, I believe, surrendered his judgment. Your way is quite different. You have too little initiative and, therefore, whenever you get someone to whom you can look up, what little you have deserts you. Because too much reading has dulled your originality, you want to be an assistant.

One may wish to work independently and yet be extremely modest. Your motive in wanting to live with me is sincere, but it is wrong. You merely wish to imitate the West. If I always keep someone with me merely in order that a record of my activities may be kept, I myself would come to behave unnaturally. It is one thing that someone may remain by my side in the usual course of things and keep notes unobtrusively, but quite another that a person should keep notes of everything of set purpose. Did anyone take notes of Rama's activities? The world has lost nothing because no one did so. If extensive notes of Johnson's talks were taken, they have conferred on the world no incomparable benefit that I know of. We do not at all look at this matter merely from the point of view of literature.

However, I do want you always to be with me. Since your grasp is so good and you are so well-equipped, I should like you to understand everything about my life and work. I have a great many ideas, but they find expression only as occasions arise. There are subtleties, sometimes, which no one follows. My unexceptionable comments on Vasantram Shastri's letter were understood neither by Kaka nor by Swami. You understood them a little better than they. My considerateness in those comments went unnoticed. The tempting thought does not leave me, therefore, that if I had a man life you by my side he could, in the course of time, take up my work. I do not wish yet to employ you exclusively on any one task, but want you, instead, to gather experience. If, moreover, you get acquainted with everyone whom I know, our work in the future will be easier. . . .

Blessings from
Bapu

THE SIN OF UNTOUCHABILITY
(from *Freedom's Battle*, 1922)

It is worthy of note that the subjects Committee accepted without any opposition the clause regarding the sin of untouchability. It is well that the National assembly passed the resolution stating that the removal of this blot on Hinduism was necessary for the attainment of Swaraj. The Devil succeeds only by receiving help from his fellows. He always takes advantage of the weakest spots in our natures in order to gain mastery over us. Even so does the Government retain its control over us through our weaknesses or vices. And if we would render ourselves proof against its machination, we must remove our weaknesses. It is for that reason that I have called noncooperation a process of purification. As soon as that process is completed, this government must fall to pieces for want of the necessary environment, just as mosquitoes cease to haunt a place whose cess-pools are filled up and dried.

Has not a just Nemesis overtaken us for the crime of untouch-ability? Have we not reaped as we have sown? Have we not practiced Dwyerism and O'Dwyerism on our own kith and kin? We have seg-regated the "pariah" and we are in turn segregated in the British Colonies. We deny him the use of public wells; we throw the leavings of our plates at him. His very shadow pollutes us. Indeed there is no charge that the "pariah" cannot fling in our faces and which we do not fling in the faces of Englishmen.

How is this blot on Hinduism to be removed? "Do unto others as you would that others should do unto you." I have often told English officials that, if they are friends and servants of India, they should come down from their pedestal, cease to be patrons, dem-onstrate by their loving deeds that they are in every respect our friends, and believe us to be equals in the same sense they believe fellow Englishmen to be their equals. After the experiences of the Punjab and the Khilafat, I have gone a step further and asked them to repent and to change their hearts. Even so is it necessary for us Hindus to repent of the wrong we have done, to alter our behavior towards those whom we have "suppressed" by a system as devilish as we believe the English system of the Government of India to be. We must not throw a few miserable schools at them; we must not adopt the air of superiority towards them. We must treat them as our blood brothers as they are in fact. We must return to them the inheritance of which we have robbed them. And this must not be the act of a few

English-knowing reformers merely, but it must be a conscious voluntary effort on the part of the masses. We may not wait till eternity for this much belated reformation. We must aim at bringing it about within this year of grace, probation, preparation and *tapasya*. It is a reform not to follow *Swaraj* but to precede it.

Untouchability is not a sanction of religion, it is a device of Satan. The devil has always quoted scriptures. But scriptures cannot transcend reason and truth. They are intended to purify reason and illuminate truth. I am not going to burn a spotless horse because the Vedas are reported to have advised, tolerated, or sanctioned the sacrifice. For me the Vedas are divine and unwritten. "The letter killeth." It is the spirit that giveth the light. And the spirit of the Vedas is purity, truth, innocence, chastity, humility, simplicity, forgiveness, godliness, and all that makes a man or woman noble and brave. There is neither nobility nor bravery in treating the great and uncomplaining scavengers of the nation as worse than dogs to be despised and spat upon. Would that God gave us the strength and the wisdom to become voluntary scavengers of the nation as the "suppressed" classes are forced to be. There are Augean stables enough and to spare for us to clean.

The Need for Humility

The spirit of non-violence necessarily leads to humility. Non-violence means reliance on God, the Rocks of ages. If we would seek His aid, we must approach Him with a humble and a contrite heart.

Non-cooperationists may not trade upon their amazing success at the Congress. We must act, even as the mango tree which drops as it bears fruit. Its grandeur lies in its majestic lowliness. But one hears of non-cooperationists being insolent and intolerant in their behavior towards those who differ from them. I know that they will lose all their majesty and glory, if they betray any inflation. Whilst we may not be dissatisfied with the progress made so far, we have little to our credit to make us feel proud. We have to sacrifice much more than we have done to justify pride, much less elation. Thousands, who flocked to the Congress pandal, have undoubtedly given their intellectual assent to the doctrine but few have followed it out in practice. Leaving aside the pleaders, how many parents have withdrawn their children from schools? How many of those who registered their vote in favor of non-cooperation have taken to hand-spinning or discarded the use of all foreign cloth?

Non-cooperation is not a movement of brag, bluster, or bluff. It is a test of our sincerity. It requires solid and silent self-sacrifice. It challenges our honesty and our capacity for national work. It is a movement that aims at translating ideas into action. And the more we do, the more we find that much more must be done than we have expected. And this thought of our imperfection must make us humble.

A non-cooperationist strives to compel attention and to set an example not by his violence but by his unobtrusive humility. He allows his solid action to speak for his creed. His strength lies in his reliance upon the correctness of his position. And the conviction of it grows most in his opponent when he least interposes his speech between his action and his opponent. Speech, especially when it is haughty, betrays want of confidence and it makes one's opponent skeptical about the reality of the act itself. Humility therefore is the key to quick success. I hope that every non-cooperationist will recognize the necessity of being humble and self-restrained. It is because so little is really required to be done because all of that little depends entirely upon ourselves that I have ventured the belief that Swaraj is attainable in less than one year.

»» For Further Thought ««

Fasting, prayer, celibacy, the preservation of the body through mindful diet and the avoidance of intoxicants—all of the disciplines that Gandhi promoted passionately early in his life were ultimately subsumed within his lifelong political goals: self-sufficiency, justice, religious and racial tolerance, and freedom for all people. In the ideal world that Gandhi envisioned, we would all assume unshakeable dominion over ourselves and thereby gain control over the world. We would all help to effect change for the better.

Read back over Chapter One and find a passage that resonates strongly for you. Then write about why these particular words of Gandhi's, written nearly a century ago, have immediacy and meaning for you today. Here are a few passages to consider, among many others:

To bring a man here on starvation wages, to hold him under bondage, and when he shows the least signs of liberty, or, is in a position to live less miserably, to wish to send him back to his home where he would become comparatively a stranger and perhaps unable to earn a living, is hardly a mark of fair play or justice.... *(page 63)*

The time has now passed when the followers of one religion can stand and say, ours is the only true religion and all others are false. *(page 102)*

A great many people, we find, are inclined to imitate America. Men are dazzled by her industry. But, on deeper reflection, we shall see that there is not much in America worthy of imitation. *(page 111)*

Self-surrender does not, should not, deprive one of one's originality. It only means that the person has realized his littleness and, therefore, relies on somebody in whom he has faith. *(page 148)*

Chapter Two

SWADESHI: SELF-SUFFICIENCY

"Just as the cult of patriotism teaches us today that the individual has to die for the family, the family for the village, the village for the district, the district for the province, and the province for the country, so a country has to be free in order that it may die, if necessary, for the benefit of the world."

Before encountering Gandhi's work, you were probably unfamiliar with the term *swadeshi*—but it is key to understanding both his philosophy and his politics. It derives from a conjunction of two Sanskrit words (*swa* and *desh*) meaning "own country." Gandhi used it to emphasize the importance of his nation's self-sufficiency—of remaining "of one's own country."

In his promotion of swadeshi, Gandhi dictated national pride; respect for the mother tongue; preservation of Indian history, rites, and traditions; and—perhaps most notably—the consumption of homegrown and homemade goods only. His personal vow to use only homespun cloth (and his advocacy of personal spinning wheels for all) became a potent symbol of the swadeshi movement.

This chapter includes some of Gandhi's most resonant commentary on the importance of swadeshi, as well as his recommended methods for achieving and maintaining it.

FAMINE IN INDIA

(*Indian Opinion*, November 11, 1911)

We refer to the famine as "Famine in India" though Gujarat and Kathiawar [alone] are affected. If a part of the body is injured, the whole is injured; in the same way, a famine in Gujarat is a famine in India.

We gather from letters and newspapers from India that this year's famine will be much worse than any in the past. Men and cattle are both dying off. The last rains, it seems, have failed. One has actually to see the conditions to realize that they are beyond description. Even a day's starvation makes us irritable. If we do not get the food we are used to, there is no limit to the anger we vent upon the cook or the lady of the house. Suppose, instead, that for eight months we have had almost nothing to eat. The body is reduced to a skeleton. The belly almost touches the back. One can stand up only if helped by someone else. If we can visualize this for ourselves and suppose further that hundreds of thousands are in this state, we shall then have some idea of the conditions that obtain in India.

How can we help? The first way is to restrain our luxurious ways, our pretensions, our pride, and our sharp practices, and crave God's forgiveness for the sins we have committed. After this, if we feel that our minds have been purified, we may pray to God for relief for India in this cruelty inflicted on her.

If we proceed in this manner, money can be saved. We can use this money to provide relief to the famine-stricken. We are ready to accept money from those who cannot themselves send it, and to do so on their behalf. Already, we are in correspondence with a generous person who has come forward with the money he is willing to spend for this purpose. The money sent by us we shall pass on to this gentleman or to some public body of standing and publish the receipts.

The important thing is not how to send the money but how to collect it. It is our belief that the money sent by those who have made their minds simple and pure as we have suggested, will bear worthy fruit, as good seeds do; of this there can be no doubt.

RESPECT FOR THE MOTHER TONGUE
(Speech at Bihar Students' Conference, Bhagalpur, October 15, 1917)

You have, as it were, chained me to you by inviting me to preside over this session of the Students' Conference. For twenty-five years, I have been in close contact with students. It was in South Africa that I first came to know some. While in England, I always maintained contact with other students. After returning to India, I have been meeting students all over the country. They show me unbounded love.

By inviting me to preside over this meeting today and permitting me to speak in Hindi and conduct the proceedings, too, in Hindi, you, students, have given me evidence of your love. I shall think myself fortunate indeed if I can prove myself worthy of this love and be of some service to you. You have shown great wisdom in deciding to carry on the proceedings of this Conference in the regional language of the province—which also happens to be our national language. I congratulate you, and hope that you will continue this practice.

We have been guilty of disrespect to our mother tongue. I am sure we shall have to pay heavily for this act of sin. It has raised a wall of separation between us and our families. All those who are present at this Conference will bear witness to this fact. We do not and cannot explain to our mothers anything of what we learn. We do not and cannot give the benefit of our knowledge to others in our families.

One will never find this sad state of affairs in an English family. In England and in other countries where education is imparted through the mother tongue, students, when they return home, discuss with their parents what they learn at school; the servants in the home, and others too, become familiar with it. Thus, the other members of the family also benefit from what the children learn at school. We, on the other hand, leave behind in the school what we learn there. Knowledge, like air, can circulate in no time. But, as a miser keeps his wealth buried in the ground, so we keep our learning to ourselves and others, therefore, do not share in its benefits.

Disrespect to the mother tongue is as reprehensible as disrespect to one's mother. No one who is guilty of it deserves to be called a patriot. We hear many people saying that our languages are not rich enough in words to express our highest thinking. Gentlemen, this is no fault of the language.

It is for us to develop and enrich our language. There was a time when English was in the same condition [as our languages]. It progressed because the British made progress and strove to develop their language. If we fail to develop our languages, holding that English alone can help us to cultivate and express higher thoughts, there is not the least doubt that we shall continue to be slaves for ever. So long as our languages do not acquire the power to express all our thinking and remain incapable of serving as the medium of communication for the various sciences, the nation will not get modern knowledge. It is self-evident:

1. that the entire body of our people need this knowledge;

2. that it will never be possible for all our people to understand English;

3. that, if only an English-educated individual can acquire new knowledge, it is impossible for all the people to have it.

This means that, if the first two propositions are correct, there is no hope for the masses. For this position, however, the blame does not lie with the languages. Tulsidas was able to express his divine ideas just in Hindi. There are not many books in the world to equal his *Ramayana*. A great patriot Like Bharat Bhushan Pandit Madan Mohan Malaviya, who, though a house holder, has sacrificed his all for the country, has no difficulty in expressing himself in Hindi. He commands silvery English, but his speeches in Hindi have the brilliance of gold, like the current of the Ganga blazing like gold in sunshine as it pours down from lake Manasa. I have heard some Maulavis delivering their sermons. They find it easy enough to express their most profound ideas in their mother tongue. The language of Tulsidas is perfect, immortal. If we cannot express our thoughts in the speech which was his, surely the fault is ours.

The reason why we cannot do so is clear: the medium of education is English. All of us can help in getting this serious anomaly removed. I feel students can petition the Governments, respectfully, on this matter. There is another remedy which they can simultaneously adopt, and that is, to translate what they learn at school into Hindi, share their knowledge with others in their homes, and pledge themselves to use only their mother tongue in their intercourse with one another. I cannot bear to see one Bihari corresponding with another Bihari in English. I have heard thousands of Englishmen talking to one another. Some of them know other languages, but I have never heard two Englishmen talking in any foreign language among themselves. The inordinate folly that we are guilty of in India has no parallel in the history of the world.

A *Vedantist* poet has said that learning without thinking is useless. But owing to the reasons mentioned above, students' lives seem to be almost bankrupt of thought. They have lost all spirit and energy, are devoid of originality, and most of them appear listless and apathetic.

I do not dislike English; its riches are infinite. It is the language of administration and is rich with the wealth of knowledge. All this notwithstanding, I hold that it is not necessary for every Indian to learn it. But of this, I do not wish to speak more here. Students have been learning English, and they have no option but to do so till some other system is devised and the present schools undergo a revolution.

I shall, therefore, end this all-important subject of the mother tongue here, merely saying in conclusion that in their dealings with one another, and whenever possible, people should use only their mother tongue and that others, besides students, who are present here should strive their utmost to make the mother tongue the medium of education.

As I have earlier pointed out, most of the students look listless and devoid of energy. Many of them have asked me what they should do, how they could serve the country, and what they had best do to earn their living. I have the impression that they are most anxious about this last. Before answering these questions, it is necessary to consider what the true aim of education is. Huxley has said that education should aim at building character. Our seers aver that, if a man, though well-versed in the Vedas and the shastras, fails to realize the Self and to make himself worthy of liberation from all bonds, all his learning will have been in vain. They have also said: "He who has known the Self knows all." Self-realization is possible even without knowledge of letters. Prophet Mahomed was illiterate. Jesus Christ never went to school. But it would be foolhardy to assert, therefore, that these great souls had not attained self-realization. Though they never went to our schools and colleges to take any examination, we revere them. They had all that learning and knowledge could bring.

They were mahatmas. If, following their example in blind imitation of one another, we leave off attending school, we shall get nowhere, to be sure. But we, too, can attain knowledge of the Self only by cultivating good character. What is character, however? What are the hallmarks of a virtuous life? A virtuous man is one who strives to practice truth, non-violence, *brahmacharya*, non-possession, non-stealing fearlessness, and such other rules of conduct. He will give up his life rather than truth. He will choose to die rather than kill. He will rather suffer himself than make others suffer. He will be as a friend even to his wife and entertain no carnal thoughts towards her.

Thus the man of virtue practices brahmacharya [celibacy] and tries to conserve, as well as he can, the ultimate source of energy in the body. He does not steal, nor take bribes. He does not waste his time nor that of others. He does not accumulate wealth needlessly. He does not seek ease and comfort and does not use things he does not really need but is quite content to live a simple life. Firm in the belief that "I am the immortal spirit and not this perishable body and that none in this world can ever kill the spirit," he casts out all fear of suffering of mind and body and of worldly misfortunes and refusing to be held down even by an emperor, goes on doing his duty fearlessly.

If our schools never succeed in producing this result, the students, the system of education, and the teachers—all three must share the blame. It is, however, in the students' own hands to make good the want of character. If they are not anxious to develop character, neither teachers nor books will avail them. Thus, as I have said earlier, we must first understand the aim of education. A student who desires to cultivate and build character will learn how to do so from any good book on the subject. As Tulsidas has said:

> The Lord of Creation has made all things in this world, animate and inanimate, an admixture of good and evil. But a good man selects the good and rejects the evil even as the fabled swan is said to help himself to milk leaving out water.

Being devoted to Rama, Tulsidas beheld him even in the image of Krishna. Some of our students attend Bible classes as required by rules but they remain innocent of the teaching of the Bible.

One who reads the *Gita* with the intention of discovering errors in it may well succeed in doing so. But to him who desires liberation, the *Gita* shows the surest way thereto. Some people see nothing but imperfection in the *Koran-e-Sharif*, others, by meditating over it, fit themselves to cross the ocean of this earthly life. But I am afraid that most of the students never think as to the real aim of education.

They attend school merely because that is the normal thing to do. Some do so in order to be able to obtain employment later on.

In my humble opinion, to think of education as a means of earning a living betrays an unworthy disposition of mind. The body is the means of earning a living, while the school is a place for building character. To regard the latter as the means of fulfilling one's bodily needs is like killing a buffalo for a small piece of hide. The body should be maintained through bodily work. How can the *atman*, the spirit, be employed for this purpose? "Thou shalt earn the bread by the sweat of thy brow"—this is a *mahavakya* of Jesus Christ. The *Gita* also seems to say the same. About 99 percent of the people in this world follow this law and live without fear. "He who has given the teeth will also give the feed" is indeed a true saying. But it is not for the lazy and indolent. Students had better know from the very start that they will have to earn their living through bodily labor and not be ashamed of manual work to that end. I do not mean that all of us should always be plying the hoe. But it is necessary to understand that there is nothing wrong in plying the hoe to earn one's living even though one may be engaged in some other avocation, and that laborers are in no way inferior to us. One who has accepted this as a principle and an ideal, will reveal himself as a man of pure and exceptional character in the way he does his work, no matter what profession he follows. Such a man will not be the slave of wealth; rather, wealth will be his slave. If I am right in this, students will have to acquire the habit of doing physical labor. I have said this for the benefit of those who look upon education as the means of earning their living.

Students who attend school without taking thought as to the true aim of education, should first make sure what it should be. Such a student may resolve this very day that, henceforth, he will regard school as a place for building character. I am sure that he will effect a change for the better in his character in the course of a month and that his companions will also bear witness to his having done so. The shastras assert that we become what we think.

Many students feel that it is not necessary to make any special effort for health. However, regular exercise is absolutely necessary for the body. What can be expected of a student who is not well equipped in health? Just as milk cannot be held in a paper container, so also education is not likely to remain for long in the paper-like bodies of our students. The body is the abode of the spirit and, therefore, holy like a place of pilgrimage. We must see that it is well protected.

Walking regularly and energetically for an hour and a half in the morning and for the same period in the evening in open air keeps it healthy and the mind fresh. The time thus spent is not wasted. Such exercise, coupled with rest, will invigorate both the body and the intellect, enabling one to learn things more quickly. I think games like cricket have no place in a poor country like India.

We have a number of inexpensive games of our own which afford innocent joy. The daily life of the student should be above reproach. He alone can experience true delight whose mind is pure. Indeed, to ask such a man to seek delight in worldly pleasures is to deprive him of the real delight which is his. He who has resolved to rise does indeed rise.

Ramachandra, in his innocence, wished for the moon, and he got it. From one point of view, the world seems to be an illusion; from another, it seems real enough. For students, the world does indeed exist, for it is they who have to strive for great achievement in it. He who declares the world to be illusory without knowing what that really means, indulges in pleasures as the fancy takes him and then claims to have renounced the world, is welcome to call himself a *sannyasi*, but in reality he is a deluded man.

This brings me to the subject of *dharma* [order, righteousness, duty]. Where there is no dharma, there can be neither knowledge nor wealth, nor health, nor anything else. Where there is no dharma, life is devoid of all joy, is mere emptiness. We have had to go without instruction in dharma; we are in much the same position as the bridegroom's party at a wedding without the bridegroom. Students cannot have innocent joy without a knowledge of dharma. That they may have such joy, it is necessary for them to study the *shastras*, to reflect over their teaching and bring their conduct in conformity with their ideals. Smoking a cigarette the first thing in the morning or idle gossip does good to nobody. Nazir has said that, even the sparrows as they twitter, sing the name of the Lord morning and evening, when we are still lying in our beds fulllength.

It is the duty of every student to acquire the knowledge of dharma in any manner he can. Whether or not dharma is taught in schools, it is my prayer to students who have assembled here that they introduce its essential principles in their life. What exactly is dharma?

In what manner can instruction in religion be imparted? This is not the place for a discussion of this subject. But I shall give you this practical advice, based on my own experience, that you should take to the *Ramacharitamanasa* [of Tulsidas] and the *Bhagavad Gita* in love and reverence. You have a real jewel in the latter; seize it. But see that you study these two books in order to learn the secret of dharma. The seers who wrote these works did not set out to write history but only to teach dharma and morals. Millions of people read these books and lead pure lives. They read them with a guileless heart and live in this world full of innocent joy. It never occurs to them even in a dream to ask whether or not Ravana was a historical figure or whether they might not kill their enemies as Rama killed Ravana. Even when face to face with enemies, they pray for Ramachandra's protection and remain unafraid. Tulsidas, the author of the *Ramayana*, had nothing but compassion by way of a weapon. He desired to kill none. He who creates, destroys. Rama was God; He had created Ravana and so had the right to kill him. When any of us becomes God, he may consider whether he is fit to have the power to destroy. I have ventured to say this by way of introduction to these great books. I was, myself, a sceptic once and lived in fear of being destroyed. I have grown out of that stage and become a believer. I have thought it fit here to describe the influence which these books have had on me. For Muslim students, the Koran is the best book in this respect. I would counsel them as well that they study this book in a spirit of devotion. They should understand its true message. I feel, too, that both Hindus and Muslims should study each other's religious scriptures with due respect and try to understand them.

From this most absorbing subject, I shall pass on to a topic of more worldly interest. It is often asked whether it is proper for students to take part in politics. I will let you know my opinion about it without going into the reasons. Politics has two aspects, theoretical study and practical activity. It is essential that students be introduced to the former, but it is harmful for them to concern themselves with the latter. They may attend political meetings or the sessions of the Congress in order to learn the science of politics. Such gatherings are useful as object-lessons. Students should have complete freedom to attend them and every effort should be made to get the recent ban on them removed. Students may not speak or vote at such meetings but may serve as volunteers if that does not interfere with their studies. No student can afford to miss an opportunity of serving Malaviyaji if one comes his way. Students should keep away from party politics. They should remain detached and cultivate respect for the leaders of the nation. It is not for them to judge the latter. Students easily respond to excellences of character; they adore them.

They say it is the duty of students to look upon elders with reverence and respect their words. This is well said. He who has not learnt to respect others cannot hope for respect for himself. An attitude of insolence ill becomes students. In this respect, an unusual situation has come about in India. Older folk are careless how they behave, or fail to maintain their dignity.

What are the students to do in these circumstances? As I imagine, a student should have regard for dharma. Such a student, when faced with a moral dilemma, should recall the instance of Prahlad. Placed in circumstances in which this boy respectfully disobeyed the commands of his father, we can act in like manner towards elders resembling the latter. But any disrespect shown to them beyond this will be wrong. It will ruin the community. An elder is so not merely by virtue of his age, but by virtue of the knowledge, experience and wisdom which age brings. Where these are absent, the elder's position depends simply on his age. Nobody, however, worships age as such.

Another question is: How can students serve the country? The simple answer is that a student should study well, safeguarding his health meanwhile and cherishing the aim of using the fruits of his study in the service of the country. I am quite sure he will thereby serve his country. By living a purposeful life and taking care to be unmindful of our own interests and to work for others, we can achieve much with little effort. I want to tell you of one task of this kind. You must have seen my letter in the newspapers about the difficulties of third-class passengers. I suppose most of you travel third. These passengers spit in the compartment; they also spit out the remains of betel leaves and tobacco which they chew right in the carriage, and likewise throw the skins of bananas, etc., and other leavings on the floor of the carriage; they are careless in the use of the latrine and foul it. They smoke *bidis* and cigarettes without any regard for the convenience of fellow-passengers. We can explain to the other passengers in our compartment the harm that results from their dirtying the place. Most passengers respect students and listen to them. They should not then miss these excellent opportunities of explaining the rules of hygiene to the masses. The eatables sold at stations are dirty. It is the duty of students, when they find the things dirty, to draw the attention of the traffic manager to the fact, whether he replies or no. And take care that you write to him in Hindi. When he receives many such letters, he will be forced to heed them. This is easy work to do but it will yield important results.

I have spoken about the habits of chewing betel leaves and tobacco. In my humble opinion, these habits are both harmful and unclean. Most of us, men and women, have become their slaves. We must be free of this slavery. A stranger visiting India will surely think that we are always eating some thing or the other. That the betel leaf, possibly, helps to digest food may be conceded, but food eaten in the proper quantity and manner is digested without any help from things like the betel leaf. Moreover, it does not have even an agreeable taste. And tobacco chewing must be given up as well. Students should always practice self-control. It is also necessary to consider the habit of smoking. Our rulers have set a bad example in this respect. They smoke cigarettes anywhere and everywhere. This has led us to consider smoking a fashion, and to turn our mouths into chimneys.

Many books have been written to show that smoking is harmful. We call this age *Kaliyuga*. Christians believe that Jesus Christ will come again when selfishness, immorality, addiction to drugs and drink, etc., become rife. I shall not consider to what extent we may accept this as true. But I do feel that the world has been suffering a great deal from evils such as drinking, smoking, addiction to opium, *ganja*, hemp and so on. All of us are caught in this snare and so we cannot truly measure the magnitude of its unhappy consequences. It is my prayer that you, the students, keep away from them.

This Conference has entered its seventeenth year. The speeches of the Presidents in previous years were sent to me; I have gone through them. What is the object behind arranging these speeches? If it is that you may learn something from them, ask yourselves what you have learnt. If it is just to hear a beautiful flow of English words and enhance the prestige of the Conference, I feel sorry for you. I take it that these speeches are arranged with the idea that you may learn something from them and put it into practice. How many of you followed Smt. Besant's advice and adopted the Indian mode of dress, simplified your food habits and gave up unclean talk or acted on Prof. Jadunath Sarkar's advice and spent your vacations in teaching the poor, free of charge? I can put many questions. I do not ask for a reply. You may answer these questions to your own conscience. The worth of your learning will be judged by your actions. Stuffing your brains with the contents of hundreds of books may bring its reward but action is of much greater value by far. One's stock of learning is of no more value than the action it leads to. The rest is an unnecessary burden. I would, therefore, always request you and urge you to practice what you learn and what appears to you to be right. That is the only way to progress.

⟫ For Further Thought ⟪

Gandhi was by any definition a learned man—a reader, writer, and thinker. So it might have surprised you to read his views on the value and purpose of education. "Self-realization is possible even without knowledge of letters," he said while addressing a students' conference in 1917. "Prophet Mahomed was illiterate. Jesus Christ never went to school." Reading on, it's clear that, far from denigrating education, he was attempting to broaden its definition—to take it beyond the realm of the classroom and into the world. "The worth of your learning will be judged by your actions. Stuffing your brains with the contents of hundreds of books may bring its reward but action is of much greater value by far."

Gandhi was exhorting the young people of India to be citizens as well as scholars, and it is hard to disagree with this point of view. Think about your own most valuable learning experiences. Aside from in school, what experiences and encounters have changed your point of view or taught you lessons you couldn't have learned from books or lectures—educated you about the world and yourself?

_____

_____

_____

THE SWADESHI VOW

(*The Bombay Chronicle*, April 18, 1919;
also *New India*, April 22, 1919)

I

Although the desire for swadeshi animating a large number of people at the present moment is worthy of all praise, it seems to me that they have not fully realized the difficulty in the way of its observance.

Vows are always taken only in respect of matters otherwise difficult of accomplishment. When after a series of efforts we fail in doing certain things, by taking a vow to do them we draw a cordon round ourselves, from which we may never be free and thus we avoid failures. Anything less than such inflexible determination cannot be called a vow. It is not a pledge or vow when we say we shall so far as possible do certain acts. If by saying that we shall so far as we can only use swadeshi articles, we can be deemed to have taken the swadeshi vow, then from the Viceroy down to the laboring man very few people would be found who could not be considered to have taken the pledge, but we want to go outside this circle and aim at a much higher goal. And there is as much difference between the act contemplated by us and the acts above described as there is between a right angle and all other angles. And if we decide to take the swadeshi vow in this spirit, it is clear that it is well nigh impossible to take an all-comprehensive vow.

After having given deep consideration to the matter for a

number of years, it is sufficiently demonstrated to me that we can take the full swadeshi vow only in respect of our clothing, whether made of cotton, silk, or wool. Even in observing this vow, we shall have to face many difficulties in the initial stages and that is only proper. By patronizing foreign cloth we have committed a deep sin. We have condoned an occupation which in point of importance is second only to agriculture, and we are face to face with a total disruption of a calling to which Kabir was born and which he adorned. One meaning of the swadeshi vow suggested by me is that in taking it we desire to do penance for our sins, that we desire to resuscitate the almost lost art of hand-weaving, and that we are determined to save our Hindustan crores of rupees which go out of it annually in exchange for the cloth we receive. Such high results cannot be attained without difficulties; there must be obstacles in the way. Things easily obtained are practically of no value, but however difficult of observance that pledge may be, some day or other there is no escape from it if we want our country to rise to its full height. And we shall then accomplish the vow when we shall deem it a religious duty to use only that cloth which is entirely produced in the country and refrain from using any other.

A Hasty Generalization

Friends tell me that at the present moment we have not enough swadeshi cloth to supply our wants and that the existing mills are too few for the purpose. This appears to me to be a hasty generalization.

We can hardly expect such good fortune as to have thirty crores of covenanters for swadeshi. A hardened optimist dare not expect more than a few lakhs, and I anticipate no difficulty in providing them with swadeshi cloth, but where there is a question of religion, there is no room for thoughts of difficulties. The general climate of India is such that we require very little clothing. It is no exaggeration tosay that three-fourths of the middle class population use much unnecessary clothing. Moreover, when many men take the vow, there would be set up many spinning wheels and handlooms. India can produce innumerable weavers. They are merely awaiting encouragement. Mainly two things are needful, viz., self-denial and honesty. It is self-evident that the covenanter must possess these two qualities, but in order to enable people to observe such a great vow comparatively easily, our merchants also will need to be blessed with these qualities.

An honest and self-denying merchant will spin his yarn only from Indian cotton and confine weaving only to such cotton. He will only use those dyes which are made in India. When a man desires to do a thing he cultivates the necessary ability to remove difficulties in his path.

Destroy All Foreign Clothing

It is not enough that we manage if necessary with as little clothing as possible, but for a full observance it is further necessary to destroy all foreign clothing in our possession. If we are satisfied that we erred in making use of foreign cloth, that we have done an immense injury to India, that we have all but destroyed the race of weavers, cloth stained with such sin is only fit to be destroyed. In this connection, it is necessary to understand the distinction between swadeshi and boycott. Swadeshi is a religious conception. It is the natural duty imposed upon every men. The well-being of people depends upon it, and the swadeshi vow cannot be taken in a punitive or revengeful spirit. The swadeshi vow is not derived from any extraneous happening, whereas boycott is a purely worldly and political weapon. It is rooted in ill will and a desire for punishment, and I can see nothing but harm in the end for a nation that resorts to boycott. One who wishes to be a satyagrahi forever cannot participate in any boycott movement, and a perpetual satyagraha is impossible without swadeshi. This is the meaning I have understood to be given to boycott. It has been suggested that we should boycott British goods till the Rowlatt legislation is withdrawn and that the boycott should terminate with the removal of that legislation. In such a scheme of boycott, it is open to us to take Japanese or other foreign goods even though they may be rotten. If I must use foreign goods, having political relations with England, I would only take English goods and consider such conduct to be proper.

In proclaiming a boycott of British goods, we expose ourselves to the charge of desiring to punish the English but we have no quarrel with them; our quarrel is with the governors. And, according to the law of satyagraha, we may not harbor any ill will even against the rulers, and as we may harbor no ill will, I cannot see the propriety of resorting to boycott.

The Swadeshi Pledge

For a complete observance of the restricted swadeshi vow suggested above, I would advise the following text: "With God as my witness, I solemnly declare that from today I shall confine myself, for my personal requirements, to the use of cloth manufactured in India from Indian cotton, silk and wool; and I shall altogether abstain from using foreign cloth, and I shall destroy all foreign cloth in my possession."

I hope that many men and women will be ready to take this vow, and the public taking of the pledge will be desirable only if many men and women are ready for it. Even a few men and women may publicly take the pledge, but in order to make swadeshi a national movement, it is necessary that many should join it. Those who approve of the proposed movement should, in my opinion, lose no time in taking effective steps to begin it. It is necessary to interview merchants. At the same time, there need be no undue haste. The foundation of swadeshi should be well and truly laid. This is the right time for it as I have found that when a purifying movement like satyagraha is going on allied activities have an easy chance of success.

English-Owned Mills

I am told that there are in India English-owned mills which do not admit Indian share-holders. If this information be true, I would consider cloth manufactured in such mills to be foreign cloth. Moreover, such cloth bears the taint of ill will. However well made such cloth may be, it should be avoided. The majority do not give thought to such matters. All cannot be expected to consider whether their actions promote or retard the welfare of their country, but it behooves those, who are learned, those who are thoughtful, whose intellects are trained or who are desirous of serving their country, to test every action of theirs, whether public or private, in the manner aforesaid, and when ideals which appear to be of national importance and which have been tested by practical experience should be placed before the people as has been said in the Divine Song, "the multitude will copy the actions of the enlightened." Even thoughtful men and women have not hitherto generally carried on the above-mentioned self-examination. The nation has therefore suffered by reason of this neglect. In my opinion, such self-examination is only possible where there is religious perception.

Thousands of men believe that by using cloth woven in Indian mills, they comply with the requirements of the swadeshi vow. The fact is that most fine cloth is made of foreign cotton spun outside.

Therefore the only satisfaction to be derived from the use of such cloth is that it is woven in India. Even on handlooms for very fine cloth only foreign yarn is used. The use of such cloth does not amount to an observance of swadeshi. To say so is simple self-deception.

Satyagraha, i.e., insistence on truth is necessary even in swadeshi. When men will say, "we shall confine ourselves to pure swadeshi cloth, even though we may have to remain satisfied with a mere loin cloth," and when women will resolutely say, "we shall observe pure swadeshi even though we may have to restrict ourselves to clothing just enough to satisfy the sense of modesty," then shall we be successful in the observance of the great swadeshi vow. If a few thousand men and women were to take the swadeshi vow in this spirit, others will try to imitate them so far as possible. They will then begin to examine their wardrobes in the light of swadeshi. Those who are not attached to pleasures and personal adornment, I venture to say, can give a great impetus to swadeshi.

Key to Economic Salvation

Generally speaking, there are very few villages in India without weavers. From time immemorial, we have had village farmers and village weavers, as we have village carpenters, shoemakers, blacksmiths, etc., but our farmers have become poverty-stricken, and our weavers have patronage only from the poor classes. By supplying them with Indian cloth spun in India, we can obtain the cloth we may need. For the time being it may be coarse, but by constant endeavors, we can get our weavers to weave out of fine yarn, and so doing we shall raise our weavers to a better status, and if we would go a step still further, we can easily cross the sea of difficulties lying in our path.

We can easily teach our women and our children to spin and weave cotton, and what can be purer than cloth woven in our own home? I tell it from my experience that acting in this way we shall be saved from many a hardship, we shall be ridding ourselves of many an unnecessary need, and our life will be one song of joy and beauty. I always hear divine voices telling me in my ears that such life was a matter of fact once in India, but even if such an India be the idle dream of the poet, it does not matter. Is it not necessary to create such an India now, does not our purushartha lie therein? I have been traveling throughout India.

I cannot bear the heart-rending cry of the poor. The young and old all tell me, "We cannot get cheap cloth, we have not the means wherewith to purchase dear cloth. Everything is dear—provisions, cloth and all. What are we to do?" And they heave a sigh of despair.

It is my duty to give these men a satisfactory reply. It is the duty of every servant of the country but I am unable to give a satisfactory reply. It should be intolerable for all thinking Indians that our raw materials should be exported to Europe and that we have to pay heavy prices therefor. The first and the last remedy for this is swadeshi. We are not bound to sell our cotton to anybody, and when Hindustan rings with the echoes of swadeshi, no producer of cotton will sell it for its being manufactured in foreign countries. When swadeshi pervades the country, everyone will be set a-thinking why cotton should not be refined and spun and woven in the place where it is produced, and when the swadeshi mantra resounds in every ear, millions of men will have in their hands the key to the economic salvation of India.

Training for this does not require hundreds of years. When the religious sense is awakened, people's thoughts undergo a revolution in a single moment. Only selfless sacrifice is the sine qua non. The spirit of sacrifice pervades the Indian atmosphere at the present moment. If we fail to preach swadeshi at this supreme moment, we shall have to wring our hands in despair. I beseech every Hindu, Mussulman, Sikh, Parsi, Christian, and Jew, who believes that he belongs to this country, to take the swadeshi vow and to ask others also to do likewise. It is my humble belief that if we cannot do even this little for our country, we are born in it in vain. Those who think deep will see that such swadeshi contains pure economics. I hope that every man and woman will give serious thought to my humble suggestion. Imitation of English economics will spell our ruin.

THE VOW OF HINDU-MUSLIM UNITY
(Young India, May 7, 1919)

In the huge mass meeting of Hindus and Mahomedans held in the Sonapur Masjid compound on Sunday, the 6th April, the day of humiliation and prayer, a vow of Hindu-Muslim unity was proposed to be taken as in the case of swadeshi proposed at the Chowpatty meeting, and I had to utter a note of warning on both the occasions. At times in a fit of joyous passion we are spurred on to certain courses of action for which we have afterwards to repent. A vow is a purely religious act which cannot be taken in a fit of passion. It can be taken only with a mind purified and composed and with God as witness.

Most of what I have said whilst writing about the swadeshi vow applies here. Acts which are not possible by ordinary self-denial become possible with the aid of vows which require extraordinary self-denial.

It is hence believed that vows can only uplift us. If the Hindu and Muslim communities could be united in one bond of mutual friendship, and if each could act towards the other even as children of the same mother, it would be a consummation devoutly to be wished.

But before this unity becomes a reality, both the communities will have to give up a good deal, and will have to make radical changes in ideas held heretofore. Members of one community when talking about those of the other at times indulge in terms so vulgar that they but acerbate the relations between the two. In Hindu society we do not hesitate to indulge in unbecoming language when talking of the Mahomedans and *vice versa*. Many believe that an ingrained and ineradicable animosity exists between the Hindus and Mahomedans.

In many places we see that each community harbors distrust against the other. Each fears the other. It is an undoubted fact that this anomalous and wretched state of things is improving day by day. The Time-Spirit is ceaselessly working on unchecked, and willy-nilly we have to live together. But the object of taking a vow is speedily to bring about, by the power of self-denial, a state of things which can only be expected to come in the fulness of time. How is this possible?

Meetings should be called of Hindus—I mean the orthodox Hindus—where this question should be seriously considered. The standing complaint of the Hindus against the Mussulmans is that the latter are beef-eaters and that they purposely sacrifice cows on the *Bakr-i-ld* day. Now it is impossible to unite the Hindus and Mahomedans so long as the Hindus do not hesitate to kill their Mahomedan brethren in order to protect a cow. For I think it is futile to expect that our violence will ever compel the Mahomedans to refrain from cowslaughter.

I do not believe the efforts of our cow-protection societies have availed in the least to lessen the number of cows killed every day. I have had no reason to believe so. I believe myself to be an orthodox Hindu and it is my conviction that no one who scrupulously practices the Hindu religion may kill a cow-killer to protect a cow. There is one and only one means open to a Hindu to protect a cow and that is that he should offer himself a sacrifice if he cannot stand its slaughter.

Even if a very few enlightened Hindus thus sacrificed themselves, I have no doubt that our Mussulman brethren would abandon cowslaughter.

But this is satyagraha; this is equity; even as, if I want my brother to redress a grievance, I must do so by taking upon my head a certain amount of sacrifice and not by inflicting injury on him. I may not demand it as of right. My only right against my brother is that I can offer myself a sacrifice.

It is only when the Hindus are inspired with a feeling of pure love of this type that Hindu-Muslim unity can be expected. As with the Hindus, so with the Mussulmans. The leaders among the latter should meet together and consider their duty towards the Hindus.

When both are inspired by a spirit of sacrifice, when both try to do their duty towards one another instead of pressing their rights, then and then only would the long-standing differences between the two communities cease. Each must respect the other's religion, must refrain from even secretly thinking ill of the other. We must politely dissuade members of both the communities from indulging in bad language against one another. Only a serious endeavor in this direction can remove the estrangement between us. Our vow would have value only when masses of Hindus and Mussulmans join in the endeavor. I think I have now made sufficiently clear the seriousness and magnitude of this vow. I hope that on this auspicious occasion and surely the occasion must be auspicious when a wave of satyagraha is sweeping over the whole country—we could all take this vow of unity. For this it is further necessary that leading Hindus and Mahomedans should meet together and seriously consider the question and then pass a unanimous resolution at a public meeting.

This consummation will certainly be reached if our present efforts are vigorously continued. I think the vow may be taken individually even now and I expect that numerous people will do so every day. My warnings have reference to the taking of the vow publicly by masses of men. If it is taken by the masses, it should, in my humble opinion, be as follows:

> With God as witness we Hindus and Mahomedans declare that we shall behave towards one another as children of the same parents, that we shall have no

differences, that the sorrows of each shall be the sorrows of the other and that each shall help the other in removing them. We shall respect each other's religion and religious feelings and shall not stand in the way of our respective religious practices. We shall always refrain from violence to each other in the name of religion.

THE MUSIC OF THE SPINNING-WHEEL
(*Young India*, July 21, 1920)

Slowly but surely the music of perhaps the most ancient machine of India is once more permeating society. Pandit Malaviyaji has stated that he is not going to be satisfied until the ranis and the maharanis of India spin yarn for the nation, and the ranas and the maharanas sit behind the handlooms and weave cloth for the nation.

They have the example of Aurangzeb who made his own caps. A greater emperor—Kabir—as himself a weaver and has immortalized the art in his poems. The queens of Europe before Europe was caught in Satan's trap, spun yarn and considered it a noble calling. The very words, spinster and wife, prove the ancient dignity of the art of spinning and weaving. "When Adam delved and Eve span, who was then a gentleman" also reminds one of the same fact. Well may Panditji hope to persuade the royalty of India to return to the ancient calling of this sacred land of ours. Not on the clatter of arms depends the revival of her prosperity and true independence. It depends most largely upon reintroduction, in every home, of the music of the spinning-wheel. It gives sweeter music and is more profitable than the execrable harmonium, concertina and the accordion.

Whilst Panditji is endeavoring in his inimitably suave manner to persuade the Indian royalty to take up the spinning-wheel, Shrimati Saraladevi Chaudhrani, who is herself a member of the Indian nobility, has learnt the art and has thrown herself heart and soul into the movement. From all the accounts received from her and others, swadeshi has become a passion with her. She says she feels uncomfortable in her muslin saris and is content to wear her khaddar saris even in the hot weather. Her khaddar saris continue to preach true swadeshi more eloquently than her tongue. She had spoken to audiences in Amritsar, Ludhiana, and elsewhere, and has succeeded in enlisting the services, for her spinning committee at Amritsar, of Mrs. Ratanchand and Bugga Chaudhri and the famous Ratandevi who during the frightful night of the 13th April despite the curfew order of General Dyer sat, all alone in the midst of the hundreds of the dead and dying, with her dead husband's cold head in her lap. I venture to tender my congratulations to these ladies. May they find solace in the music of the spinning-wheel and in the thought that they are doing national work. I hope that the other ladies of Amritsar will help Saraladevi in her efforts and that the men of Amritsar will realize their own duty in the matter.

In Bombay the readers are aware that ladies of noted families have already taken up spinning. Their ranks have been joined by Dr. Mrs. Manekbai Bahadurji who has already learnt the art and who is now trying to introduce it in the Sevasadan. Her Highness the Begum Saheba of Janjira and her sister Mrs. Atia Begum Rahman have also undertaken to learn the art. I trust that these good ladies will, having learnt spinning, religiously contribute to the nation their daily quota of yarn.

I know that there are friends who laugh at this attempt to revive this great art. They remind me that in these days of mills, sewing machines or typewriters, only a lunatic can hope to succeed in reviving the rusticated spinning-wheel. These friends forget that the needle has not yet given place to the sewing machine nor has the hand lost its cunning in spite of the typewriter. There is not the slightest reason why the spinning-wheel may not coexist with the spinning mills even as the domestic kitchen coexists with the hotels. Indeed typewriters and sewing machines may go, but the needle and the reed pen will survive. The mills may suffer destruction. The spinning-wheel is a national necessity. I would ask sceptics to go to the many poor homes where the spinning-wheel is again supplementing their slender resources and ask the inmates whether the spinning-wheel has not brought joy to their homes.

Thank God, the reward issued by Mr. Revashanker Jagjiwan bids fare to bear fruit. In a short time India will possess a renovated spinning-wheel—a wonderful invention of a patient Deccan artisan. It is made out of simple materials. There is no great complication about it. It will be cheap and capable of being easily mended. It will give more yarn than the ordinary wheel and is capable of being worked by a five-year-old boy or girl. But whether the new machine proves what it claims to be or it does not, I feel convinced that the revival of hand-spinning and hand-weaving will make the largest contribution to the economic and the moral regeneration of India. The millions must have a simple industry to supplement agriculture. Spinning was the cottage industry years ago and if the millions are to be saved from starvation, they must be enabled to reintroduce spinning in their homes, and every village must repossess its own weaver.

MY LOIN-CLOTH
(*The Hindu*, October 15, 1921)

All the alterations I have made in my course of life have been effected by momentous occasions; and they have been made after such a deep deliberation that I have hardly had to regret them. And I did them, as I could not help doing them. Such a radical alteration—in my dress—I effected in Madura.

I had first thought of it in Barisal. When, on behalf of the famine-stricken at Khulna, I was twitted that I was burning cloth utterly regardless of the fact that they were dying of hunger and nakedness, I felt that I should content myself with a mere loincloth and send on my shirt and dhoti to Dr. Roy, for the Khulna people.

But I restrained my emotion. It was tinged with egotism. I knew that the taunt was groundless. The Khulna people were being helped, and only a single zemindar could have sent all the relief necessary. I needed therefore nothing to do there.

The next occasion came when my friend Maulana Mahomed Ali was arrested before my very eyes. I went and addressed a meeting soon after his arrest. I thought of dispensing with my cap and shirt that moment, but then I restrained myself fearing that I might create a scene.

The third occasion came during my Madras tour. People began to tell me that they had not enough khadi to start with and that if khadi was available, they had no money. "If the laborers burn their foreign clothing where are they to get khadi from?" That stuck into my heart. I felt there was truth in the argument. The plea for the poor overpowered me. I expressed grief to Maulana Azad Sobhani, Mr. Rajagopalachariar, Doctor Rajan and others, and proposed that I should thenceforth go about with a loin cloth. The Maulana realized my grief and entirely fell in with my idea. The other co-workers were uneasy. They felt that such radical change might make people uneasy, some might not understand it; some might take me to be a lunatic, and that all would find it difficult if not impossible, to copy my example.

For four days I revolved these thoughts, and ruminated the arguments, I began telling people in my speeches: "If you don't get khadi, you will do with mere loin-cloth but discard foreign clothing."

But I know that I was hesitating whilst I uttered those words. They lacked the necessary force, as long as I had my dhoti and my shirt on.

The dearth of swadeshi in Madras, also continued to make me uneasy. The people seemed to be overflowing with love but it appeared to be all froth.

I again turned to my proposal, again discussed with friends.

They had no new argument to advance, and September was very nearly closing. What should I do to complete the boycott the close of September? That was what was for ever troubling me.

Thus we reached Madura on the night of the 22nd. I decided that I should content myself with only a loin-cloth until at least the 31st of October. I addressed a meeting of the Madura weavers early next morning in loin-cloth. Today is the third day.

The Maulana has liked the idea so much that he has made as much alteration in his dress as the *Shariat* permits. Instead of the trousers, he puts on a *lungi*, and wears a shirt of which the sleeves do not reach beyond the elbow. Only at the time of the prayers, he wears a cap, as it is essential.

The other co-workers are silently watching. The masses in Madras watch me with bewilderment.

But if India calls me a lunatic, what then? If the co-workers do not copy my example, what then? Of course this is not meant to be copied by co-workers. It is meant simply to hearten the people, and to make my way clear. Unless I went about with a loin-cloth, how might I advise others to do likewise? What should I do where millions have to go naked? At any rate why not try the experiment for a month and a quarter? Why not satisfy myself that I left not a stone unturned?

It is after all this thinking that I took this step. I feel so very easy. For eight months in the year, you do not need a shirt here. And so far as Madras is concerned, it may be said that there is no cold season at all, and even the respectable class in Madras wears hardly anything more than a dhoti.

The dress of the millions of agriculturists in India is really only the loin-cloth, and nothing more. I have seen it with my own eyes wherever I have gone.

I want the reader to measure from this the agony of my soul. I do not want either my co-workers or readers to adopt the loincloth.

But I do wish that they should thoroughly realize the meaning of the boycott of foreign cloth and put forth their best effort to get it boycotted, and to get khadi manufactured. I do wish that they may understand that swadeshi means everything.

To Every Englishman in India

(from *Freedom's Battle*, 1922)

Dear Friend,

I wish that every Englishman will see this appeal and give thoughtful attention to it.

Let me introduce myself to you. In my humble opinion no Indian has co-operated with the British Government more than I have for an unbroken period of twenty-nine years of public life in the face of circumstances that might well have turned any other man into a rebel. I ask you to believe me when I tell you that my cooperation was not based on the fear of the punishments provided by your laws or any other selfish motives. It was free and voluntary cooperation based on the belief that the sum total of the activity of the British Government was for the benefit of India. I put my life in peril four times for the sake of the Empire—at the time of the Boer war when I was in charge of the Ambulance corps whose work was mentioned in General Buller's dispatches, at the time of the Zulu revolt in Natal when I was in charge of a similar corps at the time of the commencement of the late war when I raised an Ambulance corps and as a result of the strenuous training had a severe attack of pleurisy, and lastly, in fulfilment of my promise to Lord Chelmsford at the War Conference in Delhi. I threw myself in such an active recruiting campaign in Kuira District involving long and trying marches that I had an attack of dysentry which proved almost fatal.

I did all this in the full belief that acts such as mine must gain for my country an equal status in the Empire. So late as last December I pleaded hard for a trustful cooperation, I fully believed that Mr. Lloyd George would redeem his promise to the Mussulmans and that the revelations of the official atrocities in the Punjab would secure full reparation for the Punjabis. But the treachery of Mr. Lloyd George and its appreciation by you, and the condonation of the Punjab atrocities have completely shattered my faith in the good intentions of the Government and the nation which is supporting it.

But though, my faith in your good intentions is gone, I recognize your bravery and I know that what you will not yield to justice and reason, you will gladly yield to bravery.

See what this Empire means to India.

> Exploitation of India's resources for the benefit of Great Britain.

> An ever-increasing military expenditure, and a civil service the most expensive in the world.

> Extravagant working of every department in utter disregard of India's poverty.

> Disarmament and consequent emasculation of a whole nation lest an armed nation might imperil the lives of a handful of you in our midst. Traffic

in intoxicating liquors and drugs for the purposes of sustaining a top-heavy administration.

Progressively representative legislation in order to suppress an evergrowing agitation seeking to give expression to a nation's agony.

Degrading treatment of Indians residing in your dominions, and

You have shown total disregard of our feelings by glorifying the Punjab administration and flouting the Mussulman sentiment.

I know you would not mind if we could fight and wrest the scepter form your hands. You know that we are powerless to do that, for you have ensured our incapacity to fight in open and honorable battle. Bravery on the battlefield is thus impossible for us. Bravery of the soul still remains open to us. I know you will respond to that also. I am engaged in evoking that bravery. Non-cooperation means nothing less than training in self-sacrifice. Why should we cooperate with you when we know that by your administration of this great country we are being daily enslaved in an increasing degree. This response of the people to my appeal is not due to my personality. I would like you to dismiss me, and for that matter the Ali Brothers too, from your consideration. My personality will fail to evoke any response to anti-Muslim cry if I were foolish enough to rise it, as the magic name of the Ali Brothers would fail to inspire the Mussulmans with enthusiasm if they were madly to raise in anti-Hindu cry. People flock in their thousands to listen to us because we today represent the voice of a nation groaning under iron heels. The Ali Brothers were your friends as I was, and still am. My religion forbids me to bear any ill will towards you. I would not raise my hand against you even if I had the power. I expect to conquer you only by my suffering. The Ali Brothers will certainly draw the sword, if they could, in defense of their religion and their country. But they and I have made common cause with the people of India in their attempt to voice their feelings and to find a remedy for their distress.

You are in search of a remedy to suppress this rising ebullition of national feeling. I venture to suggest to you that the only way to suppress it is to remove the causes. You have yet the power. You can repent of the wrongs done to Indians. You can compel Mr. Lloyd George to redeem his promises. I assure you he has kept many escape doors. You can compel the Viceroy to retire in favor of a better one, you can revise your ideas about Sir Michael O'Dwyer and General Dyer. You can compel the Government to summon a conference of the recognized lenders of the people, duly elected by them and representing all shades of opinion so as to devise means for granting *Swaraj* in accordance with the wishes of the people of India. But this you cannot do unless you consider every Indian to be in reality your equal and brother. I ask for no patronage; I merely point out to you, as a friend, as honorable solution of a grave problem. The other solution, namely repression is open to YOU. I prophesy that it will fail. It has begun already. The Government has already imprisoned two brave men of Panipat for holding and expressing their opinions freely. Another is on his trial in Lahore for having expressed similar opinion. One in the Oudh District is already imprisoned. Another awaits judgment. You should know what is going on in your midst. Our propaganda is being carried on in anticipation of repression. I invite you respectfully to choose the better way and make common cause with the people of India whose salt you are eating. To seek to thwart their inspirations is disloyalty to the country.

⇾ For Further Thought ⇽

"Swadeshi is a religious conception," said Gandhi—but he devised a practical means to achieve it. As outlined in the powerful Swadeshi Vow, he encouraged all of his countrymen to take: "With God as my witness, I solemnly declare that from today I shall confine myself, for my personal requirements, to the use of cloth manufactured in India from Indian cotton, silk and wool; and I shall altogether abstain from using foreign cloth, and I shall destroy all foreign cloth in my possession."

It seems odd, the idea that a nation could achieve sovereignty via homespun cloth—but this is quintessential Gandhi: he believed that small, peaceful gestures could bring about massive change.

As you become steeped in Gandhi's way of thinking and acting, does it inspire you to think of simple things you can do to be more self-sufficient and better your own world? Those active in the current "locavore movement," for example, endeavor to safeguard the environment and local economies by consuming only food grown or raised within a few miles of where it is consumed. Is that something you might be willing to do? What other things can you think of that an individual in this day and age can do to help achieve swadeshi?

_____

_____

_____

_____

_____

_____

_____

Chapter Three

SWARAJ: INDEPENDENCE

"A nation that is capable of limitless sacrifice is capable of rising to limitless heights. The purer the sacrifice the quicker the progress."

Another word that was probably unfamiliar to you before you began studying Gandhi's ideas is *swaraj*, which literally means "self-rule." It is rarely used to describe anything other than Gandhi's own call for Indian independence from foreign oversight, interference, and trade.

To outline this concept, Gandhi wrote *Hind Swaraj* ("Home Rule") in November 1909, while traveling from London to South Africa. It was distributed widely as a pamphlet and is considered to be the blueprint for India's freedom movement. Much like the Socratic dialogues of Plato (with which Gandhi was no doubt familiar), it takes the form of a conversation between two characters, the Reader and the Editor. The Reader plays the role of a typical Indian, voicing the common beliefs and arguments of the time concerning his country's independence. Gandhi, as the Editor, responds.

In this important work, and other pieces collected in this chapter, Gandhi's path to Indian independence is set forth, leading to his inevitable conclusion that India can never be free unless it rejects Western civilization completely. In *Hind Swaraj*, as well, are the seeds of his most significant contribution to political thought and action: nonviolent resistance.

Hind Swaraj [Home Rule]
(Pamphlet, 1909)

The Congress and Its Officials

READER: Just at present there is a Home Rule wave passing over India. All our countrymen appear to be pining for National Independence. A similar spirit pervades them even in South Africa. Indians seem to be eager to acquire rights. Will you explain your views in this matter?

EDITOR: You have put the question well, but the answer is not easy. One of the objects of a newspaper is to understand popular feeling and to give expression to it; another is to arouse among the people certain desirable sentiments; and the third is fearlessly to expose popular defects. The exercise of all these three functions is involved in answering your question. To a certain extent the people's will has to be expressed; certain sentiments will need to be fostered, and defects will have to be brought to light. But, as you have asked the question, it is my duty to answer it.

READER: Do you then consider that a desire for Home Rule has been created among us?

EDITOR: That desire gave rise to the National Congress. The choice of the word "National" implies it.

READER: That surely, is not the case. Young India seems to ignore the Congress. It is considered to be an instrument for perpetuating British Rule.

EDITOR: That opinion is not justified. Had not the Grand Old Man of India prepared the soil, our young men could not have even spoken about Home Rule. How can we forget what Mr. Hume has written, how he has lashed us into action, and with what effort he has awakened us, in order to achieve the objects of the Congress? Sir William Wedderburn has given his body, mind, and money to the same cause. His writings are worthy of perusal to this day. Professor Gokhale in order to prepare the nation, embraced poverty and gave twenty years of his life. Even now, he is living in poverty. The late Justice Budruddin Tyebji was also one of those who, through the Congress, sowed the seed of Home Rule. Similarly, in Bengal, Madras, the Punjab and other places, there have been lovers of India and members of the Congress, both Indian and English.

READER: Stay, stay; you are going too far, you are straying away from my question. I have asked you about Home- or Self-Rule; you are discussing foreign rule. I do not desire to hear English names, and you are giving me such names. In these circumstances, I do not think we can ever meet. I shall be pleased if you will confine yourself to Home Rule. All other talk will not satisfy me.

EDITOR: You are impatient. I cannot afford to be likewise. If you will bear with me for a while, I think you will find that you will obtain what you want. Remember the old proverb that the tree does not grow in one day. The fact that you have checked me and that you do not want to hear about the well-wishers of India shows that, for you at any rate, Home Rule is yet far away. If we had many like you, we would never make any advance. This thought is worthy of your attention.

READER: It seems to me that you simply want to put me off by talking round and round. Those whom you consider to be well-wishers of India are not such in my estimation. Why, then, would I listen to your discourse on such people? What has he whom you consider to be the Father of the Nation done for it? He says that the English Governors will do justice and that we should cooperate with them.

EDITOR: I must tell you, with all gentleness, that it must be a matter of shame for us that you should speak about that great man in terms of disrespect. Just look at his work. He has dedicated his life to the service of India. We have learned what we know from him. It was the respected Dadabhai who taught us that the English had sucked our life-blood. What does it matter that, today, his trust is still in the English nation? Is Dadabhai less to be honored because, in the exuberance of youth, we are prepared to go a step further? Are we, on that account, wiser than he? It is a mark of wisdom not to kick away the very step from which we have risen higher. The removal of a step from a staircase brings down the whole of it. When, out of infancy, we grow into youth, we do not despise infancy, but, on the contrary, we recall with affection the days of our childhood. If after many years of study, a teacher were to teach me something, and if I were to build a little more on the foundation laid by that teacher, I would not, on that account, be considered wiser than the teacher. He would always command my respect. Such is the case with the Grand Old Man of India. We must admit that he is the author of nationalism.

READER: You have spoken well. I can now understand that we must look upon Mr. Dadabhai with respect. Without him and men like him, we should probably not have the spirit that fires us. How can the same be said of Professor Gokhale? He has constituted himself a great friend of the English; he says that we have to learn a great deal from them, that we have to learn their political wisdom, before we can talk of Home Rule. I am tired of reading his speeches.

EDITOR: If you are tired, it only betrays your impatience. We believe that those, who are discontented with the slowness of their parents and are angry because the parents would not run with their children, are considered disrespectful to their parents. Professor Gokhale occupies the place of a parent. What does it matter if he cannot run with us? A nation that is desirous of securing Home Rule cannot afford to despise its ancestors. We shall become useless, if we lack respect for our elders. Only men with mature thoughts are capable of ruling themselves and not the hasty-tempered. Moreover, how many

Indians were there like Professor Gokhale, when he gave himself to Indian education? I verily believe that whatever Professor Gokhale does, he does with pure motives and with a view of serving India. His devotion to the Motherland is so great that he would give his life for it, if necessary. Whatever he says is said not to flatter anyone but because he believes it to be true. We are bound, therefore, to entertain the highest regard for him.

READER: Are we, then, to follow him in every respect?

EDITOR: I never said any such thing. If we conscientiously differed from him, the learned Professor himself would advise us to follow the dictates of our conscience rather than him. Our chief purpose is not to decry his work, but to believe that he is infinitely greater then we are, and to feel assured that compared with his work for India, ours is infinitesimal. Several newspapers write disrespectfully of him. It is our duty to protest against such writings. We should consider men like Professor Gokhale to be the pillars of Home Rule. It is bad habit to say that another man's thoughts are bad and ours only are good and that those holding different views from ours are the enemies of the country.

READER: I now begin to understand somewhat your meaning. I shall have to think the matter over. But what you say about Mr. Hume and Sir William Wedderburn is beyond my comprehension.

EDITOR: The same rule holds good for the English as for the Indians. I can never subscribe to the statement that all Englishmen are bad. Many Englishmen desire Home Rule for India. That the English people are somewhat more selfish than others is true, but that does not prove that every Englishman is bad. We who seek justice will have to do justice to others. Sir William does not wish ill to India; that should be enough for us. As we proceed, you will see that, if we act justly, India will be sooner free. You will see, too, that if we shun every Englishman as an enemy, Home Rule will be delayed. But if we are just to them, we shall receive their support in our progress towards the goal.

READER: All this seems to me at present to be simply nonsensical. English support and the obtaining of Home Rule are two contradictory things. How can the English people tolerate Home Rule for us? But I do not want you to decide this question for me just yet. To spend time over it is useless. When you have shown how we can have Home Rule, perhaps I shall understand your views. You have prejudiced me against you by discoursing on English help. I would, therefore, beseech you not to continue this subject.

EDITOR: I have no desire to do so. That you are prejudiced against me is not a matter for much anxiety. It is well that I should say unpleasant things at the commencement. It is my duty patiently to try to remove your prejudice.

READER: I like that last statement. It emboldens me to say what I like. One thing still puzzles me. I do not understand how the Congress laid the foundation of Home Rule.

EDITOR: Let us see. The Congress brought together Indians from different parts of India, and enthused us with the idea of nationality. The Government used to look upon it with disfavor. The Congress has always insisted that the Nation should control revenue and expenditure. It has always desired self-government after the Canadian model. Whether we can get it or not, whether we desire it or not, and whether there is not something more desirable, are different questions. All I have to show is that the Congress gave us a foretaste of Home Rule. To deprive it of the honor is not proper, and for us to do so would not only be ungrateful, but retard the fulfillment of our object. To treat the Congress as an institution inimical to our growth as a nation would disable us from using that body.

What Is Swaraj?

READER: I have now learnt what the Congress has done to make India one nation, how the Partition has caused an awakening, and how discontent and unrest have spread through the land. I would now like to know your views on Swaraj. I fear that our interpretation is not the same as yours.

EDITOR: It is quite possible that we do not attach the same meaning to the term. You and I and all Indians are impatient to obtain Swaraj, but we are certainly not decided as to what it is. To drive the English out of India is a thought heard from many mouths, but it does not seem that many have properly considered why it should be so. I must ask you a question. Do you think that it is necessary to drive away the English, if we get all we want?

READER: I should ask of them only one thing, that is: "Please leave our country." If, after they have complied with this request, their withdrawal from India means that they are still in India. I should have no objection. Then we would understand that, in their language, the word "gone" is equivalent to "remained."

EDITOR: Well then, let us suppose that the English have retired. What will you do then?

READER: That question cannot be answered at this stage. The state after withdrawal will depend largely upon the manner of it. If, as you assume, they retire, it seems to me we shall still keep their constitution and shall carry on the Government. If they simply retire for the asking we should have an army, etc., ready at hand. We should, therefore, have no difficulty in carrying on the Government.

EDITOR: You may think so; I do not. But I will not discuss the matter just now. I have to answer your question, and that I can do well by asking you several questions. Why do you want to drive away the English?

READER: Because India has become impoverished by their Government. They take away our money from year to year. The most important posts are reserved for themselves. We are kept in a state of slavery. They behave insolently towards us and disregard our feelings.

EDITOR: If they do not take our money away, become gentle, and give us responsible posts, would you still consider their presence to be harmful?

READER: That question is useless. It is similar to the question whether there is any harm in associating with a tiger if he changes his nature. Such a question is sheer waste of time. When a tiger changes his nature, Englishmen will change theirs. This is not possible, and to believe it to be possible is contrary to human experience.

EDITOR: Supposing we get Self-Government similar to what the Canadians and the South Africans have, will it be good enough?

READER: That question also is useless. We may get it when we have the same powers; we shall then hoist our own flag. As is Japan, so must India be. We must own our navy, our army, and we must have our own splendor, and then will India's voice ring through the world.

EDITOR: You have drawn the picture well. In effect it means this; that we want English rule without the Englishman. You want the tiger's nature, but not the tiger; that is to say, you would make India English. And when it becomes English, it will be called not Hindustan but Englistan. This is not the Swaraj that I want.

READER: I have placed before you my idea of Swaraj as I think it should be. If the education we have received be of any use, if the works of Spencer, Mill, and others be of any importance, and if the English Parliament be the Mother of Parliaments, I certainly think that we should copy the English people, and this to such an extent that, just as they do not allow others to obtain a footing in their country, so we should not allow them or others to obtain it in ours. What they have done in their own country has not been done in any other country. It is, therefore, proper for us to import their institutions. But now I want to know your views.

EDITOR: There is need for patience. My views will develop of themselves in the course of this discourse. It is as difficult for me to understand the true nature of Swaraj as it seems to you to be easy. I shall therefore, for the time being, content myself with endeavoring to show that what you call Swaraj is not truly Swaraj.

Civilization

READER: Now you will have to explain what you mean by civilization.

EDITOR: It is not a question of what I mean. Several English writers refuse to call that civilization which passes under that name. Many books have been written upon that subject. Societies have been formed to cure the nation of the evils of civilization. A great English writer has written a work called Civilization: Its Cause and Cure. Therein he has called it a disease.

READER: Why do we not know this generally?

EDITOR: The answer is very simple. We rarely find people arguing against themselves. Those who are intoxicated by modern civilization are not likely to write against it. Their care will be to find out facts and arguments in support of it and this they do unconsciously, believing it to be true. A man whilst he is dreaming, believes in his dream; he is undeceived only when he is awakened from his sleep. A man laboring under the bane of civilization is like a dreaming man. What we usually read are the works of defenders of modern civilization, which undoubtedly claims among its votaries very brilliant and even some very good men. Their writings hypnotize us. And so, one by one, we are drawn into the vortex.

READER: This seems to be very plausible. Now will you tell me something of what you have read and thought of this civilization?

EDITOR: Let us first consider what state of things is described by the word "civilization." Its true test lies in the fact that people living in it make bodily welfare the object of life. We will take some examples. The people of Europe today live in better-built houses than they did a hundred years ago. This is considered an emblem of civilization, and this is also a matter to promote bodily happiness. Formerly, they wore skins, and used spears as their weapons. Now, they wear long trousers, and, for embellishing their bodies, they wear a variety of clothing, and, instead of spears, they carry with them revolvers containing five or more chambers. If people of a certain country, who have hitherto not been in the habit of wearing much clothing, boots, etc., adopt European clothing, they are supposed to have become civilized out of savagery. Formerly, in Europe, people ploughed their lands mainly by manual labor. Now, one man can plough a vast tract by means of steam engines and can thus amass great wealth. This is called a sign of civilization. Formerly, only a few men wrote valuable books. Now, anybody writes and prints anything he likes and poisons people's minds. Formerly, men traveled in wagons. Now, they fly through the air in trains at the rate of four hundred and more miles per day. This is considered the height of civilization. It has been stated that, as men progress, they shall be able to travel in airship and reach any part of the world in a few hours. Men will not need the use of their hands and feet. They will press a button, and they will have their clothing by their side. They will press another button, and they will have their newspaper. A third, and a motor-car will be in waiting for them. They will have a variety of delicately dished up food. Everything will be done by machinery. Formerly, when people wanted to fight with one another, they measured between them their bodily strength; now it is possible to take away thousands of lives by one man working behind a gun from a hill. This is civilization. Formerly, men worked in the open air only as much as they liked. Now thousands of workmen meet together and for the sake of maintenance work in factories or mines. Their condition is worse than that of beasts. They are obliged to work, at the risk of their lives, at most dangerous occupations, for the sake of millionaires. Formerly, men were made slaves under physical compulsion. Now they are enslaved by temptation of money and of the luxuries that money can buy. There are now diseases of which people never dreamt before, and an army of doctors is engaged in finding out their cures, and so hospitals have increased. This is a test of civilization. Formerly, special messengers were required and much expense was incurred in order to send letters; today, anyone can abuse his fellow by means of a letter for one penny. True, at the same cost, one can send one's thanks also. Formerly, people had two or three meals consisting of home-made bread and vegetables; now, they require something to eat every two hours so that they have hardly leisure for anything else. What more need I say? All this you can ascertain from several authoritative books. There are all true tests of civilization. And if anyone speaks to the contrary, know that he is ignorant. This civilization takes note neither of morality nor of religion. Its votaries calmly state that their business is not to teach religion. Some even consider it to be a superstitious growth.

Others put on the cloak of religion, and prate about morality. But, after twenty years' experience, I have come to the conclusion that immorality is often taught in the name of morality. Even a child can understand that in all I have described above there can be no inducement to morality. Civilization seeks to increase bodily comforts, and it fails miserably even in doing so.

This civilization is irreligion, and it has taken such a hold on the people in Europe who are in it appear to be half mad. They lack real physical strength or courage. They keep up their energy by intoxication. They can hardly be happy in solitude. Women, who should be the queens of households, wander in the streets or they slave away in factories. For the sake of a pittance, half a million women in England alone are laboring under trying circumstances in factories or similar institutions. This awful fact is one of the causes of the daily growing suffragette movement.

This civilization is such that one has only to be patient and it will be self-destroyed. According to the teaching of Mahommed this would be considered a Satanic Civilization. Hinduism calls it the Black Age. I cannot give you an adequate conception of it. It is eating into the vitals of the English nation. It must be shunned. Parliaments are really emblems of slavery. If you will sufficiently think over this, you will entertain the same opinion and cease to blame the English. They rather deserve our sympathy. They are a shrewd nation, and I therefore believe that they will cast off the evil. They are enterprising and industrious, and their mode of thought is not inherently immoral. Neither are they bad at heart. I therefore respect them. Civilization is not an incurable disease, but it should never be forgotten that the English people are at present afflicted by it.

The Condition of India: Railways

READER: You have deprived me of the consolation I used to have regarding peace in India.

EDITOR: I have merely given you my opinion on the religious aspect, but when I give you my views as to the poverty of India, you will perhaps begin to dislike me because what you and I have hitherto considered beneficial for India no longer appears to me to be so.

READER: What may that be?

EDITOR: Railways, lawyers, and doctors have impoverished the country so much so that, if we do not wake up in time, we shall be ruined.

READER: I do now, indeed, fear that we are not likely to agree at all. You are attacking the very institutions which we have hitherto considered to be good.

EDITOR: It is necessary to exercise patience. The true inwardness of the evils of civilization you will understand with difficulty. Doctors assure us that a consumptive clings to life even when he is about to die. Consumption does not produce apparent hurt? It even produces a seductive color about a patient's face so as to induce the belief that all is well. Civilization is such a disease, and we have to be very wary.

READER: Very well, then. I shall hear you on the railways.

EDITOR: It must be manifest to you that, but for the railways, the English could not have such a hold on India as they have. The railways, too, have spread the bubonic plague. Without them, the masses could not move from place to place. They are the carriers of plague germs. Formerly we had natural segregation. Railways have also increased the frequency of famines because, owing to facility of means of locomotion, people sell out their grain and it is sent to the dearest markets. People become careless and so the pressure of famine increases. Railways accentuate the evil nature of man. Bad men fulfill their evil designs with greater rapidity. The holy places of India have become unholy. Formerly, people went to these places with very great difficulty. Generally, therefore, only the real devotees visited such places. Nowadays rogues visit them in order to practice their roguery.

READER: You have given a one-sided account. Good men can visit these places as well as bad men. Why do they not take the fullest advantage of the railways?

EDITOR: Good travels at a snail's pace. It can, therefore, have little to do with the railways. Those who want to do good are not selfish; they are not in a hurry; they know that to impregnate people with good requires a long time. But evil has wings. To build a house takes time. Its destruction takes none. So the railways can become a distributing agency for the evil one only. It may be a debatable matter whether railways spread famines, but it is beyond dispute that they propagate evil.

READER: Be that as it may, all the disadvantages of railways are more than counterbalanced by the fact that it is due to them that we see in India the new spirit of nationalism.

EDITOR: I hold this to be a mistake. The English have taught us that we were not one nation before and that it will require centuries before we become one nation. This is without foundation. We were one nation before they came to India. One thought inspired us. Our mode of life was the same. It was because we were one nation that they were able to establish one kingdom. Subsequently they divided us.

READER: This requires an explanation.

EDITOR: I do not wish to suggest that because we were one nation we had no differences, but it is submitted that our leading men traveled throughout India either on foot or in bullock-carts. They learned one another's languages, and there was no aloofness between them.

What do you think could have been the intention of those farseeing ancestors of ours who established Setubandha (Rameshwar) in the South, Jagannath in the East and Hardwar in the North as places of pilgrimage? You will admit they were no fools. They knew that worship of God could have been performed just as well at home. They taught us that those whose hearts were aglow with righteousness had the Ganges in their own homes. But they saw that India was one undivided land so made by nature. They, therefore, argued that it must be one nation. Arguing thus, they established holy places in various parts of India, and fired the people with an idea of nationality in a manner unknown in other parts of the world. And we Indians are one as no two Englishmen are. Only you and I and others who consider ourselves civilized and superior persons imagine that we are many nations. It was after the advent of railways that we began to believe in distinctions, and you are at liberty now to say that it is through the railways that we are beginning to abolish distinctions. An opium-eater may argue the advantage of opium-eating from the fact that he began to understand the evil of the opium habit after having eaten it. I would ask you to consider well what I had said on the railways.

READER: I will gladly do so but one question occurs to me even now. You have described to me the India of the pre-Mahomedan period, but now we have Mahomedans, Parsis, and Christians. How can they be one nation? Hindus and Mahomedans are old enemies. Our very proverbs prove it. Mahomedans turn to the West for worship, whilst

Hindus turn to the East. The former look down on the Hindus as idolaters. The Hindus worship the cow, the Mahomedans kill her. The Hindus believe in the doctrine of non-killing, the Mahomedans do not. We thus meet with differences at every step. How can India be one nation?

What Is True Civilization?

READER: You have denounced railways, lawyers, and doctors. I can see that you will discard all machinery. What, then, is civilization?

EDITOR: The answer to that question is not difficult. I believe that the civilization India evolved is not to be beaten in the world. Nothing can equal the seeds sown by our ancestors, Rome went, Greece shared the same fate; the might of the Pharaohs was broken; Japan has become Westernized; of China nothing can be said; but India is still, somehow or other, sound at the foundation. The people of Europe learn their lessons from the writings of the men of Greece or Rome, which exist no longer in their former glory. In trying to learn from them, the Europeans imagine that they will avoid the mistakes of Greece and Rome. Such is their pitiable condition. In the midst of all this India remains immovable and that is her glory. It is a charge against India that her people are so uncivilized, ignorant and stolid, that it is not possible to induce them to adopt any changes. It is a charge really against our merit. What we have tested and found true on the anvil of experience, we dare not change. Many thrust their advice upon India, and she remains steady. This is her beauty: it is the sheet-anchor of our hope.

Civilization is that mode of conduct which points out to man the path of duty. Performance of duty and observance of morality are convertible terms. To observe morality is to attain mastery over our mind and our passions. So doing, we know ourselves. The Gujarati equivalent for civilization means "good conduct."

If this definition be correct, then India, as so many writers have shown, has nothing to learn from anybody else, and this is as it should be. We notice that the mind is a restless bird; the more it gets the more it wants, and still remains unsatisfied. The more we indulge our passions the more unbridled they become. Our ancestors, therefore set a limit to our indulgences. They saw that happiness was largely a mental condition. A man is not necessarily happy because he is rich, or unhappy because he is poor. The rich are often seen to be unhappy, the poor to be happy. Millions will always remain poor. Observing all this, our ancestors dissuaded us from luxuries and pleasures. We have managed with the same kind of plough as existed thousands of years ago. We have retained the same kind of cottages that we had in former times and our indigenous education remains the same as before. We have had no system of life-corroding competition. Each followed his own occupation or trade and charged a regulation wage. It was not that we did not know how to invent machinery, but our forefathers knew that, if we set our hearts after such things, we would become slaves and lose our moral fiber. They, therefore, after due deliberation decided that we should only do what we could with our hands and feet. They saw that our real happiness and health consisted in a proper use of our hands and feet. They further reasoned that large cities were a snare and a useless encumbrance and that people would not be happy in them, that there would be gangs of thieves and robbers, prostitution, and vice flourishing in them and that poor men would be robbed by rich men. They were, therefore, satisfied with small villages. They saw that kings and their swords were inferior to the sword of ethics, and they, therefore, and the sovereigns of the earth to be inferior to the Rishis and the Fakirs. A nation with a constitution like this is fitter to teach others than to learn from. This nation had courts, lawyers, and doctors, but they were all within bounds. Everybody knew that these professions were not particularly superior; moreover, these vakils and vaids did not rob people; they were considered people's dependants, not their masters. Justice was tolerably fair. The ordinary rule was to avoid courts. There were no touts to lure people into them. This evil, too, was noticeable only in and around capitals. The common people lived independently and followed their agricultural occupation. They enjoyed true Home Rule.

And where this cursed modern civilization has not reached, India remains as it was before. The inhabitants of that part of India will very properly laugh at your newfangled notions. The English do not rule over them, nor will you ever rule over them. Those in whose name we speak we do not know, nor do they know us. I would certainly advise you and those like you who love the motherland to go into the interior that has yet been not polluted by the railways and to live there for six months; you might then be patriotic and speak of Home Rule.

Now you see what I consider to be real civilization. Those who want to change conditions such as I have described are enemies of the country and are sinners.

READER: It would be all right if India were exactly as you have described it, but it is also India where there are hundreds of child widows, where two-year-old babies are married, where twelve-year-old girls are mothers and housewives, where women practice polyandry, where the practice of Niyoga obtains, where, in the name of religion, girls dedicate themselves to prostitution, and in the name of religion sheep and goats are killed. Do you consider these also symbols of the civilization that you have described?

EDITOR: You make a mistake. The defects that you have shown are defects. Nobody mistakes them for ancient civilization. They remain in spite of it. Attempts have always been made and will be made to remove them. We may utilize the new spirit that is born in us for purging ourselves of these evils. But what I have described to you as emblems of modern civilization are accepted as such by its votaries. The Indian civilization, as described by me, has been so described by its votaries. In no part of the world, and under no civilization, have all men attained perfection. The tendency of the Indian civilization is to elevate the moral being, that of the Western civilization is to propagate immorality. The latter is godless, the former is based on a belief in God. So understanding and so believing, it behooves every lover of India to cling to the old Indian civilization even as a child clings to the mother's breast.

Passive Resistance

Reader: Is there any historical evidence as to the success of what you have called soul-force or truth-force? No instance seems to have happened of any nation having risen through soul-force. I still think that the evil-doers will not cease doing evil without physical punishment.

Editor: The poet Tulsidas has said: "Of religion, pity, or love, is the root, as egotism of the body. Therefore, we should not abandon pity so long as we are alive." This appears to me to be a scientific truth. I believe in it as much as I believe in two and two being four. The force of love is the same as the force of the soul or truth. We have evidence of its working at every step. The universe would disappear without the existence of that force. But you ask for historical evidence. It is, therefore, necessary to know what history means. The Gujarati equivalent means: "It so happened." If that is the meaning of history, it is possible to give copious evidence. But, if it means the doings of the kings and emperors, there can be no evidence of soul-force or passive resistance in such history. You cannot expect silver ore in a tin mine. History, as we know it, is a record of the wars of the world, and so there is a proverb among Englishmen that a nation which has no history, that is, no wars, is a happy nation. How kings played, how they became enemies of one another, how they murdered one another, is found accurately recorded in history, and if this were all that had happened in the world, it would have been ended long ago. If the story of the universe had commenced with wars, not a man would have been found alive today. Those people who have been warred against have disappeared as, for instance, the natives of Australia of whom hardly a man was left alive by the intruders. Mark, please, that these natives did not use soul-force in self-defense, and it does not require much foresight to know that the Australians will share the same fate as their victims. "Those that take the sword shall perish by the sword." With us the proverb is that professional swimmers will find a watery grave.

The fact that there are so many men still alive in the world shows that it is based not on the force of arms but on the force of truth or love. Therefore, the greatest and most unimpeachable evidence of the success of this force is to be found in the fact that, in spite of the wars of the world, it still lives on.

Thousands, indeed tens of thousands, depend for their existence on a very active working of this force. Little quarrels of millions of families in their daily lives disappear before the exercise of this force. Hundreds of nations live in peace. History does not and cannot take note of this fact. History is really a record of every interruption of the even working of the force of love or of the soul. Two brothers quarrel; one of them repents and reawakens the love that was lying dormant in him; the two again begin to live in peace; nobody takes note of this. But if the two brothers, through the intervention of solicitors or some other reason take up arms or go to law? which is another form of the exhibition of brute force? their doings would be immediately noticed in the press, they would be the talk of their neighbors and would probably go down to history. And what is true of families and communities is true of nations. There is no reason to believe that there is one law for families and another for nations. History, then, is a record of an interruption of the course of nature. Soul-force, being natural, is not noted in history.

READER: According to what you say, it is plain that instances of this kind of passive resistance are not to be found in history. It is necessary to understand this passive resistance more fully. It will be better, therefore, if you enlarge upon it.

EDITOR: Passive resistance is a method of securing rights by personal suffering; it is the reverse of resistance by arms. When I refuse to do a thing that is repugnant to my conscience, I use soul-force. For instance, the Government of the day has passed a law which is applicable to me. I do not like it. If by using violence I force the Government to repeal the law. I am employing what may be termed body-force. If I do not obey the law and accept the penalty for its breach, I use soul-force. It involves sacrifice of self.

Everybody admits that sacrifice of self is infinitely superior to sacrifice of others. Moreover, if this kind of force is used in a cause that is unjust, only the person using it suffers. He does not make others suffer for his mistakes. Men have before now done many things which were subsequently found to have been wrong. No man can claim that he is absolutely in the right or that a particular thing is wrong because he thinks so, but it is wrong for him so long as that is his deliberate judgment. It is therefore meet that he should not do that which he knows to be wrong, and suffer the consequence whatever it may be. This is the key to the use of soul-force.

READER: You would then disregard laws? This is rank disloyalty. We have always been considered a law-abiding nation. You seem to be going even beyond the extremists. They say that we must obey the laws that have been passed, but that if the laws be bad, we must drive out the law-givers even by force.

EDITOR: Whether I go beyond them or whether I do not is a matter of no consequence to either of us. We simply want to find out what is right and to act accordingly. The real meaning of the statement that we are a law-abiding nation is that we are passive resisters. When we do not like certain laws, we do not break the heads of law-givers but we suffer and do not submit to the laws. That we should obey laws whether good or bad is a newfangled notion. There was no such thing in former days. The people disregarded those laws they did not like and suffered the penalties for their breach.

It is contrary to our manhood if we obey laws repugnant to our conscience. Such teaching is opposed to a religion and means slavery. If the Government were to ask us to go about without any clothing, should we do so? If I were a passive resister, I would say to them that I would have nothing to do with their law. But we have so forgotten ourselves and become so compliant that we do not mind degrading law.

A man who has realized his manhood, who fears only God, will fear no one else. Man-made laws are not necessarily binding on him. Even the Government does not expect any such things from us. They do not say: "You must do such and such a thing." but they say: "If you do not do it, we will punish you." We are sunk so low that we fancy that it is our duty and our religion to do what the law lays down. If man will only realize that it is unmanly to obey laws that are unjust, no man's tyranny will enslave him. This is the key to self-rule or home-rule.

It is a superstition and ungodly thing to believe that an act of a majority binds a minority. Many examples can be given in which acts of majorities will be found to have been wrong and those of minorities to have been right. All reforms owe their origin to the initiation of minorities in opposition to majorities. If among a band of robbers a knowledge of robbing is obligatory, is a pious man to accept the obligation? So long as the superstition that men should obey unjust laws exists, so long will their slavery exist. And a passive resister alone can remove such a superstition.

To use brute force, to use gunpowder, is contrary to passive resistance, for it means that we want our opponent to do by force that which we desire but he does not. And if such a use of force is justifiable, surely he is entitled to do likewise by us. And so we should never come to an agreement. We may simply fancy, like the blind horse moving in a circle round a mill, that we are making progress. Those who believe that they are not bound to obey laws which are repugnant to their conscience have only the remedy of passive resistance open to them. Any other must lead to disaster.

READER: From what you say I deduce that passive resistance is a splendid weapon of the weak, but that when they are strong they may take up arms.

EDITOR: This is gross ignorance. Passive resistance, that is, soul-force, is matchless. It is superior to the force of arms. How, then, can it be considered only a weapon of the weak? Physical-force men are strangers to the courage that is requisite in a passive resister. Do you believe that a coward can ever disobey a law that he dislikes? Extremists are considered to be advocates of brute force. Why do they, then, talk about obeying laws? I do not blame them. They can say nothing else. When they succeed in driving out the English and they themselves become governors, they will want you and me to obey their laws. And that is a fitting thing for their constitution. But a passive resister will say he will not obey a law that is against his conscience, even though he may be blown to pieces at the mouth of a cannon.

What do you think? Wherein is courage required? in blowing others to pieces from behind a cannon, or with a smiling face to approach a cannon and be blown to pieces? Who is the true warrior? He who keeps death always as a bosom-friend, or he who controls the death of others? Believe me that a man devoid of courage and manhood can never be a passive resister.

This however, I will admit: that even a man weak in body is capable of offering this resistance. One man can offer it just as well as millions. Both men and women can indulge in it. It does not require the training of an army; it needs no jiujitsu. Control over the mind is alone necessary, and when that is attained, man is free like the king of the forest and his very glance withers the enemy.

Passive resistance is an all-sided sword, it can be used anyhow; it blesses him who uses it and him against whom it is used. Without drawing a drop of blood it produces far-reaching results. It never rusts and cannot be stolen. Competition between passive resisters does not exhaust. The sword of passive resistance does not require a scabbard. It is strange indeed that you should consider such a weapon to be a weapon merely of the weak.

READER: You have said that passive resistance is a speciality of India. Have cannons never been used in India?

EDITOR: Evidently, in your opinion, India means its few princes. To me it means its teeming millions on whom depends the existence of its princes and our own.

Kings will always use their kingly weapons. To use force is bred in them. They want to command, but those who have to obey commands do not want guns; and these are in a majority throughout the would. They have to learn either body-force or soul-force. Where they learn the former, both the rulers and the ruled become like so many madmen: but where they learn soul-force, the commands of the rulers do not go beyond the point of their swords, for true men disregard unjust commands. Peasants have never been subdued by the sword, and never will be. They do not know the use of the sword, and they are not frightened by the use of it by others. That nation is great which rests its head upon death as its pillow. Those who defy death are free from all fear. For those who are laboring under the delusive charms of brute-force, this picture is not overdrawn. The fact is that, in India, the nation at large has generally used passive resistance in all departments of life. We cease to cooperate with our rulers when they displease us. This is passive resistance.

I remember an instance when, in a small principality, the villagers were offended by some command issued by the prince. The former immediately began vacating the village. The prince became nervous, apologized to his subjects and withdrew his command. Many such instances can be found in India. Real Home Rule is possible only where passive resistance is the guiding force of the people. Any other rule is foreign rule.

READER: Then you will say that it is not at all necessary for us to train the body?

EDITOR: I will certainly not say any such thing. It is difficult to become a passive resister unless the body is trained. As a rule, the mind, residing in a body that has become weakened by pampering, is also weak, and where there is no strength of mind there can be no strength of soul. We shall have to improve our physique by getting rid of infant marriages and luxurious living. If I were to ask a man with a shattered body to face a cannon's mouth I should make a laughing stock of myself.

READER: From what you say, then, it would appear that it is not a small thing to become a passive resister, and, if that is so, I should like you to explain how a man may become one.

EDITOR: To become a passive resister is easy enough but it is also equally difficult. I have known a lad of fourteen years become a passive resister; I have known also sick people do likewise: and I have also known physically strong and otherwise happy people unable to take up passive resistance. After a great deal of experience it seems to me that those who want to become passive resisters for the service of the country have to observe perfect chastity, adopt poverty, follow truth, and cultivate fearlessness.

Chastity is one of the greatest disciplines without which the mind cannot attain requisite firmness. A man who is unchaste loses stamina, becomes emasculated and cowardly. He whose mind is given over to animal passions is not capable of any great effort. This can be proved by innumerable instances. What, then, is a married person to do is the question that arises naturally; and yet it need not. When a husband and wife gratify the passions, it is no less an animal indulgence on that account. Such an indulgence, except for perpetuating the race, is strictly prohibited. But a passive resister has to avoid even that very limited indulgence because he can have no desire for progeny. A married man, therefore, can observe perfect chastity. This subject is not capable of being treated at greater length. Several questions arise: How is one to carry one's wife with one, what are her rights, and other similar questions. Yet those who wish to take part in a great work are bound to solve these puzzles.

Just as there is necessity for chastity, so is there for poverty. Pecuniary ambition and passive resistance cannot well go together. Those who have money are not expected to throw it away, but they are expected to be indifferent about it. They must be prepared to lose every penny rather than give up passive resistance.

Passive resistance has been described in the course of our discussion as truth-force. Truth, therefore, has necessarily to be followed and that at any cost. In this connection, academic questions such as whether a man may not lie in order to save a life, etc., arise, but these questions occur only to those who wish to justify lying. Those who want to follow truth every time are not placed in such a quandary; and if they are, they are still saved from a false position.

Passive resistance cannot proceed a step without fearlessness. Those alone can follow the path of passive resistance who are free from fear, whether as to their possessions, false honor. their relatives, the government, bodily injuries or death.

These observances are not to be abandoned in the belief that they are difficult. Nature has implanted in the human breast ability to cope with any difficulty or suffering that may come to man unprovoked. These qualities are worth having, even for those who do not wish to serve the country. Let there be no mistake, as those who want to train themselves in the use of arms are also obliged to have these qualities more or less. Everybody does not become a warrior for the wish. A would-be warrior will have to observe chastity and to be satisfied with poverty as his lot. A warrior without fearlessness cannot be conceived of. It may be thought that he would not need to be exactly truthful, but that quality follows real fearlessness. When a man abandons truth, he does so owing to fear in some shape or form. The above four attributes, then, need not frighten anyone. It may be as well here to note that a physical-force man has to have many other useless qualities which a passive resister never needs. And you will find that whatever extra effort a swordsman needs is due to lack of fearlessness. If he is an embodiment of the latter, the sword will drop from his hand that very moment. He does not need its support. One who is free from hatred requires no sword. A man with a stick suddenly came face to face with a lion and instinctively raised his weapon in self-defense. The man saw that he had only prated about fearlessness when there was none in him. That moment he dropped the stick and found himself free from all fear.

Machinery

READER: When you speak of driving out Western civilization, I suppose you will also say that we want no machinery.

EDITOR: By raising this question, you have opened the wound I have received. When I read Mr. Dutt's *Economic History of India*. I wept; and as I think of it again my heart sickens. It is machinery that has impoverished India. It is difficult to measure the harm that Manchester has done to us. It is due to Manchester that Indian handicraft has all but disappeared.

But I make a mistake. How can Manchester be blamed? We wore Manchester cloth, and this is why Manchester wove it. I was delighted when I read about the bravery of Bengal. There were no clothmills in that presidency. They were, therefore, able to restore the original hand-weaving occupation. It is true Bengal encourages the mill industry of Bombay. If Bengal had proclaimed a boycott of all machine-made goods, it would have been much better.

Machinery has begun to desolate Europe. Ruination is now knocking at the English gates. Machinery is the chief symbol of modern civilization; it represents a great sin.

The workers in the mills of Bombay have become slaves. The condition of the women working in the mills is shocking. When there were no mills, these women were not starving. If the machinery craze grows in our country, it will become an unhappy land. It may be considered a heresy, but I am bound to say that it were better for us to send money to Manchester and to use flimsy Manchester cloth than to multiply mills in India. By using Manchester cloth we only waste our money; but by reproducing Manchester in India, we shall keep our money at the price of our blood, because our very moral being will be sapped, and I call in support of my statement the very mill-hands as witnesses. And those who have amassed wealth out of factories are not likely to be better than other rich men. It would be folly to assume that an Indian Rockefeller would be better than the American Rockefeller. Impoverished India can become free, but it will be hard for any India made rich through immorality to regain its freedom. I fear we shall have to admit that moneyed men support British rule; their interest is bound up with its stability. Money renders a man helpless. The other thing which is equally harmful is sexual vice. Both are poison. A snake-bite is a lesser poison than these two, because the former merely destroys the body but the latter destroy body, mind and soul. We need not, therefore, be pleased with the prospect of the growth of the mill-industry.

READER: Are the mills, then, to be closed down?

EDITOR: That is difficult. It is no easy task to do away with a thing that is established. We, therefore, say that the non-beginning of a thing is supreme wisdom. We cannot condemn mill owners; we can but pity them. It would be too much to expect them to give up their mills, but we may implore them not to increase them. If they would be good they would gradually contract their business. They can establish in thousands of households the ancient and sacred handlooms and they can buy out the cloth that may be thus woven. Whether the mill owners do this or not, people can cease to use machine-made goods.

READER: You have so far spoken about machine-made cloth, but there are innumerable machine-made things. We have either to import them or to introduce machinery into our country.

EDITOR: Indeed, our gods even are made in Germany. What need, then, to speak of matches, pins, and glassware? My answer can be only one. What did India do before these articles were introduced? Precisely the same should be done today. As long as we cannot make pins without machinery so long will we do without them. The tinsel splendor of glassware we will have nothing to do with, and we will make wicks, as of old, with home-grown cotton, and use handmade earthen saucers for lamps. So doing, we shall save our eyes and money and support Swadeshi and so shall we attain Home Rule.

It is not to be conceived that all men will do all these things at one time or that some men will give up all machine-made things at once. But, if the thought is sound, we shall always find out what we can give up and gradually cease to use it. What a few may do, others will copy; and the movement will grow like the cocoanut of the mathematical problem. What the leaders do, the populace will gladly do in turn. The matter is neither complicated nor difficult. You and I need not wait until we can carry others with us. Those will be the losers who will not do it, and those who will not do it, although they appreciate the truth, will deserve to be called cowards.

READER: What, then, of the tram-cars and electricity?

EDITOR: This question is now too late. It signifies nothing. If we are to do without the railways we shall have to do without the tram-cars. Machinery is like a snake-hole which may contain from one to a hundred snakes. Where there is machinery there are large cities; and where there are large cities, there are tram-cars and railways; and there only does one see electric light. English villages do not boast of any of these things. Honest physicians will tell you that where means of artificial locomotion have increased, the health of the people has suffered. I remember that when in a European town there was a scarcity of money, the receipts of the tramway company, of the lawyers and of the doctors went down and people were less unhealthy. I cannot recall a single good point in connection with machinery. Books can be written to demonstrate its evils.

READER: Is it a good point or a bad one that all you are saying will be printed through machinery?

EDITOR: This is one of those instances which demonstrate that sometimes poison is used to kill poison. This, then, will not be a good point regarding machinery. As it expires, the machinery, as it were, says to us: "Beware and avoid me. You will derive no benefits from me and the benefit that may accrue from printing will avail only those who are infected with the machinery-craze."

Do not, therefore, forget the main thing. It is necessary to realize that machinery is bad. We shall then be able gradually to do away with it. Nature has not provided any way whereby we may reach a desired goal all of a sudden. If, instead of welcoming machinery as a boon, we should look upon it as an evil, it would ultimately go.

Conclusion

READER: From your views I gather that you would form a third party. You are neither an extremist nor a moderate.

EDITOR: That is a mistake. I do not think of a third party at all. We do not all think alike. We cannot say that all the moderates hold identical views. And how can those who want only to serve have a party? I would serve both the moderates and the extremists. Where I differ from them, I would respectfully place my position before them and continue my service.

READER: What, then, would you say to both the parties?

EDITOR: I would say to the extremists: "I know that you want Home Rule for India; it is not to be had for your asking. Everyone will have to take it for himself. What others get for me is not Home Rule but foreign rule; therefore, it would not be proper for you to say that you have obtained Home Rule if you have merely expelled the English. I have already described the true nature of Home Rule. This you would never obtain by force of arms. Brute-force is not natural to Indian soil. You will have, therefore, to rely wholly on soul-force.

You must not consider that violence is necessary at any stage for reaching our goal."

I would say to the moderates: "Mere petitioning is derogatory; we thereby confess inferiority. To say that British rule is indispensable, is almost a denial of the Godhead. We cannot say that anybody or anything is indispensable except God. Moreover, common sense should tell us that to state that, for the time being, the presence of the English in India is a necessity, is to make them conceited.

If the English vacated India, bag and baggage, it must not be supposed that she would be widowed. It is possible that those who are forced to observe peace under their pressure would fight after their withdrawal. There can be no advantage in suppressing an eruption; it must have its vent. If, therefore, before we can remain at peace, we must fight amongst ourselves, it is better that we do so. There is no occasion for a third party to protect the weak. It is this so-called protection which has unnerved us. Such protection can only make the weak weaker. Unless we realize this, we cannot have Home Rule. I would paraphrase the thought of an English divine and say that anarchy under Home Rule were better than orderly foreign rule. Only, the meaning that the learned divine attached to Home Rule is different from Indian Home Rule according to my conception. We have to learn, and to teach others, that we do not want the tyranny of either English rule or Indian rule.

If this idea were carried out, both the extremists and the moderates could join hands. There is no occasion to fear or distrust one another.

READER: What, then, would you say to the English ?

EDITOR: To them I would respectfully say: "I admit you are my rulers. It is not necessary to debate the question whether, you hold India by the sword or by my consent. I have no objection to your remaining in my country, but although you are the rulers, you will have to remain as servants of the people. It is not we who have to do as you wish, but it is you who have to do as we wish. You may keep the riches that you have drained away from this land, but you may not drain riches henceforth. Your function will be, if you so wish, to police India; you must abandon the idea of deriving any commercial benefit from us. We hold the civilization that you support to be the reverse of civilization. We consider our civilization to be far superior to yours. If you realize this truth, it will be to your advantage and, if you do not, according to your own proverb, you should only live in our country in the same manner as we do. You must not do anything that is contrary to our religions. It is your duty as rulers that for the sake of the Hindus you should eschew beef, and for the sake of Mahomedans you should avoid bacon and ham. We have hitherto said nothing because we have been cowed down, but you need not consider that you have not hurt our feelings by your conduct. We are not expressing our sentiments either through base selfishness or fear, but because it is our duty now to speak out boldly. We consider your schools and law courts to be useless. We want our own ancient schools and courts to be restored. The common language of India is not English but Hindi. You should, therefore, learn it. We can hold communication with you only in our national language.

"We cannot tolerate the idea of your spending money on railways and the military. We see no occasion for either. You may fear Russia; we do not. When she comes we shall look after her. If you are with us, we may then receive her jointly. We do not need any European cloth. We shall manage with articles produced and manufactured at home. You may not keep one eye on Manchester and the other on India. We can work together only if our interests are identical.

This has not been said to you in arrogance. You have great military resources. Your naval power is matchless. If we wanted to fight with you, on your own ground, we should be unable to do so, but if the above submissions be not acceptable to you, we cease to play the part of the ruled. You may, if you like, cut us to pieces. You may shatter us at the cannon's mouth. If you act contrary to our will, we shall not help you; and without our help, we know that you cannot move one step forward.

It is likely that you will laugh at all this in the intoxication of your power. We may not be able to disillusion you at once ; but if there be any manliness in us, you will see shortly that your intoxication is suicidal and that your laugh at our expense is an aberration of intellect. We believe that at heart you belong to a religious nation. We are living in a land which is the source of religions. How we came together need not be considered, but we can make mutual good use of our relations.

"You, English, who have come to India are not good specimens of the English nation, nor can we, almost half-Anglicized Indians, be considered good specimens of the real Indian nation. If the English nation were to know all you have done, it would oppose many of your actions. The mass of the Indians have had few dealings with you. If you will abandon your so-called civilization and search into your own scriptures, you will find that our demands are just. Only on condition of our demands being fully satisfied may you remain in India ; and if you remain under those conditions, we shall learn several things from you and you will learn many from us. So doing we shall benefit each other and the world. But that will happen only when the root of our relationship is sunk in a religious soil."

READER: What will you say to the nation?

EDITOR: Who is the nation?

READER: For our purposes it is the nation that you and I have been thinking of, that is those of us who are affected by European civilization, and who are eager to have Home Rule.

EDITOR: To these I would say, "It is only those Indians who are imbued with real love who will be able to speak to the English in the above strain without being frightened, and only those can be said to be so imbued who conscientiously believe that Indian civilization is the best and that the European is a nine days' wonder. Such ephemeral civilizations have often come and gone and will continue to do so. Those only can be considered to be so imbued who, having experienced the force of the soul within themselves, will not cower before brute-force, and will not, on any account, desire to use brute-force. Those only can be considered to have been so imbued who are intensely dissatisfied with the present pitiable condition, having already drunk the cup of poison.

"If there be only one such Indian, he will speak as above to the English and the English will have to listen to him.

"These are not demands, but they show our mental state. We shall get nothing by asking; we shall have to take what we want, and we need the requisite strength for the effort and that strength will be available to him only who will act thus:

1. He will only on rare occasions make use of the English language;

2. If a lawyer, he will give up his profession, and take up a handloom;

3. If a lawyer, he will devote his knowledge to enlightening both his people and the English;

4. If a lawyer, he will not meddle with the quarrels between parties but will give up the courts, and from his experience induce the people to do likewise;

5. If a lawyer, he will refuse to be a judge, as he will give up his profession;

6. If a doctor, he will give up medicine, and understand that rather than mending bodies, he should mend souls;

7. If a doctor, he will understand that no matter to what religion he belongs, it is better that bodies remain diseased rather than that they are cured through the instrumentality of the diabolical vivisection that is practiced in European schools of medicine;

8. Although a doctor, he will take up a hand-loom, and if any patients come to him, will tell them the cause of their diseases, and will advise them to remove the cause rather than pamper them by giving useless drugs; he will understand that if by not taking drugs, perchance the patient dies, the world will not come to grief and that he will have been really merciful to him;

9. Although a wealthy man, yet regardless of his wealth, he will speak out his mind and fear no one;

10. If a wealthy man, he will devote his money to establishing hand-looms, and encourage others to use hand-made goods by wearing them himself;

11. Like every other Indian, he will know that this is a time for repentance, expiation, and mourning;

12. Like every other Indian, he will know that to blame the English is useless, that they came because of us, and remain also for the same reason, and that they will either go or change their nature only when we reform ourselves;

13. Like others, he will understand that at a time of mourning, there can be no indulgence, and that, whilst we are in a fallen state, to be in jail or in banishment is much the best;

14. Like others, he will know that it is superstition to imagine it necessary that we should guard against being imprisoned in order that we may deal with the people;

15. Like others, he will know that action is much better than speech; that it is our duty to say exactly what we think and face the consequences and that

it will be only then that we shall be able to impress anybody with our speech;

16. Like others, he will understand that we shall become free only through suffering;

17. Like others, he will understand that deportation for life to the Andamans is not enough expiation for the sin of encouraging European civilization:

18. Like others, he will know that no nation has risen without suffering; that, even in physical warfare, the true test is suffering and not the killing of others, much more so in the warfare of passive resistance;

19. Like others, he will know that it is an idle excuse to say that we shall do a thing when the others also do it: that we should do what we know to be right, and that others will do it when they see the way; that when I fancy a particular delicacy, I do not wait till others taste it: that to make a national effort and to suffer are in the nature of delicacies; and that to suffer under pressure is no suffering."

READER: This is a large order. When will all carry it out?

EDITOR: You make a mistake. You and I have nothing to do with the others. Let each do his duty. If I do my duty, that is, serve myself, I shall be able to serve others. Before I leave you, I will take the liberty of repeating:

1. Real home-rule is self-rule or self-control.

2. The way to it is passive resistance: that is soul-force or love-force.

3. In order to exert this force, Swadeshi in every sense is necessary.

4. What we want to do should be done, not because we object to the English or because we want to retaliate but because it is our duty to do so. Thus, supposing that the English remove the salt-tax, restore our money, give the highest posts to Indians, withdraw the English troops, we shall certainly not use their machine-made goods, nor use the English language, nor many of their industries. It is worth noting that these things are, in their nature, harmful; hence we do not want them. I bear no enmity towards the English but I do towards their civilization.

In my opinion, we have used the term "Swaraj" without understanding its real significance. I have endeavored to explain it as I understand it, and my conscience testifies that my life henceforth is dedicated to its attainment.

››› For Further Thought ‹‹‹

The key ideas that Gandhi would continue to promote passionately throughout his life—and would ultimately die for—are introduced simply and effectively in this brief essay: the importance of swaraj and swadeshi, and the methods of satyagraha, or nonviolent resistance. He argues, first and foremost, for home rule—which he insists begins with self-rule; he denounces violence absolutely; and he states that India can never be free unless it rejects the values and customs of the West: "The tendency of the Indian civilization is to elevate the moral being, that of the Western civilization is to propagate immorality. The latter is godless, the former is based on a belief in God. So understanding and so believing, it behooves every lover of India to cling to the old Indian civilization even as a child clings to the mother's breast."

It's hard to imagine what Gandhi would make of today's globalized, technology-dependent world. His hope for a self-sufficient India devoid of Western influence and innovation did not come to pass (though he lived just long enough to see his homeland become an independent republic, albeit partitioned from Pakistan). Does this mean that Gandhi's ideas were flawed, or that he failed? Gandhi seemed to be against progress—and that can be hard for some of us to endorse. Do any of the ideas in *Hind Swaraj* seem relevant or useful to you today? What statements still ring true and seem to be of lasting value?

_____

_____

_____

_____

_____

_____

_____

_____

_____

_____

_____

_____

_____

_____

_____

_____

_____

_____

"PATH OF TRUTH FOR THE BRAVE ALONE"
(*Madhpudo*, July 1920)

"The path of truth is for the brave alone, never for a coward." I realize the significance of this poem more and more as days pass. I also see that it is not for grown-ups only to put the idea of this verse into practice; children and students, too, can do so. If we try to know and follow the path of truth right from childhood, then alone, on growing up, shall we be saved from following the path of untruth. Just as a disease, if neglected, becomes chronic and incurable, so also untruth, if permitted to take rot in us from childhood, will later grow into a serious disease and, becoming incurable, gradually ruin our health. It is for this reason that we find untruth increasing in us. So the highest lesson to be learnt during one's student-life is that one should know truth and act on it.

This path has always been for the brave because a much greater effort is required to go up the steep slope of truth than to climb the Himalayas. If at all, therefore, we want to work in this direction and serve ourselves, we should give the first place to truth and march forward with unshakable faith in it. Truth is God.

The Fear of Death

(*Young India*, October 13, 1921)

I have been collecting descriptions of swaraj. One of these would be: Swaraj is the abandonment of the fear of death. A nation which allows itself to be influenced by the fear of death cannot attain swaraj, and cannot retain it if somehow attained.

English people carry their lives in their pockets. Arabs and Pathans consider death as nothing more than an ordinary ailment; they never weep when a relation dies. Boer women are perfectly innocent of this fear. In the Boer war, thousands of young Boer women became widowed. They never cared. It did not matter in the least if the husband or the son was lost; it was enough and more than enough that the country's honor was safe. What booted the husband if the country was enslaved? It was infinitely better to bury a son's mortal remains and to cherish his immortal memory than to bring him up as a serf. Thus did the Boer women steel their hearts and cheerfully give up their darlings to the angel of Death.

The people I have mentioned kill and get killed. But what of those who do not kill but are only ready to die themselves? Such people become the objects of a world's adoration. They are the salt of the earth.

The English and the Germans fought one another; they killed and got killed. The result is that animosities have increased. There is no end of unrest, and the present condition of Europe is pitiful.

There is more of deceit, and each is anxious to circumvent the rest. But the fearlessness which we are cultivating is of a nobler and purer order and it is therefore that we hope to achieve a signal victory within a very short time.

When we attain swaraj, many of us will have given up the fear of death; or else we shall not have attained swaraj. Till now mostly young boys have died in the cause. Those who died in Aligarh were all below twenty-one. No one knows who they were. If Government resort to firing now, I am hoping that some men of the first rank will have the opportunity of offering up the supreme sacrifice.

Why should we be upset when children or young men or old men die? Not a moment passes when someone is not born or is not dead in this world. We should feel the stupidity of rejoicing in a birth and lamenting a death. Those who believe in the soul—and what Hindu, Mussulman, or Parsi is there who does not?—know that the soul never dies. The souls of the living as well as of the dead are all one. The eternal processes of creation and destruction are going on ceaselessly.

There is nothing in it for which we might give ourselves up to joy or sorrow. Even if we extend the idea of relationship only to our countrymen and take all the births in the country as taking place in our own family, how many births shall we celebrate? If we weep for all the deaths in our country, the tears in our eyes would never dry. This train of thought should help us to get rid of all fear of death.

India, they say, is a nation of philosophers; and we have not been unwilling to appropriate the compliment. Still, hardly any other nation becomes so helpless in the face of death as we do. And in India again, no other community perhaps betrays so much of this helplessness as the Hindus. A single birth is enough for us to be beside ourselves with ludicrous joyfulness. A death makes us indulge in orgies of loud lamentation which condemn the neighborhood to sleeplessness for the night. If we wish to attain swaraj, and if having attained it we wish to make it something to be proud of, we must perfectly renounce this unseemly fright.

And what is imprisonment to the man who is fearless of death itself? If the reader will bestow a little thought upon the matter, he will find that if swaraj is delayed, it is delayed because we are not prepared calmly to meet death and inconveniences less than death.

As larger and larger numbers of innocent men come out to welcome death, their sacrifice will become the potent instrument for the salvation of all others; and there will be a minimum of suffering.

Suffering cheerfully endured ceases to be suffering and is transmuted into an ineffable joy. The man who flies from suffering is the victim of endless tribulation before it has come to him, and is half dead when it does come. But one who is cheerfully ready for anything and everything that comes escapes all pain; his cheerfulness acts as an anaesthetic.

I have been led to write about this subject because we have got to envisage even death if we will have swaraj this very year. One who is previously prepared often escapes accidents; and this may well be the case with us. It is my firm conviction that swadeshi constitutes this preparation. When once swadeshi is a success, neither this Government nor any one else will feel the necessity of putting us to any further test.

Still it is best not to neglect any contingency whatever.

Possession of power makes men blind and deaf; they cannot see things which are under their very nose, and cannot hear things which invade their ears. There is thus no knowing what this power-intoxicated Government may not do. So it seemed to me that patriotic men ought to be prepared for death, imprisonment and similar eventualities.

The brave meet death with a smile on their lips, but they are circumspect all the same. There is no room for foolhardiness in this non-violent war. We do not propose to go to jail or to die by an immoral act. We must mount the gallows while resisting the oppressive laws of this Government.

SWARAJ IN ONE YEAR

(from *Freedom's Battle*, 1922)

Much laughter has been indulged in at my expense for having told the Congress audience at Calcutta that if there was sufficient response to my program of non-cooperation Swaraj would be attained in one year. Some have ignored my condition and laughed because of the impossibility of getting Swaraj anyhow within one year. Others have spelt the "if" in capitals and suggested that if "ifs" were permissible in argument, any absurdity could be proved to be a possibility. My proposition however is based on a mathematical calculation. And I venture to say that true Swaraj is a practical impossibility without due fulfillment of my conditions. Swaraj means a state such that we can maintain our separate existence without the presence of the English. If it is to be a partnership, it must be partnership at will. There can be no Swaraj without our feeling and being the equals of Englishmen.

Today we feel that we are dependent upon them for our internal and external security, for an armed peace between the Hindus and the Mussulmans, for our education and for the supply of daily wants, nay, even for the settlement of our religious squabbles. The Rajahs are dependent upon the British for their powers and the millionaires for their millions. The British know our helplessness and Sir Thomas Holland cracks jokes quite legitimately at the expense of non-cooperationists. To get Swaraj then is to get rid of our helplessness.

The problem is no doubt stupendous even as it is for the fabled lion who having been brought up in the company of goats found it impossible to feel that he was a lion. As Tolstoy used to put it, mankind often labored under hypnotism. Under its spell continuously we feel the feeling of helplessness. The British themselves cannot be expected to help us out of it. On the contrary, they din into our ears that we shall be fit to govern ourselves only by slow educative processes. The *Times* suggested that if we boycott the councils we shall lose the opportunity of a training in Swaraj. I have no doubt that there are many who believe what the *Times* says. It even resorts to a falsehood. It audaciously says that Lord Milner's Mission listened to the Egyptians only when they were ready to lift the boycott of the Egyptian Council. For me the only training in Swaraj we need is the ability to defend ourselves against the whole world and to live our natural life in perfect freedom even though it may be full of defects.

Good Government is no substitute for self-Government. The Afghans have a bad Government but it is self-Government. I envy them. The Japanese learnt the art through a sea of blood. And if we today had the power to drive out the English by superior brute force, we would be counted their superiors, and in spite of our inexperience in debating at the Council table or in holding executive offices, we would be held fit to govern ourselves. For brute force is the only test the west has hitherto recognized. The Germans were defeated not because they were necessarily in the wrong, but because the allied Powers were found to possess greater brute strength. In the end therefore India must either learn the art of war which the British will not teach her or, she must follow her own way of discipline and self-sacrifice through non-cooperation.

It is as amazing as it is humiliating that less than one hundred-thousand white men should be able to rule three hundred and fifteen million Indians. They do so somewhat undoubtedly by force, but more by securing our cooperation in a thousand ways and making us more and more helpless and dependent on them as time goes forward. Let us not mistake reformed councils, more law courts, and even governorships for real freedom or power. They are but subtler methods of emasculation. The British cannot rule us by mere force. And so they resort to all means, honorable and dishonorable, in order to retain their hold on India. They want India's billions, and they want India's manpower for their imperialistic greed. If we refuse to supply them with men and money, we achieve our goal, namely, Swaraj, equality, manliness.

The cup of our humiliation was filled during the closing scenes in the Viceregal Council. Mr. Shustri could not move his resolution on the Punjab. The Indian victims of Jullianwala received Rs. 1,250, the English victims of mob-frenzy received lakhs. The officials, who were guilty of crimes against those whose servants they were, were reprimanded. And the councilors were satisfied. If India were powerful, India would not have stood this addition of insult, to her injury.

I do not blame the British. If we were weak in numbers as they are, we too would perhaps have resorted to the same methods as they are now employing. Terrorism and deception are weapons not of the strong but of the weak. The British are weak in numbers; we are weak in spite of our numbers. The result is that each is dragging the other down. It is common experience that Englishmen lose in character after residence in India and that Indians lose in courage and manliness by contact with Englishmen. This process of weakening is good neither for us, two nations, nor for the world.

But if we Indians take care of ourselves the English and the rest of the world would take care of themselves. Our contributions to the world's progress must therefore consist in setting our own house in order.

Training in arms for the present is out of the question. I go a step further and believe that India has a better mission for the world. It is within her to show that she can achieve her destiny by pure self-sacrifice, i.e., self-purification. This can be done only by non-cooperation. And non-cooperation is possible only when those who commenced to cooperate being the process of withdrawal. If we can but free ourselves from the threefold maya of Government-controlled schools, Government law-courts, and legislative councils, and truly control our own education regulate our disputes and be indifferent to their legislation, we are ready to govern ourselves, and we are only then ready to ask the government servants, whether civil or military, to resign, and the taxpayers to suspend payment of taxes.

And is it such an impracticable proposition to expect parents to withdraw their children from schools and colleges and establish their own institutions or to ask lawyers to suspend their practice and devote their whole time attention to national service against payment where necessary, of their maintenance, or to ask candidates for councils not to enter councils and lend their passive or active assistance to the legislative machinery through which all control is exercised. The movement of non-cooperation is nothing but an attempt to isolate the brute force of the British from all the trappings under which it is hidden and to show that brute force by itself cannot for one single moment hold India.

But I frankly confess that, until the three conditions mentioned by me are fulfilled, there is no Swaraj. We may not go on taking our college degrees, taking thousands of rupees monthly from clients for cases which can be finished in five minutes and taking the keenest delight in wasting national time on the council floor and still expect to gain national self-respect.

The last though not the least important part of the Maya still remains to be considered. That is Swadeshi. Had we not abandoned Swadeshi, we need not have been in the present fallen state. If we would get rid of the economic slavery, we must manufacture our own cloth and at the present moment only by hand-spinning and hand-weaving.

All this means discipline, self-denial, self-sacrifice, organizing ability, confidence, and courage. If we show this in one year among the classes that today count, and make public opinion, we certainly gain Swaraj within one year. If I am told that even we who lead have not these qualities in us, there certainly will never be Swaraj for India, but then we shall have no right to blame the English for what they are doing. Our salvation and its time are solely dependent upon us.

British Rule—An Evil

The *Interpreter* is however more to the point in asking, "Does Mr. Gandhi hold without hesitation or reserve that British rule in India is altogether an evil and that the people of India are to be taught so to regard it? He must hold it to be so evil that the wrongs it does outweigh the benefit it confers, for only so is non-cooperation to be justified at the bar of conscience or of Christ." My answer is emphatically in the affirmative. So long as I believed that the sum total of the energy of the British Empire was good, I clung to it despite what I used to regard as temporary aberrations. I am not sorry for having done so. But having my eyes opened, it would be sin for me to associate myself with the Empire unless it purges itself of its evil character. I write this with sorrow, and I should be pleased if I discovered that I was in error and that my present attitude was a reaction. The continuous financial drain, the emasculation of the Punjab, and the betrayal of the Muslim sentiment constitute, in my humble opinion, a threefold robbery of India. "The blessings of *pax Britanica*" I reckon, therefore, to be a curse. We would have at least remained like the other nations brave men and women, instead of feeling as we do so utterly helpless, if we had no British Rule imposing on us an armed peace. "The blessing" of roads and railways is a return no self-respecting nation would accept for its degradation. "The blessing" of education is proving one of the greatest obstacles in our progress towards freedom.

Hindu-Mahomedan Unity

Mr. Candler some time ago asked me in an imaginary interview whether if I was sincere in my professions of Hindu-Mahomedan Unity. I would eat and drink with a Mahomedean and give my daughter in marriage to a Mahomedan. This question has been asked again by some friends in another form. Is it necessary for Hindu-Mahomedan Unity that there should he interdining and intermarrying? The questioners say that if the two are necessary, real unity can never take place because crores of *Sanatanis* would never reconcile themselves to interdining, much less to intermarriage.

I am one of those who do not consider caste to be a harmful institution. In its origin caste was a wholesome custom and promoted national well-being. In my opinion the idea that interdining or intermarrying is necessary for national growth, is a superstition borrowed from the West. Eating is a process just as vital as the other sanitary necessities of life. And if mankind had not, much to its harm, made of eating a fetish and indulgence we would have performed the operation of eating in private even as one performs the other necessary functions of life in private. Indeed the highest culture in Hinduism regards eating in that light and there are thousands of Hindus still living who will not eat their food in the presence of anybody. I can recall the names of several cultured men and women who ate their food in entire privacy but who never had any ill will against anybody and who lived on the friendliest terms with all.

Intermarriage is a still more difficult question. If brothers and sisters can live on the friendliest footing without ever thinking of marrying each other, I can see no difficulty in my daughter regarding every Mahomedan brother and vice versa. I hold strong views on religion and on marriage. The greater the restraint we exercise with regard to our appetites whether about eating or marrying, the better we become from a religious standpoint. I should despair of ever cultivating amicable relations with the world, if I had to recognize the right or the propriety of any young man offering his hand in marriage to my daughter or to regard it as necessary for me to dine with anybody and everybody. I claim that I am living on terms of friendliness with the whole world. I have never quarreled with a single Mahomedan or Christian, but for years I have taken nothing but fruit in Mahomedan or Christian households. I would most certainly decline to eat food cooked from the same plate with my son or to drink water out of a cup which his lips have touched and which has not been washed. But the restraint or the exclusiveness exercised in these matters by me has never affected the closest companionship with the Mahomedan or the Christian friends or my sons.

But interdining and intermarriage have never been a bar to disunion, quarrels and worse. The Pandavas and the Kauravas flew at one another's throats without compunction although they interdined and intermarried. The bitterness between the English and the Germans has not yet died out.

The fact is that intermarriage and interdining are not necessary factors in friendship and unity though they are often emblems thereof. But insistence on either the one or the other can easily become and is today a bar to Hindu-Mahomedan Unity. If we make ourselves believe that Hindus and Mahomedans cannot be one unless they interdine or intermarry, we would be creating an artificial barrier between us which it might be almost impossible to remove. And it would seriously interfere with the flowing unity between Hindus and Mahomedans if, for example, Mahomedan youths consider it lawful to court Hindu girls. The Hindu parents will not, even if they suspected any such thing, freely admit Mahomedans to their homes as they have begun to do now. In my opinion it is necessary for Hindu and Mahomedan young men to recognize this limitation.

I hold it to be utterly impossible for Hindus and Mahomedans to intermarry and yet retain intact each other's religion. And the true beauty of Hindu-Mahomedan Unity lies in each remaining true to his own religion and yet being true to each other. For, we are thinking of Hindus and Mahomedans even of the most orthodox type being able to regard one another as natural friends instead of regarding one another as natural enemies as they have done hitherto.

What then does the Hindu-Mahomedan Unity consist in and how can it be best promoted? The answer is simple. It consists in our having a common purpose, a common goal and common sorrows. It is best promoted by cooperating to reach the common goal, by sharing one another's sorrow and by mutual toleration. A common goal we have. We wish this great country of ours to be greater and self-governing. We have enough sorrows to share and today seeing that the Mahomedans are deeply touched on the question of Khilafat and their case is just, nothing can be so powerful for winning Mahomedans friendship for the Hindu as to give his whole-hearted support to the Mahomedan claim. No amount of drinking out of the same cup or dining out of the same bowl can bind the two as this help in the Khilafat question.

And mutual toleration is a necessity for all time and for all races. We cannot live in peace if the Hindu will not tolerate the Mahomedan form of worship of God and his manners and customs or if the Mahomedans will be impatient of Hindu idolatory, cow-worship. It is not necessary for toleration that I must approve of what I tolerate. I heartily dislike drinking, meat eating, and smoking, but I tolerate all these in Hindus, Mahomedans, and Christians even as I expect them to tolerate my abstinence from all these, although they may dislike it. All the quarrels between the Hindus and the Mahomedans have arisen from each wanting to *force* the other his view.

⫸ For Further Thought ⫷

"I have been collecting descriptions of swaraj," says Gandhi. "One of these would be: Swaraj is the abandonment of the fear of death. A nation which allows itself to be influenced by the fear of death cannot attain swaraj, and cannot retain it if somehow attained." This statement, and others in a similar vein, might provoke us to brand Gandhi a radical—an extremist. It seems to indicate that there is no length to which he would not go to attain his ends. Though he would never advocate violence against others, and is revered as a man of peace, he seems to believe that even the ultimate sacrifice—of one's own life—is worthwhile in support of the cause.

By today's definition, does this make Gandhi a kind of terrorist? When translating a political idea into a call for action, how far do you think it is permissible to go? Take some time to contemplate your views on political activism and decide where you stand. Are there ideas worth killing for? Dying for? Is there any difference between the two?

_____

_____

_____

_____

Chapter Four

Satyagraha: Soul Force

*"Nonviolence should never
be used as a shield for cowardice.
It is a weapon for the brave."*

At last, we arrive at Gandhi's core concept, the source of his most profound influence on the world: *satyagraha*. Derived from the Sanskrit words *satya* and *agraha,* it literally means "insistence on truth"—but Gandhi liked to define it as "soul force" or "the Force which is born of Truth and Love or non-violence." After 1906, when he developed the term, he came to use it in place of "passive resistance"—even when writing or speaking in English. He explains:

> [In the past], I often used "passive resistance" and "satyagraha" as synonymous terms: but . . . passive resistance has admitted of violence, as in the case of the suffragettes, and has been universally acknowledged to be a weapon of the weak. Moreover, passive resistance does not necessarily involve complete adherence to truth under every circumstance. Therefore it is different from satyagraha in three essentials: Satyagraha is a weapon of the strong; it admits of no violence under any circumstance whatsoever; and it ever insists upon truth.

In this final chapter, you will read some of Gandhi's most powerful early writing on the subject of satyagraha and come to understand the deeply held beliefs for which he lived and died.

MY SECOND EXPERIENCE IN JAIL

(*Indian Opinion*, January 30, 1909)

Moral Dilemma

When I had completed about half the term of my imprisonment, there was a telegram from Phoenix saying that Mrs. Gandhi was seriously ill and asking me to go down immediately.

Everyone was unhappy at this. I had no doubt as to my duty. When the jailer asked me whether I would agree to pay the fine to obtain my release, I replied without the slightest hesitation that I would never do so, and that it was implied in our movement that we should bear separation from out kith and kin. The jailor smiled at this, but felt sorry, too. On a superficial view of the matter, this attitude would appear to be rather harsh, but personally I am convinced that that is the only right attitude to adopt. I think of my love for the motherland as an aspect of my religion. It is, of course, not the whole of religion. But religion cannot be considered to be complete without it. If necessary, we should bear separation from our family in order to be able to follow the dictates of our religion. We may even have to lose them. Not only is there no cruelty in this, but it is actually our duty to do so. If it is true that we have pledged ourselves to fight unto death, there is nothing further to think of. Lord Roberts lost his only son for a cause inferior to ours and, being on the front, could not even attend his funeral. This history of the world is full of such instances.

Quarrels Among Kaffirs

There are some dangerous murderers among the Kaffir prisoners in jail. We find these prisoners constantly engaged in disputes. After they are locked up in the cell, they quarrel among themselves. Sometimes, they openly defy the warder. One warder was twice assaulted by the prisoners. Indian prisoners are obviously in danger when locked up in the same cell with these. So far, Indians have not been placed in such a situation. But so long as Indian prisoners are classed with the Kaffirs, the danger will remain.

Illness in Jail

There was for the most part no serious illness among the prisoners. . . . There was a Tamil named Mr. Raju, who had acute dysentery. He was very much pulled down. The reason he gave for this was that he used to take 30 cups of tea [every day], and he got dysentery because he did not get them. He asked for tea. Of course, the request was rejected. But he was given some medicine, and the medical officer in the jail ordered two pounds of milk and bread [for him]. This restored him to full health. Mr. Ravikrishna Talevantsingh kept indifferent health till the end. Mr. Kazi and Mr. Bawazeer were ill all the time. Mr. Ratanshi Sodha was observing a religious vow for the four months of the rainy season, and therefore he had only one meal a day. Since the food was not quite satisfactory, he nearly starved himself and as a result got edema. A part from these, there were other cases of minor illness. On the whole, however, we found that even those Indians who fell ill were not broken in spirit. They were happy to bear this particular kind of hardship for the sake of the motherland.

Some Difficulties

It was observed that the more irritating difficulties were those of our own making rather than those created by others. There were occasions in the jail when one sensed in the air distinctions between Hindus and Muslims, between high and low castes. Indians of all communities and castes lived together in the jail, which gave one an opportunity to observe how backward we are in the matter of self-government.

It was also discovered, however, that we were not altogether incapable of self-government, for whatever difficulties cropped up were always overcome in the end.

Some Hindus said that they were not prepared to take food prepared by Muslims or by certain individuals. Men who hold such views should never stir out of India. I also observed that no objection was raised if any Kaffir or white touched our food. It so happened once that someone objected to sleeping near a certain person on the ground that the latter belonged to the scavenger caste. This again was humiliating to us. On probing deeper into the matter, it was found that the objection was raised not because the man [who had raised the objection] was himself particular about it, but because he was afraid of being declared an outcast should other members of his community in India come to hear of it. Thanks to these hypocritical distinctions of high and low and to the fear of subsequent caste tyranny, we have, I think, turned our back on truth and embraced falsehood. How can we be called satyagrahis if, knowing that it is wrong to despise the scavenger, we still do so out of an unreasonable fear of members of our caste or other men? I wish that Indians who join this movement also resort to satyagraha against their caste and their family and against evil wherever they find it. As for myself, I am convinced that it is because we do not act in this way that the successful outcome of our struggle is being delayed. If it is true that we are all Indians, how can we cling to false distinctions and so quarrel among ourselves and, at the same time, demand our rights? How can we hope to achieve success in our struggle if, out of fear of what may happen to us in India, we do not do what we believe to be right? It is the mark of a coward to shrink from anything out of mere fear, and Indians who are cowards will not hold out to the last in this great war that is being waged against the Government.

Who Can Go to Jail?

We see from these facts that those who are slaves to bad habits, who observe vain distinctions of caste and community, who are quarrelsome, who are not able to look on Hindus and Muslims with an equal eye and those who are diseased in body—such men cannot go to jail or remain in jail for any length of time. It follows therefore that those who want to go to jail as a matter of honor and with a view to the welfare of the motherland must be healthy in body, mind, and soul.

An ailing man will find himself exhausted in the end; those who are conscious of Hindu-Muslim differences, who think themselves superior to others, who are slaves to bad habits, who are possessed by a craving for tea, smoking or such other things, are incapable of fighting till the bitter end.

What I Read in Jail

Though the entire day is taken up with work, one can find time for some reading in the mornings and evenings, as also on Sundays and, since there is nothing else to tax one's attention in jail, it is possible to read with a peaceful mind. Though I had limited time on my hand, I managed to read two books by the great Ruskin, the essays of the great Thoreau, some portions of the Bible, life of Garibaldi (in Gujarati), essays of Lord Bacon (in Gujarati), and two other books about India. We can find the doctrine of satyagraha in the writings of Ruskin and Thoreau. The Gujarati books were sent by Mr. Diwan for all of us to read. Apart from these works, I read the Bhagavad Gita almost every day. All this reading had the effect of confirming my belief in satyagraha, and I can say today that life in jail is not in the least boring.

Two Attitudes

We can take two different attitudes to what I have written above.

First, why should we bear such hardships, submit ourselves, for instance, to the restrictions of jail life, wear coarse and ungainly dress, eat food which is hardly food, starve ourselves, suffer being kicked by the warder, live among the Kaffirs, do every kind of work, whether we like it or not, obey a warder who is only good enough to be our servant, be unable to receive any friends or write letters, go without things that we may need, and sleep in company with robbers and thieves? Better die than suffer this. Better pay the fine than go to jail. Let no one be punished with jail.

Such an attitude will make a man quite weak and afraid of imprisonment, and he will achieve nothing good by being in jail.

Alternatively, one may consider oneself fortunate to be in jail in the cause of the motherland, in defense of one's honor and one's religion. Jail life, one may think, involves no [real] suffering. Outside, one has to carry out the will of many, whereas one has only the warder to reckon with in jail. One has no anxieties in jail, no problem of earning one's livelihood, no worry about getting one's bread, for that is provided regularly by others. One's person is protected by the Government. None of these things has to be paid for. By way of exercise, one gets ample work to do and, without any effort on one's part, all of one's bad habits fall away. The mind enjoys a sense of freedom. One has ready to hand the benefit of being absorbed in devotions to God. The body is held in bondage, but the soul grows more free. One is in full enjoyment of the use of one's limbs. The body is looked after by those who hold it in bondage. Thus, from every point of view, one is free. One might, perhaps, be in difficulties, be manhandled by a wicked warder, but then one learns to be patient.

One feels glad to have an opportunity of dissuading [him] from such behavior. It is up to us to adopt such an attitude and think of jail as a holy and happy place and to make it such. In short, happiness and misery are states of the mind.

I hope that the reader, after reading this account of my second experience in jail, will resolve in his mind that his only happiness will be in going to jail for the sake of the motherland or his religion, in submitting himself to the suffering involved in it, or bearing hardships in other ways.

"Purest Passive Resistance Can Exist Only in Theory"

(Letter to W. J. Wybergh, *Indian Opinion*, May 21, 1910)

Dear Mr. Wybergh,

I am exceedingly obliged to you for your very full and valuable criticism of the little pamphlet on Indian Home Rule (see page 210). I shall with very great pleasure send your letter to *Indian Opinion* for publication, and shall treat this reply likewise.

I entirely reciprocate the sentiments you express in the last paragraph of your letter. I am quite aware that my views will lead to many differences of opinion between my staunchest friends and those whom I have come to regard with respect and myself, but these differences, so far as I am concerned, can neither diminish respect nor affect friendly relations.

I am painfully conscious of the imperfections and defects you point out in your letter, and I know how unworthy I am to handle the very important problems dealt with in the booklet. But, having had the position of a publicist practically forced upon me by circumstances, I felt bound to write for those for whom *Indian Opinion* caters. The choice lay between allowing the readers of *Indian Opinion*, anxious though they were for guidance, to drift away in the matter of the insane violence that is now going on in India, or giving them, no matter how humble, a lead that they were asking for. The only way I saw of mitigating violence was the one sketched in the pamphlet.

I share your views that a superficial reader will consider the pamphlet to be a disloyal production, and I admit, too, that those who will not distinguish between men and measures, between modern civilization and its exponents, will come to that conclusion. And I accept your proposition that I discourage violence only because I think it to be both wrong and ineffective, and not because the object sought to be attained is wrong, that is to say, if it were ever possible, which I hold it is not, to detach the object from the means adopted to attain it. I hold that Home Rule obtained by violence would be totally different in kind from that obtained by the means suggested by me.

I have ventured utterly to condemn modern civilization because I hold that the spirit of it is evil. It is possible to show that some of its incidents are good, but I have examined its tendency in the scale of ethics. I distinguish between the ideals of individuals who have risen superior to their environment, as also between Christianity and modern civilization. Its activity is by no means confined to Europe. Its blasting influence is now being exhibited in full force in Japan. And it now threatens to overwhelm India. History teaches us that men who are in the whirlpool, except in the cases of individuals, will have to work out their destiny in it but I do submit that those who are still outside its influence, and those who have a well-tried civilization to guide them, should be helped to remain where they are, if only as a measure of prudence. I claim to have tested the life which modern civilization has to give, as also that of the ancient civilization, and I cannot help most strongly contesting the idea that the Indian population requires to be roused by "the lash of competition and the other material and sensuous, as well as intellectual, stimuli"; I cannot admit that these will add a single inch to its moral stature. Liberation in the sense in which I have used the term is undoubtedly the immediate aim of all humanity. It does not, therefore, follow that the whole of it can reach it in the same time. But if that liberation is the best thing attainable by mankind, then, I submit, it is wrong to lower the ideal for anyone. All the Indian Scriptures have certainly preached incessantly liberation as an immediate aim, but we know that this preaching has not resulted in "activity in the lower worlds" being abandoned.

I admit that the term "passive resistance" is a misnomer. I have used it because, generally speaking, we know what it means. Being a popular term, it easily appeals to the popular imagination. The underlying principle is totally opposed to that of violence. It cannot, therefore, be that "the battle is transferred from the physical to the mental plane." The function of violence is to obtain reform by external means; the function of passive resistance, that is, soul-force, is to obtain it by growth from within; which, in its turn, is obtained by self-suffering, self-purification. Violence ever fails; passive resistance is ever successful. The fight of a passive resister is none the less spiritual because he fights to win. Indeed, he is obliged to fight to win, that is, to obtain the mastery of self. Passive resistance is always moral, never cruel; and any activity, mental or otherwise, which fails in this test is undoubtedly not passive resistance.

Your argument tends to show that there must be complete divorce between politics and religion or spirituality. That is what we see in everyday life under modern conditions. Passive resistance seeks to rejoin politics and religion and to test every one of our actions in the light of ethical principles. That Jesus refused to use soul-force to turn stones into bread only supports my argument. Modern civilization is at present engaged in attempting that impossible feat.

The use of soul-force for turning stones into bread would have been considered, as it is still considered, as black magic. Nor can I hold with you that motives alone can always decide the question of a particular act being right or wrong. An ignorant mother may, from the purest motives, administer a dose of opium to her child. Her motives will not cure her of her ignorance, nor, in the moral world purge her of the offense of killing her child. A passive resister, recognizing this principle and knowing that, in spite of the purity of his motives, his action may be utterly wrong, leaves judgment to the Supreme Being, and, in attempting to resist what he holds to be wrong, suffers only in his own person.

Throughout the *Bhagavad Gita*, I can see no warrant for holding that a man who can only control "the organs of action" but cannot help "dwelling in his mind on the objects of the senses" had better use the organs of action until the mind, too, is under control. In ordinary practices, we call such use an indulgence, and we know, too, that, if we can control the flesh even while the spirit is weak, always wishing that the spirit were equally strong, we will certainly arrive at a right correspondence. I think the text you have quoted refers to a man who, for making a show, appears to be controlling the organs of action, whilst deliberately in his mind dwelling on the objects of the senses.

I agree with you entirely that a pure passive resister cannot allow himself to be regarded as a martyr nor can he complain of the hardships of prison or any other hardships, nor may he make political capital out of what may appear to be injustice or ill-treatment, much less may he allow any matter of passive resistance to be advertised. But all action unfortunately is mixed. Purest passive resistance can exist only in theory. The anomalies you point out only emphasize the fact that the Indian passive resisters of the Transvaal are, after all, very fallible human beings and yet very weak, but I can assure you that their object is to make their practice correspond with pure passive resistance as nearly as possible, and, as the struggle progresses, pure spirits are certainly rising in our midst.

I am free to admit also that all passive resisters are not fired with the spirit of love or of truth. Some of us are undoubtedly not free from vindictiveness and the spirit of hatred; but the desire in us all is to cure ourselves of hatred and enmity. I have noticed, too, that those who simply became passive resisters under the glamour of the newness of the movement or for selfish reasons have fallen away. Pretended self-suffering cannot last long. Such men never were passive resisters.

It is necessary to discuss the subject of passive resistance somewhat impersonally. If you say that physical sufferings of soldiers have vastly exceeded those of the Transvaal passive resisters, I agree with you entirely; but the sufferings of world-known passive resisters who deliberately walked into funeral pyres or into boiling cauldrons were incomparably greater than those of any soldier it is possible to name.

I cannot pretend to speak for Tolstoy, but my reading of his works has never led me to consider that, in spite of his merciless analysis of institutions organized and based upon force, that is, governments, he in any way anticipates or contemplates that the whole world will be able to live in a state of philosophical anarchy. What he has preached, as, in my opinion, have all world-teachers, is that every man has to obey the voice of his own conscience, and be his own master, and seek the Kingdom of God from within. For him there is no government that can control him without his sanction. Such a man is superior to all government. And can it be ever dangerous for a lion to tell a number of other lions who in their ignorance consider themselves to be merely lambs that they, too, are not lambs but lions?

Some very ignorant lions will no doubt contest the knowing lion's proposition. There will, no doubt, on that account be confusion also, but, no matter how gross the ignorance may be, it will not be suggested that the lion who knows should sit still and not ask his fellow-lions to share his majesty and freedom.

It has indeed occurred to me that an anti-Asiatic league which from pure though entirely misguided motives wishes to deport Asiatics from the Transvaal, because it may consider them to be an evil, would be certainly justified, from its own viewpoint, in violently attaining its object.

It is not open to passive resisters, if they are not weak, to complain of such, in their opinion, high-handed action, but for them deportation and worse must be a welcome relief from having to submit to a course of action which is repugnant to their conscience.

I hope you will not fail to see the beauty of passive resistance in your own illustration. Supposing that these deportees were capable of offering physical violence against forcible deportation, and yet from pure choice elected to be deported rather than resist deportation, will it not show superior courage and superior moral fiber in them?

Yours sincerely,
M. K. Gandhi

TRIUMPH OF SATYAGRAHA

(*Indian Opinion*, October 28, 1911)

During Diwali, some Hindus burst [fire]crackers. The Durban police went into a huff over this. A leading Hindu gentleman was arrested.

They all decided not to let the matter rest at that. It reached the ears of Mr. Dawad Mahomed and Mr. Parsee Rustomjee. They hurried off to the Mayor, and argued that, after all, the whites also exploded crackers during Christmas. Why then should the Hindus [they asked] not do so during their festivals? Why should they have to take special permission for this purpose? No one seeks such permission during Christmas. "If, in spite of this, you wish to harass Hindus for exploding crackers, we shall also join them in this as a mark of sympathy. You may then arrest anyone that you like."

The matter is not serious and the victory not much of a triumph. The significance of the event, however, is great. Because we boldly came forward to suffer the consequences of doing what was right, we had, it transpired, nothing to suffer and our self-respect was preserved. This is satyagraha.

Another, more significant, feature of this case is the fact that a Muslim and a Parsi rushed to help in a matter which concerned Hindus alone. The outcome was indeed happy. If the right course is followed in one case, it is bound to happen that it will be adopted on other occasions as well. If one knot in a tangled piece of sting can be unraveled, the other too can easily be undone.

How can Hindus, Muslims, Parsis, and Christians all be united? Mr. Mahomed and Mr. Rustomjee have provided the answer.

If Muslims come forward to sympathize with Hindus in what concerns the latter alone, if Hindus do the same and if both these communities act in this manner towards Parsis, will there be anyone so bereft of reason as to seek to come in the way of affection developing among them?

Let people's religions be different. You worship a Being—a single Entity—as Allah and another adores Him as Khuda. I worship Him as Ishwar. How does anyone stand to lose [by this arrangement]? You worship facing one way and I worship facing the other. Why should I become your enemy for that reason? We all belong to the human race; we all wear the same skin; we hail from the same land.

When the facts are as simple as that, it will be nothing but folly and short-sightedness to bear implacable enmity towards one another.

The moderns make a key which will open many kinds of locks. They call it the "master-key." Likewise, satyagraha is the master-key to our innumerable hardships. How much could be achieved if only all the Indians would use that key! Satyagraha is not a difficult term to understand. It only means adherence to truth. Whatever else the ethical life may mean, it cannot be ethical if it is not based on truth.

Truth is easy enough to follow once we know its meaning.

How to Organize the Struggle

(Indian Opinion, September 20, 1913)

This third campaign will embrace the whole of South Africa. We believe, therefore, that going to jail will be an easy matter. It does not mean that this time the sufferings in jail will be less.

They may even be more. Only, it will not be difficult, as it was before, to find ways of going to jail. So far, people courted imprisonment by entering the Transvaal. There is no need to do that this time. If, in every town and every province, a few Indians at least take intelligent interest in the fight, they will be able to participate in it in some measure, however small, and help it. The easiest way is for the hawkers. Those who are hawkers by profession, as also those who are not, can get arrested by hawking without licenses. For this, the imprisonment will be only for a short term. It will involve no risk of goods being auctioned. Moreover, they can pause and rest when tired. If we can have such a movement in every town, we shall have put up a big fight. It will agitate the whole of South Africa and compel the most serious attention from those in power.

Even those who hold licenses can act in this manner. The police demand licenses from time to time. If, having them, we do not produce them, it will be their duty to arrest us. Storekeepers and even their assistants can do this and so get arrested. As we think of it, we see that this is the easiest way and the simplest. It will involve comparatively little of suffering, the initiative will always be with us and we shall be able to have rest whenever we want. The hawkers and storekeepers should remember that their interests are deeply involved in the struggle. Both the Government and the whites feel sore over trade more than anything else. If we were not to engage in trade, we would provoke much less envy. Trade is our very life here. One should always remember that our sufferings will diminish in the measure in which we command increased respect. We hope, therefore, that the business community will utilize this excellent opportunity which will cost them so little. We need hardly say that even one single Indian in a town can put up such a fight. If there is any such hero, he should send us his name before going to jail. Those who get arrested by crossing the border must bear in mind that they will not thereby acquire any rights for themselves. Satyagraha is not meant for acquiring rights for oneself. Selfishness and satyagraha can never go together.

How to Help in Other Ways

We have seen above that it is only by going to jail that we can best help the struggle. But we know that all Indians do not have the pluck for this. We need them to consider what such Indians should do.

We give below the ideas that occur to us.

> 1. One may look after the business of those who go to jail and care for their families or see to the maintenance of their dependents.

2. This time we are not going to ask for money from India. At the same time, we are left at present with very little money; it is up to everyone to send contributions to the satyagraha fund.

3. Those who cannot afford to give money, may send food grains.

4. In every town of every province, meetings should be held and resolutions passed approving of Mr. Cachalia's letter and these resolutions should be dispatched, by telegram or post, both to the local and the Imperial Governments.

5. Telegrams welcoming the fight should be sent to the [British Indian] Association.

6. Wherever meetings cannot be held, telegrams and letters should be sent to the Government on behalf of public bodies.

7. The matter should be discussed with the whites of one's town and they should be kept well-informed through issues of *Indian Opinion* having a bearing on the struggle.

8. Shaking off lethargy, every Indian must acquaint himself with the aims of the campaign and the nature of the issues involved.

9. Issues of *Indian Opinion* pertaining to the struggle should be procured and sent to different places in India and England.

10. One should help in the collection of funds for the London Committee.

11. Every Indian should set apart some time for the fight and engage himself during that period in some work or other connected with it.

Most of these things may be done by every Indian and by every organization. Every individual and every association must undertake as many of them as possible. What can be done right now is to hold meetings at every place, pass resolutions and send them to both Governments.

"Ashram Vows"

(Speech at the Y.M.C.A, Madras, February 16, 1916)

Mr. Chairman and Dear Friends,

I have so often said that I am not myself fond of hearing my own voice, and I assure you that this morning also I retained the same position. It was only, if you will believe me, my great regard for the students, whom I love, whom I respect, and who I consider are the hope of future India that moved me to accept this invitation to speak to you this morning. I did not know what subject to choose.

To many of the students who came here last year to converse with me, I said I was about to establish an institution—an Ashram—somewhere in India, and it is about that place that I am going to talk to you this morning. I feel and I have felt during the whole of my public life that what we need, what any nation needs, but we perhaps of all the nations of the world need just now, is nothing else and nothing less than character-building. And this is the view propounded by that great patriot, Mr. Gokhale. (Cheers.) As you know, in many of his speeches, he used to say that we would get nothing, we would deserve nothing unless we had character to back what we wished for.

Hence his founding of that great body, the Servants of India Society. And as you know, in the prospectus that has been issued in connection with the Society, Mr. Gokhale has deliberately stated that it was necessary to spiritualize the political life of the country. You know also that he used to say so often that our average was less than the average of so many European nations. I do not know whether that statement by him, whom, with pride, I consider to be my political guru, has really foundation in fact, but I do believe that there is much to be said to justify it in so far as educated India is concerned; not because we, the educated portion of the community, have blundered, but because we have been creatures of circumstances. Be that as it may, this is the maxim of life which I have accepted, namely, that no work done by any man, no matter how great he is, will really prosper unless he has a religious backing.

But what is religion? the question will be immediately asked. I, for one, would answer, not the religion which you will get after reading all the scriptures of the world; it is not really a grasp by the brain, but it is a heart-grasp. It is a thing which is not alien to us, but it is a thing which has to be evolved out of us. It is always within us, with some consciously so; with others, quite unconsciously. But it is there; and whether we wake up this religious instinct in us through outside assistance or by inward growth, no matter how it is done, it has got to be done if we want to do anything in the right manner and anything that is going to persist.

Our scriptures have laid down certain rules as maxims of life and as axioms which we have to take for granted as self-demonstrated truths. The shastras tell us that without living according to those maxims, we are incapable even of having a reasonable perception of religion. Believing in these implicitly for all these long years and having actually endeavored to reduce to practice these injunctions of the shastras, I have deemed it necessary to seek the association of those who think with me in founding this institution. And I shall venture this morning to place before you the rules that have been drawn up and that have to be observed by everyone who seeks to be a member of that Ashram.

Five of these are known as Yamas, and the first and the foremost is, the:

Vow of Truth

Not truth simply as we ordinarily understand it, that as far as possible we ought not to resort to a lie, that is to say, not truth which merely answers the saying, "Honesty is the best policy"—implying that if it is not the best policy, we may depart from it. But here Truth, as it is conceived, means that we have to rule our life by this law of Truth at any cost. And in order to satisfy the definition, I have drawn upon the celebrated illustration of the life of Prahlad. For the sake of Truth, he dared to oppose his own father, and he defended himself, not by retaliation by paying his father back in his own coin, but in defense of Truth, as he knew it, he was prepared to die without caring to return the blows that he had received from his father or from those who were charged with his father's instructions. Not only that: he would not in any way even parry the blows. On the contrary, with a smile on his lips, he underwent the innumerable tortures to which he was subjected, with the result that at last, Truth rose triumphant, not that Prahlad suffered the tortures because he knew that some day or other in his very lifetime he would be able to demonstrate the infallibility of the law of Truth. That fact was there; but if he had died in the midst of torture, he would still have adhered to Truth. That is the Truth that I would like us to follow. There was an incident I noticed yesterday. It was a trifling incident, but I think these trifling incidents are like straws which show which way the wind is blowing.

The incident was this: I was talking to a friend who wanted to talk to me aside, and we were engaged in a private conversation. A third friend dropped in and he politely asked whether he was intruding.

The friend to whom I was talking said: "Oh, no, there is nothing private here." I felt taken-aback a little, because, as I was taken aside, I knew that so far as this friend was concerned, the conversation was private. But he immediately, out of politeness, I would call it over-politeness, said there was no private conversation and that he (the third friend) could join. I suggest to you that this is a departure from my definition of Truth. I think that the friend should have, in the gentlest manner possible, but still openly and frankly, said: "Yes, just now, as you properly say, you would be intruding" without giving the slightest offense to the person if he was himself a gentleman— and we are bound to consider everybody to be a gentleman unless he proves to be otherwise. But I may be told that the incident, after all, proves the gentility of the nation. I think that it is over-proving the case. If we continue to say these things out of politeness, we really become a nation of hypocrites.

I recall a conversation I had with an English friend. He was comparatively a stranger. He is a Principal of a College and has been in India for several years. He was comparing notes with me, and he asked me whether I would admit that we, unlike most Englishmen, would not dare to say "No" when it was "No" that we meant. And I must admit that I immediately said "Yes." I agree with that statement. We do hesitate to say "No," frankly and boldly, when we want to pay due regard to the sentiments of the person whom we are addressing. In this Ashram, we make it a rule that we must say "No" when we mean "No," regardless of consequences. This, then, is the first rule. Then we come to the:

Doctrine of Ahimsa

Literally speaking, *ahimsa* means non-killing. But to me it has a world of meaning and takes me into realms much higher, infinitely higher, than the realm to which I would go, if I merely understood by ahimsa non-killing. Ahimsa really means that you may not offend anybody, you may not harbor an uncharitable thought even in connection with one who may consider himself to be your enemy.

Pray notice the guarded nature of this thought; I do not say "whom you consider to be your enemy," but "who may consider himself to be your enemy." For one who follows the doctrine of ahimsa, there is no room for an enemy; he denies the existence of an enemy. But there are people who consider themselves to be his enemies, and he cannot help that circumstance. So, it is held that we may not harbor an evil thought even in connection with such persons. If we return blow for blow, we depart from the doctrine of ahimsa. But I go further. If we resent a friend's action or the so-called enemy's action, we still fall short of this doctrine. But when I say we should not resent, I do not say that we should acquiesce; but by resenting I mean wishing that some harm should be done to the enemy, or that he should be put out of the way, not even by any action of ours, but by the action of somebody else, or, say, by Divine agency. If we harbor even this thought, we depart from this doctrine of ahimsa. Those who join the Ashram have to literally accept that meaning. That does not mean that we practice that doctrine in its entirety. Far from it.

It is an ideal which we have to reach, and it is an ideal to be reached even at this very moment, if we are capable of doing so. But it is not a proposition in geometry to be learnt by heart: it is not even like solving difficult problems in higher mathematics; it is infinitely more difficult than solving those problems. Many of you have burnt the midnight oil in solving those problems. If you want to follow out this doctrine, you will have to do much more than burn the midnight oil.

You will have to pass many a sleepless night, and go through many a mental torture and agony before you can reach, before you can even be within measurable distance of this goal. It is the goal, and nothing less than that, you and I have to reach if we want to understand what a religious life means. I will not say much more on this doctrine than this: that a man who believes in the efficacy of this doctrine finds in the ultimate stage, when he is about to reach the goal, the whole world at his feet, not that he wants the whole world at his feet, but it must be so. If you express your love— ahimsa—in such a manner that it impresses itself indelibly upon your so-called enemy, he must return that love. Another thought which comes out of this is that, under this rule, there is no room for organized assassinations, and there is no room for murders even openly committed, and there is no room for any violence even for the sake of your country, and even for guarding the honor of precious ones that may be under your charge. After all, that would be a poor defense of honor. This doctrine of ahimsa tells us that we may guard the honor of those who are under our charge by delivering ourselves into the hands of the man who would commit the sacrilege. And that requires far greater physical and mental courage than the delivering of blows. You may have some degree of physical power—I do not say courage—and you may use that power.

But after that is expended, what happens? The other man is filled with wrath and indignation, and you have made him more angry by matching your violence against his; and when he has done you to death, the rest of his violence is delivered against your charge. But if you do not retaliate, but stand your ground, between your charge and the opponent, simply receiving the blows without retaliating, what happens? I give you my promise that the whole of the violence will be expended on you, and your charge will be left unscathed. Under this plan of life, there is no conception of patriotism which justifies such wars as you witness today in Europe. Then there is the:

Vow of Celibacy

Those who want to perform national service, or those who want to have a glimpse of the real religious life, must lead a celibate life, no matter if married or unmarried. Marriage but brings a woman closer together with the man, and they become friends in a special sense, never to be parted either in this life or in the lives that are to come. But I do not think that, in our conception of marriage, our lusts should necessarily enter. Be that as it may, this is what is placed before those who come to the Ashram. I do not deal with that at any length. Then we have the:

Vow of Control of the Palate

A man who wants to control his animal passions easily does so if he control his palate. I fear this is one of the most difficult vows to follow. I am just now coming after having inspected the Victoria Hostel. I saw there, not to my dismay, though it should be to my dismay, but I am used to it now, that there are so many kitchens, not kitchens that are established in order to serve caste restrictions, but kitchens that have become necessary in order that people can have the condiments, and the exact weight of the condiments, to which they are used in the respective places from which they come. And therefore we find that for the Brahmins themselves there are different compartments and different kitchens catering for the delicate tastes of all these different groups, I suggest to you that this is simply slavery to the palate, rather than mastery over it. I may say this: Unless we take our minds off from this habit, and unless we shut our eyes to the tea shops and coffee shops and all these kitchens, and unless we are satisfied with foods that are necessary for the proper maintenance of our physical health, and unless we are prepared to rid ourselves of stimulating, heating, and exciting condiments that we mix with our food, we will certainly not be able to control the overabundant, unnecessary, exciting stimulation that we may have. If we do not do that, the result naturally is, that we abuse ourselves and we abuse even the sacred trust given to us, and we become less than animals and brutes. Eating, drinking, and indulging passions we share in common with the animals, but have you ever seen a horse or a cow indulging in the abuse of the palate as we do? Do you suppose that it is a sign of civilization, a sign of real life that we should multiply our eatables so far that we do not even know where we are; and seek; dish after dish until at last we have become absolutely mad and run after the newspaper sheets which give us advertisements about these dishes? Then we have the:

Vow of Non-Thieving

I suggest that we are thieves in a way. If I take anything that I do not need for my own immediate use, and keep it, I thieve it from somebody else. I venture to suggest that it is the fundamental law of Nature, without exception, that Nature produces enough for our wants from day to day, and if only everybody took enough for himself and nothing more, there would be no pauperism in this world, there would be no man dying of starvation in this world. But so long as we have got this inequality, so long we are thieving. I am no socialist and I do not want to dispossess those who have got possessions; but I do say that, personally, those of us who want to see light out of darkness have to follow the rule. I do not want to dispossess anybody. I should then be departing from the rule of ahimsa. If somebody else possesses more than I do, let him. But so far as my own life has to be regulated, I do say that I dare not possess anything which I do not want. In India we have got three millions of people having to be satisfied with one meal a day, and that meal consisting of a *chapati* containing no fat in it, and a pinch of salt. You and I have no right to anything that we really have until these three million are clothed and fed better. You and I, who ought to know better, must adjust our wants, and even undergo voluntary starvation in order that they may be nursed, fed and clothed. Then there is the vow of non-possession which follows as a matter of course. Then I go to the:

Vow of Swadeshi

The vow of swadeshi is a necessary vow. But you are conversant with the swadeshi life and the swadeshi spirit. I suggest to you we are departing from one of the sacred laws of our being when we leave our neighbor and go out somewhere else in order to satisfy our wants. If a man comes from Bombay here and offers you wares, you are not justified in supporting the Bombay merchant or trader so long as you have got a merchant at your very door, born and bred in Madras. That is my view of swadeshi. In your village, so long as you have got your village-barber, you are bound to support him to the exclusion of the finished barber who may come to you from Madras. If you find it necessary that your village-barber should reach the attainment of the barber from Madras, you may train him to that. Send him to Madras by all means, if you wish, in order that he may learn his calling. Until you do that, you are not justified in going to another barber. That is swadeshi. So, when we find that there are many things that we cannot get in India, we must try to do without them. We may have to do without many things which we may consider necessary, but believe me, when you have that frame of mind, you will find a great burden taken off your shoulders, even as the Pilgrim did in that inimitable book, *Pilgrim's Progress*: There came a time when the mighty burden that the Pilgrim was carrying on his shoulders unconsciously dropped from him, and he felt a freer man than he was when he started on the journey. So will you feel freer men than you are now, immediately you adopt this swadeshi life. We have also the:

Vow of Fearlessness

I found, throughout my wanderings in India, that India, educated India, is seized with a paralyzing fear. We may not open our lips in public; we may not declare our confirmed opinion in public; we may hold those opinions; we may talk about them secretly; and we may do anything we like within the four walls of our house—but those are not for public consumption. If we had taken a vow of silence, I would have nothing to say. When we open our lips in public, we say things which we do not really believe in. I do not know whether this is not the experience of almost every public man who speaks in India. I then suggest to you that there is only one Being, if Being is the proper term to be used, whom we have to fear, and that is God. When we fear God, we shall fear no man, no matter how high-placed he may be. And if you want to follow the vow of truth in any shape or form, fearlessness is the necessary consequence. And so you find, in the Bhagavad Gita, fearlessness is declared as the first essential quality of a Brahmin. We fear consequences, and therefore we are afraid to tell the truth. A man who fears God will certainly not fear any earthly consequence. Before we can aspire to the position of understanding what religion is, and before we can aspire to the position of guiding the destinies of India, do you not see that we should adopt this habit of fearlessness? Or shall we over-awe our countrymen even as we are over-awed? We thus see how important this "fearlessness vow" is. And we have also the:

Vow Regarding the Untouchables

There is an ineffaceable blot that Hinduism today carries with it. I have declined to believe that it has been handed to us from immemorial times. I think that this miserable, wretched, enslaving spirit of "untouchableness" must have come to us when we were in the cycle of our lives, at our lowest ebb, and that evil has still stuck to us and it still remains with us. It is, to my mind, a curse that has come to us, and as long as that curse remains with us, so long I think we are bound to consider that every affliction that we labor under in this sacred land is a fit and proper punishment for this great and indelible crime that we are committing. That any person should be considered untouchable because of his calling passes one's comprehension; and you, the student world, who receive all this modern education, if you become a party to this crime, it were better that you received no education whatsoever.

Of course, we are laboring under a very heavy handicap.

Although you may realize that there cannot be a single human being on this earth who should be considered to be untouchable, you cannot react upon your families, you cannot react upon your surroundings, because all your thought is conceived in a foreign tongue, and all your energy is devoted to that. And so we have also introduced a rule in this Ashram that we shall receive our:

Education Through the Vernaculars

In Europe, every cultured man learns, not only his language, but also other languages, certainly three or four. And even as they do in Europe, in order to solve the problem of language in India, we, in this Ashram, make it a point to learn as many Indian vernaculars as we possibly can. And I assure you that the trouble of learning these languages is nothing compared to the trouble that we have to take in mastering the English language. We never master the English language; with some exceptions, it has not been possible for us to do so; we can never express ourselves as clearly as we can in our own mother tongue. How dare we rub out of our memory all the years of our infancy? But that is precisely what we do when we commence our higher life, as we call it, through the medium of a foreign tongue. This creates a breach in our life for bridging which we shall have to pay dearly and heavily. And you will see now the connection between these two things—education and untouchableness—this persistence of the spirit of untouchableness even at this time of the day in spite of the spread of knowledge and education. Education has enabled us to see the horrible crime. But we are seized with fear also and, therefore, we cannot take this doctrine to our homes. And we have got a superstitious veneration for our family traditions and for the members of our family. You say, "My parents will die if I tell them that I, at least, can no longer partake of this crime." I say that Prahlad never considered that his father would die if he pronounced the sacred syllables of the name of Vishnu. On the contrary, he made the whole of that household ring, from one corner to another, by repeating that name even in the sacred presence of his father. And so you and I may do this thing in the sacred presence of our parents.

If, after receiving this rude shock, some of them expire, I think that would be no calamity. It may be that some rude shocks of the kind might have to be delivered. So long as we persist in these things which have been handed down to us for generations, these incidents may happen. But there is a higher law of Nature, and in due obedience to that higher law, my parents and myself should make that sacrifice, and then we follow:

Hand-Weaving

You may ask: "Why should we use our hands?" and say "the manual work has got to be done by those who are illiterate. I can only occupy myself with reading literature and political essays." I think that we have to realize the dignity of labor. If a barber or shoe-maker attends a college, he ought not to abandon the profession of barber or shoe-maker. I consider that a barber's profession is just as good as the profession of medicine. Last of all, when you have conformed to these rules, I think then, and not till then, you may come to:

Politics

and dabble in them to your heart's content, and certainly you will then never go wrong. Politics, divorced of religion, have absolutely no meaning. If the student-world crowd the political platforms of this country, to my mind it is not necessarily a healthy sign of national growth; but that does not mean that you, in your student-life, ought not to study politics. Politics are a part of our being; we ought to understand our national institutions, and we ought to understand our national growth and all those things. We may do it from our infancy.

So, in our Ashram, every child is taught to understand the political institutions of our country, and to know how the country is vibrating with new emotions, with new aspirations, with a new life.

But we want also the steady light, the infallible light, of religious faith, not a faith which merely appeals to the intelligence, but a faith which is indelibly inscribed on the heart. First, we want to realize that religious consciousness, and immediately we have done that, I think the whole department of life is open to us, and it should then be a sacred privilege of students and everybody to partake of that whole life, so that, when they grow to manhood, and when they leave their colleges, they may do so as men properly quipped to battle with life. Today what happens is this: much of the political life is confined to student life; immediately the students leave their colleges and cease to be students, they sink into oblivion, they seek miserable employments, carrying miserable emoluments, rising no higher in their aspirations, knowing nothing of God, knowing nothing of fresh air or bright light, and nothing of that real vigorous independence that comes out of obedience to these laws that I have ventured to place before you.

Conclusion

I am not here asking you to crowd into the Ashram, there is no room there. But I say that every one of you may enact that Ashram life individually and collectively. I shall be satisfied with anything that you may choose from the rules I have ventured to place before you and act up to it. But if you think that these are the outpourings of a mad man, you will not hesitate to tell me that it is so, and I shall take that judgment from you undismayed.

⫸ For Further Thought ⫷

"The function of violence is to obtain reform by external means," Gandhi wrote. "The function of passive resistance, that is, soul-force, is to obtain it by growth from within; which, in its turn, is obtained by self-suffering, self-purification. Violence ever fails; passive resistance is ever successful." In 1917, Gandhi established an ashram—a kind of live-in school to practice "group life in a religious spirit"—near Ahmedebad, India. It's purpose was to propagate the spirit of satyagraha.

As you read through the various vows that Gandhi asked its residents to adopt—including dietary restrictions, celibacy, and swadeshi, as well as fearlessness, honesty, and religious tolerance—do you feel you could or would have wanted to join this collective? Gandhi understood that not everyone could retire to an ashram, but believed that all could "enact Ashram life individually" by choosing to live by as many of its rules as possible. Which of Gandhi's vows and expectations do you feel drawn to upholding in your own life? Have his ideas inspired you to make changes? Use this space to reflect on how Gandhi's admittedly stringent ideals have affected your own day-to-day choices and behavior—or how you hope they might in the future.

_____

_____

_____

_____

_____

_____

_____

_____

_____

THE SECRET OF SATYAGRAHA IN SOUTH AFRICA

(Pamphlet, July 27, 1916)

In brief, the significance of satyagraha consists in the quest for a principle of life. We did not say to anyone in so many words that our fight was in pursuance of this quest. If we had said so, the people there would only have laughed at us. We only made known the secondary aim of our movement, which was that the Government there, thinking us lowly and mean, was making laws to oust us from the country, and that it was right for us to defy these laws and show that we were brave.

Suppose the Government passes a law saying that Colored persons shall wear yellow caps; in fact, a law of this kind was made in Rome for the Jews. If the Government intended to treat us in a similar fashion and made a Law that appeared to humiliate us, it was for us to make it clear to the Government that we would not obey such a law. If a child says to his father: "Please put on your turban the wrong side up for me," the father understands that the child wants to have a laugh at his expense and at once obeys the command. But when someone else, with uncharitable motives, says the same thing, he clearly answers, "Look, brother, so long as my head is on my shoulders, you cannot humiliate me in this manner. You conquer my head first and then make me wear my turban in any fashion you please." The Government there in a similar way, thinking the Indians lowly, wanted to treat them as slaves and as far as possible to prevent their coming into the country. And with this end in view, it began inventing ever new laws such as putting names of Indians in a separate register, making them give fingerprints in the manner of thieves and bandits, forcing them to live in particular areas, forbidding their movement beyond a specified boundary, making rules for them to walk on particular footpaths and board specified carriages in trains, treating their wives as concubines if they could not produce marriage certificates, levying from them an annual tax of forty-five rupees per capita, etc., etc. Often a disease manifests itself in the body in various forms. The disease in this case, as has been explained, was the evil purpose of the Government of South Africa, and all the rules and regulations mentioned above were the various forms that it took. We, therefore, had to prepare ourselves to fight against these.

There are two ways of countering injustice. One way is to smash the head of the man who perpetrates injustice and to get your own head smashed in the process. All strong people in the world adopt this course. Everywhere wars are fought and millions of people are killed.

The consequence is not the progress of a nation but its decline. Soldiers returning from the front have become so bereft of reason that they indulge in various anti-social activities. One does not have to go far for examples. In the Boer War, when the British won a victory at Mafeking, the whole of England, and London in particular, went so mad with joy that for days on end everyone did nothing but dance night and day! They freely indulged in wickednesses and rowdyism and did not leave a single bar with a drop of liquor in it. *The*

Times, commenting, said that no words could describe the way those few days were spent, that all that could be said was that "the English nation went amafficking [a-Mafeking]." Pride makes a victorious nation bad-tempered. It falls into luxurious ways of living. Then for a time, it may be conceded, peace prevails. But after a short while, it comes more and more to be realized that the seeds of war have not been destroyed but have become a thousand times more nourished and mighty. No country has ever become, or will ever become, happy through victory in war. A nation does not rise that way, it only falls further. In fact, what comes to it is defeat, not victory. And if, perchance, either our act or our purpose was ill-conceived, it brings disaster to both belligerents.

But through the other method of combating injustice, we alone suffer the consequences of our mistakes, and the other side is wholly spared. This other method is satyagraha. One who resorts to it does not have to break another's head; he may merely have his own head broken. He has to be prepared to die himself suffering all the pain. In opposing the atrocious laws of the Government of South Africa, it was this method that we adopted. We made it clear to the said Government that we would never bow to its outrageous laws. No clapping is possible without two hands to do it, and no quarrel without two persons to make it. Similarly, no State is possible without two entities [the rulers and the ruled]. You are our sovereign, our Government, only so long as we consider ourselves your subjects.

When we are not subjects, you are not the sovereign either. So long as it is your endeavor to control us with justice and love, we will let you to do so. But if you wish to strike at us from behind, we cannot permit it. Whatever you do in other matters, you will have to ask our opinion about the laws that concern us. If you make laws to keep us suppressed in a wrongful manner and without taking us into confidence, these laws will merely adorn the statute-books. We will never obey them. Award us for it what punishment you like, we will put up with it. Send us to prison and we will live there as in a paradise.

Ask us to mount the scaffold and we will do so laughing. Shower what sufferings you like upon us, we will calmly endure all and not hurt a hair of your body. We will gladly die and will not so much as touch you. But so long as there is yet life in these our bones, we will never comply with your arbitrary laws.

It all began on a Sunday evening in Johannesburg when I sat on a hillock with another gentleman called Hemchandra. The memory of that day is so vivid that it might have been yesterday. At my side lay a Government *Gazette*. It contained the several clauses of the law concerning Indians. As I read it, I shook with rage. What did the Government take us for? Then and there I produced a translation of that portion of the *Gazette* which contained the said laws and wrote under it: "I will never let these laws govern me." This was at once the time that even a single Indian would be capable of the unprecedented heroism the Indians revealed or that the satyagraha movement would gain the momentum it did.

Immediately, I made my view known to fellow Indians, and many of them declared their readiness for satyagraha. In the first conflict, people took part under the impression that our aim would be gained after only a few days of suffering. In the second conflict, there were only a very few people to begin with but later many more came along. Afterwards when, on the visit of Mr. Gokhale, the Government of South Africa pledged itself to a settlement, the fight ceased. Later, the Government treacherously refused to honor its pledge; on which a third satyagraha battle became necessary. Gokhale at that time asked me how many people I thought would take part in the satyagraha. I wrote saying they would be between 30 and 60. But I could not find even that number. Only 16 of us took up the challenge. We were firmly decided that so long as the Government did not repeal its atrocious laws or make some settlement, we would accept every penalty but would not submit. We had never hoped that we should find many fellow fighters. But the readiness of one person without self-interest to offer himself for the cause of truth and country always has its effect. Soon there were twenty thousand people in the movement. There was no room for them in the prisons, and the blood of India boiled. Many people say that if Lord Hardinge had not intervened, a compromise would have been impossible. But these people forget to ask themselves why it was that Lord Hardinge intervened. The sufferings of the Canadian Indians were far greater than those of the South African Indians. Why did he not use his good offices there? Where the spiritual might of thousands of men and women has been mustered, where innumerable men and women are eager to lay down their lives, what indeed is impossible? There was no other course open for Lord Hardinge than to offer mediation, and he only showed his wisdom in adopting it. What transpired later is well known to you: the Government of South Africa was compelled to come to terms with us. All of which goes to show that we can gain everything without hurting anybody and through soul-force or satyagraha alone. He who fights with arms has to depend on arms and on support from others. He has to turn from the straight path and seek tortuous tracks. The course that a satyagrahi adopts in his fight is straight and he need look to no one for help. He can, if necessary, fight by himself alone. In that case, it is true, the outcome will be somewhat delayed. If I had not found as many comrades in the South African fight as I did, all that would have happened is that you would not have seen me here in your midst today. Perhaps all my life would have had to be spent in the struggle there. But what of that? The gain that has been secured would only have been a little late in coming. For the battle of satyagraha one only needs to prepare oneself. We have to have strict self-control. If it is necessary for this preparation to live in forests and caves, we should do so.

The time that may be taken up in this preparation should not be considered wasted. Christ, before he went out to serve the world, spent forty days in the wilderness, preparing himself for his mission.

Buddha too spent many years in such preparation. Had Christ and Buddha not undergone this preparation, they would not have been what they were. Similarly, if we want to put this body in the service of truth and humanity, we must first raise our soul by developing virtues like celibacy, non-violence and truth. Then alone may we say that we are fit to render real service to the country.

In brief, the aim of the satyagraha struggle was to infuse manliness in cowards and to develop the really human virtues, and its field was the passive resistance against the Government of South Africa.

SATYAGRAHA—NOT PASSIVE RESISTANCE
(Pamphlet, September 2, 1917)

The force denoted by the term "passive resistance" and translated into Hindi as *nishkriya pratirodha* is not very accurately described either by the original English phrase or by its Hindi rendering. Its correct description is "satyagraha." Satyagraha was born in South Africa in 1908.

There was no word in any Indian language denoting the power which our countrymen in South Africa invoked for the redress of their grievances. There was an English equivalent, namely, "passive resistance," and we carried on with it. However, the need for a word to describe this unique power came to be increasingly felt, and it was decided to award a prize to anyone who could think of an appropriate term. A Gujarati-speaking gentleman submitted the word "satyagraha," and it was adjudged the best.

"Passive resistance" conveyed the idea of the suffragette movement in England. Burning of houses by these women was called "passive resistance" and so also their fasting in prison. All such acts might very well be 'passive resistance' but they were not "satyagraha." It is said of "passive resistance" that it is the weapon of the weak, but the power which is the subject of this article can be used only by the strong. This power is not "passive" resistance; indeed it calls for intense activity. The movement in South Africa was not passive but active. The Indians of South Africa believed that Truth was their object, that Truth ever triumphs, and with this definiteness of purpose they persistently held on to Truth. They put up with all the suffering that this persistence implied. With the conviction that Truth is not to be renounced even unto death, they shed the fear of death. In the cause of Truth, the prison was a palace to them and its doors the gateway to freedom.

What Is Satyagraha?

Satyagraha is not physical force. A satyagrahi does not inflict pain on the adversary; he does not seek his destruction. A satyagrahi never resorts to firearms. In the use of satyagraha, there is no ill will whatever.

Satyagraha is pure soul-force. Truth is the very substance of the soul. That is why this force is called satyagraha. The soul is informed with knowledge. In it burns the flame of love. If someone gives us pain through ignorance, we shall win him through love. "Nonviolence is the supreme dharma" is the proof of this power of love.

Non-violence is a dormant state. In the waking state, it is love. Ruled by love, the world goes on. In English there is a saying, "Might is Right." Then there is the doctrine of the survival of the fittest. Both these ideas are contradictory to the above principle. Neither is wholly true. If ill will were the chief motive-force, the world would have been destroyed long ago; and neither would I have had the opportunity to write this article, nor would the hopes of the readers be fulfilled. We are alive solely because of love. We are all ourselves the proof of this. Deluded by modern western civilization, we have forgotten our ancient civilization and worship the might of arms.

Worship of Armed Might

We forget the principle of non-violence, which is the essence of all religions. The doctrine of arms stands for irreligion. It is due to the sway of that doctrine that a sanguinary war is raging in Europe. In India also we find worship of arms. We see it even in that great work of Tulsidas. But it is seen in all the books that soul-force is the supreme power.

Rama and Ravana

Rama stands for the soul and Ravana for the non-soul. The immense physical might of Ravana is as nothing compared to the soul-force of Rama. Ravana's ten heads are as straw to Rama. Rama is a yogi; he has conquered self and pride. He is "placid equally in affluence and adversity," he has "neither attachment, nor greed nor the intoxication of status." This represents the ultimate in satyagraha.

The banner of satyagraha can again fly in the Indian sky, and it is our duty to raise it. If we take recourse to satyagraha, we can conquer our conquerors the English, make them bow before our tremendous soul-force, and the issue will be of benefit to the whole world. It is certain that India cannot rival Britain or Europe in force of arms. The British worship the war-god and they can all of them become, as they are becoming, bearers of arms. The hundreds of millions in India can never carry arms. They have made the religion of non-violence their own. It is impossible for the *varnashram* system to disappear from India.

Historical Evidence

People demand historical evidence in support of satyagraha. History is for the most part a record of armed activities. Natural activities find very little mention in it. Only uncommon activities strike us with wonder. Satyagraha has been used always and in all situations.

The father and the son, the man and the wife are perpetually resorting to satyagraha, one towards the other. When a father gets angry and punishes the son, the son does not hit back with a weapon; he conquers his father's anger by submitting to him. The son refuses to be subdued by the unjust rule of his father, but he puts up with the punishment that he may incur through disobeying the unjust father.

We can similarly free ourselves of the unjust rule of the Government by defying the unjust rule and accepting the punishments that go with it. We do not bear malice towards the Government. When we set its fears at rest, when we do not desire to make armed assaults on the administrators, nor to unseat them from power, but only to get rid of their injustice, they will at once be subdued to our will.

The question is asked why we should call any rule unjust. In saying so, we ourselves assume the function of a judge. It is true. But in this world, we always have to act as judges for ourselves. That is why the satyagrahi does not strike his adversary with arms. If he has Truth on his side, he will win, and if his thought is faulty, he will suffer the consequences of his fault.

What is the good, they ask, of only one person opposing injustice; for he will be punished and destroyed, he will languish in prison or meet an untimely end through hanging. The objection is not valid. History shows that all reforms have begun with one person. Fruit is hard to come by without *tapasya*. The suffering that has to be undergone in satyagraha is *tapasya* in its purest form. Only when the *tapasya* is capable of bearing fruit, do we have the fruit. This establishes the fact that when there is insufficient *tapasya*, the fruit is delayed. The *tapasya* of Jesus Christ, boundless though it was, was not sufficient for Europe's need. Europe has disapproved Christ. Through ignorance, it has disregarded Christ's pure way of life. Many Christs will have to offer themselves as sacrifice at the terrible altar of Europe, and only then will realization dawn on that continent. But Jesus will always be the first among these. He has been the sower of the seed and his will therefore be the credit for raising the harvest.

Educating Ignorant Peasants in Satyagraha

It is said that it is a very difficult, if not an altogether impossible, task to educate ignorant peasants in satyagraha and that it is full of perils, for it is a very arduous business to transform unlettered ignorant people from one condition into another. Both the arguments are just silly. The people of India are perfectly fit to receive the training of satyagraha. India has knowledge of dharma, and where there is knowledge of dharma, satyagraha is a very simple matter. The people of India have drunk of the nectar of devotion. This great people overflows with faith. It is no difficult matter to lead such a people on to the right path of satyagraha. Some have a fear that once people get involved in satyagraha, they may at a later stage take to arms. This fear is illusory. From the path of satyagraha [clinging to Truth], a transition to the path of *a-satyagraha* [clinging to untruth] is impossible. It is possible of course that some people who believe in armed activity may mislead the satyagrahis by infiltrating into their ranks and later making them take to arms. This is possible in all enterprises. But as compared to other activities, it is less likely to happen in satyagraha, for their motives soon get exposed and when the people are not ready to take up arms, it becomes almost impossible to lead them on to that terrible path. The might of arms is directly opposed to the might of satyagraha. Just as darkness does not abide in light, soulless armed activity cannot enter the sunlike radiance of soul-force. Many Pathans took part in satyagraha in South Africa abiding by all the rules of satyagraha.

Then it is said that much suffering is involved in being a satyagrahi and that the entire people will not be willing to put up with this suffering. The objection is not valid. People in general always follow in the footsteps of the noble. There is no doubt that it is difficult to produce a satyagrahi leader. Our experience is that a satyagrahi needs many more virtues like self-control, fearlessness, etc., than are requisite for one who believes in armed action. The greatness of the man bearing arms does not lie in the superiority of the arms, nor does it lie in his physical prowess. It lies in his determination and fearlessness in face of death. General Gordon was a mighty warrior of the British Empire. In the statue that has been erected in his memory he has only a small baton in his hand. It goes to show that the strength of a warrior is not measured by reference to his weapons but by his firmness of mind. A satyagrahi needs millions of times more of such firmness than does a bearer of arms. The birth of such a man can bring about the salvation of India in no time. Not only India but the whole world awaits the advent of such a man. We may in the meanwhile prepare the ground as much as we can through satyagraha. . . .

Instructions to Satyagrahis
(The Bombay Chronicle, September 4, 1919)

We are now in a position to expect to be arrested any moment. It is, therefore, necessary to bear in mind that, if anyone is arrested, he should without causing any difficulty allow himself to be arrested and, if summoned to appear before a court, he should do so. No defense should be offered and no pleaders engaged in the matter. If a fine is imposed with the alternative of imprisonment, imprisonment should be accepted. If only a fine is imposed, it ought not to be paid but that his property, if he has any, should be allowed to be sold.

There should be no demonstration of grief or otherwise made by the remaining satyagrahis by reason of the arrest and imprisonment of their comrade. It cannot be too often repeated that we court imprisonment and we may not complain of it when we actually receive it. When once imprisoned, it is our duty to conform to all prison regulations, as prison reform is no part of our campaign at the present moment. A satyagrahi may not resort to surreptitious practices, of which ordinary prisoners are often found to be guilty. All a satyagrahi does can only and must be done openly.

Satyagraha Is Impossible So Long as There Is Ill Will

(Pamphlet, May 4, 1919)

Brothers and Sisters,

We have seen in our last leaflet that the actions of a satyagrahi should not be prompted by fear from without but by the voice from within, and that a satyagrahi should not think of attaining his objects by harboring ill will towards his opponent but should win him over by his friendliness. I see that many hesitate to accept the second proposition. They argue: "How can we help being angry with wrongdoers? It is against human nature to do otherwise. How can we separate the wrong from the wrong-doer? How is it possible to direct our anger against the wrong without directing it against the wrong-doer?" A father, far from getting angry with his son, often expresses his disapproval of wrong action by taking suffering on his own person. Only on such mutual conduct is continuance of friendly relations between father and son possible. These relations cease with the ceasing of such conduct. It is our daily lot to go through these experiences and hence the proverb, "Let quarrels perish." We can live in peace and be free from our fearful position only if we apply the domestic law to our relations with the Government. The doubt need not be raised whether the domestic law can at all be extended to our relations with the Government, and whether the law of love does not for its operation require reciprocity. In satyagraha, both the parties need not be satyagrahis. Where both the parties are satyagrahis, there is no play for satyagraha, no opportunity for the test of love.

Insistence on truth can come into play only when one party practices untruth or injustice. Only then can love be tested. True friendship is put to the test only when one party disregards the obligations of friendship. We stand to lose everything when we are angry against the Government. Mutual distrust and mutual ill will are thereby augmented. But if we act without in the least being angry with the Government, but also without being cowed down by their armed force, and without submitting to what we believe to be injustice, injustice would of itself be removed and we would easily attain the equality which is our goal. This equality does not depend on our power to answer their brute force with brute force, but on our ability to stand our ground without fear of brute force, and real fearlessness is not possible without love. A clear victory for satyagraha is impossible so long as there is ill will. But those who believe themselves to be weak are incapable of loving. Let then our first act every morning be to make the following resolve for the day: "I shall not fear anyone on earth. I shall fear only God; I shall not bear ill will towards anyone. I shall not submit to injustice from anyone. I shall conquer untruth by truth and in resisting untruth I shall put up with all suffering."

IN CASE OF MY ARREST

(June 30, 1919)

As my arrest may come upon me unawares, I wish to leave the following as my message.

I appeal to all my countrymen and countrywomen throughout India to observe absolute calmness and to refrain from violence to person and property in any shape or form. The greatest injury that can be done to me is deeds of violence after my arrest and for my sake. Those who love me will show their true affection only by becoming satyagrahis, i.e., believers in Truth and *ahimsa* (non-violence) and self-suffering as the only means for securing redress of grievances. To the Government of India, I respectfully wish to submit that they will never establish peace in India by ignoring the causes of the present discontent. Satyagraha has not bred lawlessness and violence. It is a vital force, and it has certainly hastened the crisis that was inevitable. But it has also acted as a restraining force of the first magnitude. Government as well as the people should recognize this fact and feel thankful for it. Without the purifying and soothing effect of satyagraha, violence would have been infinitely greater, for mutual retaliation would have produced nothing but chaos. Mahomedans are deeply resentful of what they believe to be England's attitude towards the question of Turkey, Palestine, and Mecca Sharif. The people are deeply distrustful of England's attitude towards the forthcoming Reforms, and they want repeal of the Rowlatt legislation. No repression can possibly avail to secure even a shadow of peace in the land.

Substantial peace can only be had by conciliating Mahomedan religious sentiments by granting reforms in a liberal and trusting spirit, even as was done by the late Sir Henry Campbell-Bannerman in the case of South Africa and by recognizing the sacredness of public opinion by immediate repeal of the Rowlatt legislation. But the British Government all the world over have demanded proof of a people's earnestness. The chosen European method of expressing earnestness is to create disorder by violence. The Government have given a crushing reply to this method. It may prosper in Europe, but not in India. To satyagraha, there can be no reply but that of acceding to satyagraha demands. Government of a country is possible when people support it by contributing revenue, by filling public services and such like actions symbolic of approval.

When a Government does justice, i.e., is broadbased upon the will of a people, such support is a duty in spite of its temporary aberrations. Withdrawal—total or partial—of such support becomes equally a duty when Government is carried on in defiance of people's will, and such withdrawal of support is pure satyagraha when it is unaccompanied by violence in any shape or form and unadulterated by untruth. Satyagrahis, then, knowing the sanctity and invincibility of satyagraha will not lend themselves to violence and untruth and will refrain from offering civil disobedience until they are assured that there will be no violence on the part of the people, whether such a state of things was brought about by the peoples' willing acceptance of the doctrine of Truth and non- the whole of

India will have participated in the joy of satyagraha and will have given a lesson to the world. In the latter case, the Government will realize that no physical force that they can summon to their aid will ever bend the spirit of satyagrahis.

"LET US BE HARD ON OURSELVES"
(*Young India*, July 28, 1921)

It is my conviction that we are in sight of the promised land, but the danger is the greatest when victory seems the nearest. No victory worth the name has ever been won without a final effort, more serious than all the preceding ones. God's last test is ever the most difficult. Satan's last temptation is ever the most seductive. We must stand God's last test and resist Satan's last temptation, if we would be free.

Non-violence is the most vital and integral part of non-cooperation. We may fail in everything else and still continue our battle if we remain non-violent. But we capitulate miserably if we fail in adhering to non-violence. Let it be remembered that violence is the keystone of the Government edifice. Since violence is its sheet-anchor and its final refuge, it has rendered itself almost immune from violence on our side by having prepared itself to frustrate all violent effort by the people. We therefore cooperate with the Government in the most active manner when we resort to violence. Any violence on our part must be a token of our stupidity, ignorance and impotent rage. To exercise restraint under the gravest provocation is the truest mark of soldiership. The veriest tyro in the art of war knows that he must avoid the ambushes of his adversary. And every provocation is a dangerous ambush into which we must resolutely refuse to walk.

The story of Aligarh is an illustration in point. It seems clear enough that sufficient provocation was given by the police. We have long recognized that it is their business to do so. The people of Aligarh walked into the trap laid for them. They allowed themselves to be provoked, and resorted to arson. It is not yet clear who killed the constable in mufti. The burden is on the people to show that they did not.

Let us be hard on ourselves. If we wish to walk along the straight and narrow path (which is necessarily the shortest), we must not be self-indulgent. We may not throw the blame for any mishap on the badmashes. We must be responsible for their acts. Or we declare ourselves unfit for swaraj. We must gain control even over them. Even they must realize the necessity of not interfering with the national and the religious work we are engaged in. In a movement of purification, the whole country is lifted up not excluding the wicked and the fallen. Let there be no mistake, that is our deliberate claim. If it is merely a lip claim, we shall prove ourselves guilty of having set up a system more Satanic than the one we condemn as such.

Therefore whilst we are following the course of non-violent non-cooperation, we are bound in honor to live up to it in thought, word and deed. Let us make the frank confession if we are too weak or too incredulous to live up to our creed.

The reader must not run away with the idea that I feel we are not standing the test. On the contrary I believe that we have obtained a marvelous hold over the people, that they have understood the necessity of non-violence as they have never done before.

But it would be wrong for us not to take due warning from the slightest deviation from the path deliberately chosen by us. I find it necessary too to utter the word of caution, because the provocation by the Government is on the increase. It is the greatest in the U.P. The arrest of Mr. Sherwani at 5 o'clock in the morning, his swift trial, conviction, sentence and removal the same day are enough to irritate the most sober-minded. The details of the trial show that the magistrate knew little of law and cared less. The evidence before him, if all of it has been given to the Press, was quite insufficient for a conviction. It almost seems that the conviction and sentence were prearranged. The production of evidence in that case was a huge farce. We are having a rehearsal of trials under the ordinary law.

Where is the difference between an executive order and a judicial trial? The latter is more deadly as it is more difficult to expose. To say that a man had no trial carries greater conviction of injustice than to have to say that the trial was farcical. Repressive laws may be repealed; it does not follow therefore that repression will be done away with. The substance will be the same though the form is changed. What we want is a change of substance, of spirit, of heart.

And if we desire that change, we must first change ourselves, i.e., be proof against repression. Just as we may not retort with violence, so may we not weaken under repression no matter how severe or trying it may be.

An authentic rumor comes from the U.P. that at least three more or less noted workers found the jail life too trying, gave undertakings to refrain from certain acts and procured their discharge. If this is true, it is sad. We must be firm as a rock. There must be no going back. We must be able cheerfully to bear any torture that may be our lot in the jails of India. We may expect no quarter from the Government. We must expect it to do the worst it can whether within or without the law. Its one purpose is to bend us, since it will not mend itself.

I am not passing harsh judgment on the Government. Dharwar and Aligarh are the latest instances of Government's defiance of propriety. If I am to credit another rumor, in a U.P. jail a brave Mussulman prisoner was put in a dark cell and locked up in it for three days in the midst of foul stenches. My informant asked me, what a man who could not bear these stenches was to do. the harsh but deliberate answer I gave was, that he was even then not to apologize, he was free to dash his head against the walls of the prison rather than submit to the wish of the tyrant. This is not an idle expression of opinion, but a titbit from my South African experiences. The jail life in South Africa was not a bed of roses.

Many a prisoner had to undergo solitary confinement. Hundreds had to do sanitary work. Several fasted. One woman was discharged a skeleton because the authorities would not allow her the only food she would eat. But she had a proud and resolute spirit. Out of the thousands who suffered imprisonment in South Africa, with one or two exceptions in the early stages I do not recall a single instance of a prisoner having weakened and apologized to purchase his freedom.

Some like Parsi Rustomji, Imam Kadir Bavazir, Thambi Naidu, and many others whose names I could set down never flinched but repeatedly sought imprisonment. The Temple of Freedom is not erected without the blood of sufferers. Non-violent method is the quickest, the surest, and the best. Let us be true to our solemn oath taken at Congress and Khilafat gatherings, and triumph is at hand.

THE HINDU DHARMA

(from *Freedom's Battle*, 1922)

The age of misunderstanding and mutual warfare among religions is gone. If India has a mission of its own to the world, it is to establish the unity and the truth of all religions. This unity is established by mutual help and understanding between the various religions. It has come as a rare privilege to the Hindus in the fulfillment of this mission of India to stand up in defense of Islam against the onslaught of the earth-greed of the military powers of the west.

The Dharma of Hinduism in this respect is placed beyond all doubt by the Bhagavad Gita.

> Those who are the votaries of other Gods and worship them with faith—even they, O Kaunteya, worship me alone, though not as the Shastra requires.

> Whoever being devoted wishes in perfect faith to worship a particular form, of such a one I maintain the same faith unshaken.

Hinduism will realize its fullest beauty when in the fulfillment of this cardinal tenet, its followers offer themselves as sacrifice for the protection of the faith of their brothers, the Mussulmans.

If Hindus and Mussulmans attain the height of courage and sacrifice that is needed for this battle on behalf of Islam against the greed of the West, a victory will be won not alone for Islam, but for Christianity itself. Militarism has robbed the crucified God of his name and his very cross and the World has been mistaking it to be Christianity. After the battle of Islam is won, Islam and Hinduism together can emancipate Christianity itself from the lust for power and wealth which have strangled it now and the true Christianity of the Gospels will be established. This battle of non-cooperation with its suffering and peaceful withdrawal of service will once for all establish its superiority over the power of brute force and unlimited slaughter.

What a glorious privilege it is to play our part in this history of the world, when Hinduism and Christianity will unite on behalf of Islam, and in that strife of mutual love and support each religion will attain its own truest shape and beauty.

The Alternative

(from *Freedom's Battle*, 1922)

Is violence or total surrender the only choice open to any people to whom Freedom or Justice is denied? Violence at a time when the whole world has learnt from bitter experience the futility of violence is unworthy of a country whose ancient people's privilege, it was, to see this truth long ago.

Violence may rid a nation of its foreign masters but will only enslave it from inside. No nation can really be free which is at the mercy of its army and its military heroes. If a people rely for freedom on its soldiers, the soldiers will rule the country, not the people. Till the recent awakening of the workers of Europe, this was the only freedom which the powers of Europe really enjoyed. True freedom can exist only when those who produce, not those who destroy or know only to live on other's labor, are the masters.

Even were violence the true road to freedom, is violence possible to a nation which has been emasculated and deprived of all weapons, and the whole world is hopelessly in advance of all our possibilities in the manufacture and the wielding of weapons of destruction.

Submission or withdrawal of cooperation is the real and only alternative before India. Submission to injustice puts on the tempting garb of peace and, gradual progress, but there is no surer way to death than submission to wrong.

HOW TO WORK NON-COOPERATION

(from *Freedom's Battle*, 1922)

Perhaps the best way of answering the fears and criticism as to non-cooperation is to elaborate more fully the scheme of non-cooperation. The critics seem to imagine that the organizers propose to give effect to the whole scheme at once. The fact however is that the organizers have fixed definite, progressive four stages.

The first is the giving up of titles and resignation of honorary posts. If there is no response or if the response received is not effective, recourse will be had to the second stage. The second stage involves much previous arrangement. Certainly not a single servant will be called out unless he is either capable of supporting himself and his dependents or the Khilafat Committee is able to bear the burden. All the classes of servants will not be called out at once and never will any pressure be put upon a single servant to withdraw himself from the Government service. Nor will a single private employee be touched for the simple reason that the movement is not anti-English. It is not even anti-Government. Cooperation is to be withdrawn because the people must not be party to a wrong—a broken pledge—a violation of deep religious sentiment. Naturally, the movement will receive a check, if there is any undue influence brought to bear upon any Government servant or if any violence is used or countenanced by any member of the Khilafat Committee.

The second stage must be entirely successful, if the response is at all on an adequate scale. For no Government—much less the

Indian Government—can subsist if the people cease to serve it. The withdrawal therefore of the police and the military—the third stage—is a distant goal. The organizers however wanted to be fair, open and above suspicion. They did not want to keep back from the Government or the public a single step they had in contemplation even as a remote contingency. The fourth, i.e., suspension of taxes is still more remote. The organizers recognize that suspension of general taxation is fraught with the greatest danger. It is likely to bring a sensitive class in conflict with the police. They are therefore not likely to embark upon it, unless they can do so with the assurance that there will be no violence offered by the people.

I admit as I have already done that non-cooperation is not unattended with risk, but the risk of supineness in the face of a grave issue is infinitely greater than the danger of violence ensuing form organizing non-cooperation. To do nothing is to invite violence for a certainty.

It is easy enough to pass resolutions or write articles condemning non-cooperation. But it is no easy task to restrain the fury of a people incensed by a deep sense of wrong. I urge those who talk or work against non-cooperation to descend from their chairs and go down to the people, learn their feelings and write, if they have the heart against non-cooperation. They will find, as I have found that the only way to avoid violence is to enable them to give such expression to their feelings as to compel redress. I have found nothing save non-cooperation. It is logical and harmless. It is the inherent right of a subject to refuse to assist a Government that will not listen to him.

Non-cooperation as a voluntary movement can only succeed, if the feeling is genuine and strong enough to make people suffer to the utmost. If the religious sentiment of the Mahomedans is deeply hurt and if the Hindus entertain neighborly regard towards their Muslim brethren, they will both count no cost too great for achieving the end. Non-cooperation will not only be an effective remedy but will also be an effective test of the sincerity of the Muslim claim and the Hindu profession of friendship.

There is however one formidable argument urged by friends against my joining the Khilafat movement. They say that it ill-becomes me, a friend of the English and an admirer of the British constitution, to join hands with those who are today filled with nothing but ill will against the English. I am sorry to have to con-fess that the ordinary Mahomedan entertains today no affection for Englishmen. He considers, not without some cause, that they have not played the game. But if I am friendly towards Englishmen, I am no less so towards my countrymen, the Mahomedans. And as such they have a greater claim upon my attention than Englishmen. My personal religion however enables me to serve my countrymen without hurting Englishmen or for that matter anybody else. What I am not prepared to do to my blood-brother I would not do to an Englishman, I would not injure him to gain a kingdom. But I would withdraw cooperation from him if it becomes necessary as I had withdrawn from my own brother (now deceased) when it became necessary.

I serve the Empire by refusing to partake in its wrong. William

Stead offered public prayers for British reverses at the time of the Boer War because he considered that the nation to which he belonged was engaged in an unrighteous war. The present Prime Minister risked his life in opposing that war and did everything he could to obstruct his own Government in its prosecution. And today if I have thrown in my lot with the Mahomedans, a large number of whom, bear no friendly feelings towards the British, I have done so frankly as a friend of the British and with the object of gaining justice and of thereby showing the capacity of the British constitution to respond to every honest determination when it is coupled with suffering, I hope by my "alliance" with the Mahomedans to achieve a three-fold end—to obtain justice in the face of odds with the method of Satyagraha and to show its efficacy over all other methods, to secure Mahomedan friendship for the Hindus and thereby internal peace also, and last but not least to transform ill will into affection for the British and their constitution which in spite of the imperfections weathered many a storm. I may fail in achieving any of the ends. I can but attempt. God alone can grant success. It will not be denied that the ends are all worthy. I invite Hindus and Englishman to join me in a full-hearted manner in shouldering the burden the Mahomedans of India are carrying. Theirs is admittedly a just fight. The Viceroy, the Secretary of State, the Maharaja of Bikuner and Lord Sinha have testified to it. Time has arrived to make good the testimony. People with a just cause are never satisfied with a mere protest. They have been known to die for it. Are a high-spirited people like the Mahomedans expected to do less?

PARENTS AND NON-COOPERATION

(from *Freedom's Battle*, 1922)

I have suggested yet another difficulty—to withdraw our children from the Government schools and to ask collegiate students to withdraw from the College and to empty Government aided schools. How could I do otherwise? I want to gauge the national sentiment. I want to know whether the Mahomedans feel deeply. If they feel deeply they will understand in the twinkling of an eye, that it is not right for them to receive schooling from a Government in which they have lost all faith; and which they do not trust at all. How can I, if I do not want to help this Government, receive any help from that Government. I think that the schools and colleges are factories for making clerks and Government servants. I would not help this great factory for manufacturing clerks and servants if I want to withdraw cooperation from that Government. Look at it from any point of view you like. It is not possible for you to send your children to the schools and still believe in the doctrine of non-cooperation.

➤➤ For Further Thought ◄◄

Here is a statement that simply and powerfully sums up Gandhi's vision of satyagraha:

> There are two ways of countering injustice. One way is to smash the head of the man who perpetrates injustice and to get your own head smashed in the process. . . . Th[e] other method is satyagraha. One who resorts to it does not have to break another's head; he may merely have his own head broken. He has to be prepared to die himself suffering all the pain.

What do you think of this declaration? You have now taken a journey through some of Gandhi's seminal writing. You have immersed yourself in his philosophy as it took shape in his own mind. No less a mind than Albert Einstein said, "Taken on the whole, I would believe that Gandhi's views were the most enlightened of all the political men of our time." Do you agree? Do you think that his ideas are useful in today's social and political climate?

Think about the building blocks of Gandhi's worldview as you now understand them: Self, Swadeshi, Swaraj, and Satyagraha. Gandhi set high standards for all of us and attempted to serve as a model for what we could achieve. Have his thoughts and ideas changed your views? If so, in what ways? What would you ask or say to Gandhi if you could sit down with him right now?

GLOSSARY

AHIMSA: Non-violence; love for all living things.

ASHRAM: A place for disciplined community living; a collective in which to practice "group life in a religious spirit."

BAPU: "Father"; a term of affection used for Gandhi.

BRAHMACHARYA: Celibacy; control over all of the senses and organs.

DHARMA: Righteousness; the Hindu religious code of ethics and duty.

KARMA: Destiny or fate based on the actions of this and previous states of existence.

KHILAFAT MOVEMENT: Efforts by Muslims in India to secure favorable treatment from the British government (1919–24).

MAHATMA: "Great Soul"; a title of respect conferred upon Gandhi.

SADAVRAT: Charity.

SATYA: Truth.

SATYAGRAHA: "Soul Force"; nonviolent resistance.

SWADESHI: "Of one's own country"; self-sufficiency.

SWARAJ: "Self-rule"; independence.

INDEX

A

addictions, 113–120, 174–175

adversity, uses of, 89–93

African Americans, 93–98

Africans, 33, 41, 44, 119

ahimsa, 308–311, 313

alcohol, 11, 14, 28, 108–110, 113–114

America. *See* United States of America

anger, 310, 327, 333, 338–339, 343, 351

animals, 27, 190, 312

Arabs, 48–49

architecture, 49–51

arms (weapons), 111–112, 233–234, 237–239, 242, 332–336, 349

arrest, 337, 340–342, 344. *See also* jails and prisons

Aryans, 42–43, 47

Ashram vows, 304–320

Asiatics, 111–112, 296

astronomy, 48

B

Bengal, India, 211, 243

Bhagavad Gita, 167–168, 171, 294, 315, 347

Birdwood, George, 54

body. *See also* diet; discipline; health

  bodily labor, 168

  body-force, 234

  spirituality and, 122–125

  training of, 239–240

  weakness of, 140–142

  welfare of, 221–223

Boer war, 199, 263, 325, 353

boycott, 183, 197–198, 243, 268

brahmacharya, 142–143, 166

Brahmins, 44, 48–49, 51, 312, 315

bravery, 105–106, 152, 200–201, 262, 266, 282, 324. *See also* courage

British Empire, 81, 199–203, 272, 352–353. *See also* England

British Indian Association, 108

Buddhism, 49, 56, 329

C

Carnegie, Andrew, 50, 96

caste system, 127–130, 273, 286–287

celibacy, 11, 142–148, 154, 166, 240–241, 320, 330

Chamberlain, Joseph, 74, 81–83

character, 166–167, 304

charity, 92

chastity. *See* celibacy

children, 27, 143–145, 354

Christianity, 27, 33–34, 40, 60–63, 102–104, 227, 274, 292, 298–299, 348

cigarettes. See tobacco

citizenship, 33–34, 40–41, 72

civil disobedience, 8, 341. *See also* non-cooperation; political activism

civilization, 53, 57, 148–150, 220–225, 228–232, 249–252, 257, 292–293

clothing, 181–188, 195–198, 203

coffee, 11, 14, 117–120

Colenso, battle of, 84–85, 90

cooperation, 199. *See also* non-cooperation

cotton, 181–187, 203, 245

courage, 90, 237–238, 271. *See also* bravery

courts, 12–13, 59, 75, 270–271, 344

cows, protection of, 190

D

death, fear of, 263–266, 277, 336

Devil, 124–125, 150–152.
See also Satan

dharma, 170, 173, 335, 347–348

diet, 14–18, 20–26, 28, 113–120, 154, 320. *See also* eating; health; vegetarianism

discipline, 10–11, 28, 144, 239–242, 271

discrimination, 60–63, 70–75, 89–93, 111–112, 324–325. *See also* racial prejudice

disease. *See* health

dramatic arts, 51–52

E

eating, 20–26, 113, 128–129, 190, 249, 273–276, 311–312. *See also* vegetarianism

economics, 70–74, 186–188

education, 18–19, 66, 94–98, 129, 134–137, 161–176, 270–271, 304–305, 316–317, 335–336, 354

Einstein, Albert, 8, 355

elders, respect for, 172–173, 213

electricity, 246

enemies, 308–311

England. *See also* British Empire
government of, 218–219
military power of, 250

relations with India, 64–65,
    199–203, 215, 249–257, 267
Esoteric Christian Union, 35
European colonists, 77–83
exercise, 19, 169
expulsion
    of English from India, 217–219,
        247–248
    of Indians from colonies, 63–64
extremists, 247–248

F

factories. *See* machinery
family, 284, 317–318. *See also*
    children; marriage
famine, 160–161, 225
fasting, 11, 131–133, 154
fearlessness, 241–242, 315
fines, 284, 289, 337
food. *See* diet; eating; vegetarianism
force, brute, 236–239, 247, 252,
    268–269, 271, 339, 348
freedom, 62, 94, 111, 123, 135,
    154–155, 209, 349. *See also swaraj*

G

God, 122–125, 131–132, 134, 152,
    171, 227, 315

Goethe, Johann Wolfgang von, 51
Gokhale, Gopal Krishna, 211,
    213–214, 304–305, 328
Grand Old Man of India, 211–213

H

habits, 82, 107, 110, 174–175, 227,
    287–289, 312. *See also* addictions
Hampton Normal and Agricultural
    Institute, 94–95
hand-weaving. *See* weaving
hartal, 133
health, 14–26, 28, 113–125, 169,
    246, 285–288, 312
Heber, Bishop, 53
helplessness, 265, 267–268
Hindi, 161–165, 249
Hind Swaraj (Home Rule),
    209–258
Hinduism, 104, 150–152, 223. *See
    also* caste system; untouchables
Hindu-Muslim conflicts,
    286–288
Hindu-Muslim unity, 132–133,
    188–192, 273–276
Hindus, 50, 108–109, 171, 227–228,
    265, 298–299, 347–348, 352
holy places, 225, 227

homegrown and homemade goods, 159, 181–188, 203. *See also* spinning wheels; weaving

Home Rule, 209–258, 291–292

Hugo, Victor, 55

human rights, 10–13

Hume, Allan Octavian, 211, 214

humiliation, 269, 324–325

humility, 152–154

Hunter, W. W., 54–55

    Indian Empire, 42–44, 52

hygiene, 173–174

I

illness. *See* health

ill will, 338–339

imprisonment. *See* jails and prisons

independence. *See* swaraj

India, 42–59, 66, 89–90, 99, 134–137. *See also* satyagraha; swadeshi; swaraj

Indian Ambulance Corps, 84–88, 99, 199

Indian Empire (Hunter), 42–44, 52

Indians, American. *See* Native Americans

injustice, 333–334, 339, 355. *See also* justice

inter-dining, 273–276

intermarriage, 273–276

intoxicants, 113–120, 154

Islam. *See* Muslims

J

Jacolliot, M. Louis, 55

jails and prisons, 284–290, 300–301, 337, 345–346

Jesus Christ, 329, 334–335

justice, 40, 60–63, 154–155, 349. *See also* injustice

K

Kaffirs, 285–286

Khilafat movement, 132, 151, 276, 350, 352

King, Martin Luther Jr., 8

Kingsford, Anna, 16

L

labor

    bodily labor, 168

    in British colonies, 63–64

    indentured, 41, 57, 78, 119

    manual, 318

languages, 58–59, 161–165, 252, 317–318

laws, 47, 51, 71–72, 81–82, 340–341
  discriminatory, 324–327
  disobeying of, 235–237, 326–327
liberation, 165, 167, 293
loin-cloth, 195–198
love, 92, 295, 308–311, 332
lying, 57–59

M

machine-made goods, 243–245
machinery, 222, 242–247
Mahommed, 223
Mandela, Nelson, 8
manners, 12–13
marriage, 120–121, 128–129,
  138–139, 144–148, 273–276,
  311
martyrs, 295
materialism, 35–36, 91–92
mathematics, 48
meat. *See* vegetarianism
medical science, history of, 48–49
military, 351. *See also* arms
  (weapons); wars
mill-industry, 181, 184–185, 194,
  243–244
moderates, 247–248

money, 160–161, 302–303
morality, 40, 57–58, 60–63, 125,
  222–223, 231
Müller, Max, 45
Munro, Thomas, 53
Muslims, 104, 108–109, 132–133,
  171, 227–228, 272, 286, 298–299,
  340–341, 347–348, 352–353. *See
  also* Hindu-Muslim unity
mythology, 47

N

Naoroji, Dadabhai, "Grand Old Man
  of India," 211–213
Natal Colony, 70–73, 84–88
  Indians in, 37–65, 76–83
National Congress (India), 172,
  210–211, 216, 267
nationalism, 202, 210–211, 213, 226
Native Americans, 94–95
non-cooperation, 150, 153–154, 201,
  267, 269–271, 342–346, 348–354
non-killing, 308–311
non-thieving, vow of, 313
nonviolent resistance, 8, 66, 152,
  166, 209, 257, 266, 282–283,
  330–334, 340–346. *See also* non-
  cooperation; passive resistance

O

Orange River Free State, 73

P

palate, vow of control over, 311–312
pariahs, 151. *See also* untouchables
Parsis, 227, 298–299
passive resistance, 232–242, 283,
    291–297, 320, 330–331. *See
    also* non-cooperation; nonviolent
    resistance
patience, 90, 212–213, 213–214, 219
patriotism, 87–88, 158–159, 266
peace, 54, 66, 83, 132, 203, 224,
    233, 248, 267, 272, 276–277, 288,
    326, 338, 340–341, 348–349
peasants, 136–137, 239, 335–336
philosophy, 44–47
political activism, 277, 300–303
political power, 32–34, 72–73
politics, 172, 294, 318–319
possessions, 106, 313
poverty, 143, 187, 196, 224, 241
power, 8, 266, 269, 310, 330–332, 348
Prahlad, 306–307, 317
prayer, 131–133, 154
prejudice, 66, 77–83, 99. *See also*
    racial prejudice

prison. *See* jails and prisons
progress, 257–258
property, 72–73, 79–80, 120, 337,
    340
provocation, restraint under,
    343–344
Punjab, 140, 151, 200, 269, 272

R

racial epithets, 60–61, 73, 107
racial prejudice, 10–13, 32–34,
    37–65, 89–90, 107, 111–112. *See
    also* discrimination
railways, 224–228, 246
Rama (soul), 332–333
Ramayana (Tulsidas), 137, 163–164,
    171
Ravana (non-soul), 332–333
reading, 288
religions, 35–36, 44, 102–105,
    154–155, 171–172, 188–192,
    222–223, 273–276, 294, 305, 319
    unity among, 298–299,
    347–348
Richardson, Benjamin Ward, 16
rights, 10–13, 32–34, 72–73
role models, 99
Rowatt legislation, 340–341

S

sacrifice, 187, 190–191, 201, 265, 270–271, 277

Satan, 124, 152, 192, 223, 342–343

satya, 283

satyagraha, 121, 183, 185, 190, 257, 282–320, 324–355. *See also* non violent resistance; passive resistance; soul-force
origin of, 330–331

schools, withdrawal from, 354

Schopenhauer, Arthur, 46

science, 46–47

self-control, 128, 144, 294–295, 336

self-realization, 176

self-rule. *See* Home Rule

self-sufficiency, 154, 203–204

self-surrender, 148–149, 155

Servants of India Society, 304–305

Shakuntala, 51–52

Shiva, 125

slaves, 93–94

smoking. *See* tobacco

social equality, 81–83

soldiers, 84–88

soul, 123, 264

soul-force, 232–242, 247, 294, 320, 329–333, 336. *See also satyagraha*
defined, 283

South Africa, 24, 41, 44, 66, 70–75, 89–93, 108–110, 300–301, 324–331, 345–346

spinning wheels, 182, 186–187, 192–195

spirituality, 28, 35–36, 294

starvation, 143–144, 160

suffering, 131–132, 166, 265, 289–290, 295–296, 327–328, 340, 345–346

suffragettes. *See* voting

swadeshi, 158–159, 180–188, 197, 245, 257, 265–266, 271, 320
vow of, 184, 203, 314

swaraj, 127, 150, 202, 208–258, 263–277, 343
defined, 216–219

T

Taj of Agra, 50–51

tapasya, 334

taxes, 105–106, 270, 351

tea, 11, 14, 117–120

technology, 221–222, 257

terrorism, 269, 277

tobacco, 28, 87, 114–116, 174–175

toleration, 102–105, 154–155, 276

Tolstoy, Leo, 116, 268, 296

trade, 70–74, 300–301

Transvaal, 24, 74, 105–106, 108, 295, 300

Trevelyan, Sri C., 54

truth, 166, 262, 283, 295, 299, 306–308, 330–331, 334–335, 339, 341

truth-force, 232–242

Tulsidas, 167, 332

  Ramayana, 137, 163–164, 171

Turkey, 111, 132

Tuskegee, 95–97

Tyebji, Budruddin, 211

U

United States of America, 111–112, 155

untouchables, 150–152, 316–317

Upanishads, 46

V

Vedas, 152, 165

vegetarianism, 11, 14–19, 25, 28

violence, 190, 234, 248, 292–293, 310–311, 320, 340–342, 349, 351. *See also* arms (weapons); force, brute

virtue, 166, 330, 336

vital food, 20–26

voting, 105–106, 330

vows, 184, 203, 304–320

W

wars, 84–88, 90, 199, 232–233, 263, 325–326, 332, 353

Washington, Booker T., 93–99

weakness, 22–23, 116–117, 140–143, 150, 237–240, 269–270, 283, 331, 344–346

weapons. *See* arms (weapons)

weaving, 182, 186–187, 195, 318

Wedderburn, William, 211, 214

widows, 120–121, 138–139

women, 105–106, 114, 140–142, 193–194, 223, 231, 243. *See also* marriage

writing, 134–137

Y

Yamas, 306

Z

Zululand, 73